'*Future Freedoms* is a unique and wonderful blending of political theory and the interpretation of literary and material texts. Markovits's initial argument is that the reason modern Western theorists find it so difficult to think about intergenerational justice is because they are blinded by a pair of disabling fantasies: the fantasy of sovereignty (both individual and collective), and the fantasy of inevitable historical progress toward such sovereignty. The way out of this dead-end, Markovits argues, drawing on Arendt, is not by formulating yet another abstract analytic theory, but by focusing on stories or narratives that link past, present, and future in "untimely" and unsettling ways that challenge our imagination of who we are and what we should want as individuals and citizens. Her insightful readings of two types of such narratives, ancient Athenian drama and modern public art, mark out new paths for thinking not only about the meaning of intergenerational justice but of democratic politics as well.'

– *Stephen Salkever, Bryn Mawr College*

'*Future Freedoms* is a truly impressive work. With a nuanced approach to narrative as political theory, Markovits simultaneously offers innovative readings of ancient comedy and tragedy and pushes the boundaries of our thinking about intergenerational politics. *Future Freedoms* is a must read for students of the ancient Greeks and for contemporary democratic theorists.'

– *John Zumbrunnen, University of Wisconsin*

'What kind of world will be left for future generations? Elizabeth K. Markovits' *Future Freedoms* invites you to consider this question as a *democratic* one, drawing on a tradition of ancient and modern thought to envision how people can sustain democracy into the future. Lucid, imaginative, and cogent, this book is a necessary riposte to the de-democratizing forces dominant at the present moment as well as an exhortation to become the change you want to see.'

– *Joel Alden Schlosser, Bryn Mawr College*

'*Future Freedoms* draws on important contemporary research on aesthetics, sovereignty, and recognition but is unique in its application of these concepts to some of the richest comedies and tragedies of the classical era. The facility and fluidity with which Markovits marries these seemingly incongruous texts is nothing short of remarkable. She does the field an essential service by bringing the rich potentiality of Aristophanes, Euripides, and Aeschylus to the surface once again and allowing the contours of their arguments to further shape contemporary debates on democratic practice and intergenerational responsibility.'

– *Smita A. Rahman, DePauw University*

FUTURE FREEDOMS

What do present generations owe the future? In *Future Freedoms*, Elizabeth Markovits asks readers to consider the fact that while democracy holds out the promise of freedom and autonomy, citizens are always bound by the decisions made by previous generations. Motivated by the contemporary political and theoretical landscape, Markovits examines the relationship between democratic citizenship and time by engaging ancient Greek tragedy and comedy. She reveals the ways in which democratic thought in the West has often hinged on ignoring intergenerational relationships and the obligations they create in favor of an emphasis on freedom as sovereignty. She claims that democratic citizens must develop a set of self-directed practices that better acknowledge citizens' connections across time, cultivating a particular orientation toward themselves as part of much larger transgenerational assemblages. As celebrations and critiques of Athenian political identity, the ancient plays at the core of *Future Freedoms* remind readers that intergenerational questions strike at the heart of the democratic sensibility.

This invaluable book will be of interest to students, researchers, and scholars of political theory, the history of political thought, classics, and social and political philosophy.

Elizabeth K. Markovits is Associate Professor of Politics and Director of the Teaching & Learning Initiative at Mount Holyoke College. Her research interests range from ancient Greek thought to contemporary feminist and democratic theory. She is the author of *The Politics of Sincerity: Frank Speech, Plato, and Democratic Judgment* (2008). She has also published scholarly articles on Greek comedy and tragedy, rhetoric, and on women, carework, and democracy, as well as numerous op-eds.

FUTURE FREEDOMS

Intergenerational Justice, Democratic Theory, and Ancient Greek Tragedy and Comedy

Elizabeth K. Markovits

NEW YORK AND LONDON

First published 2018
by Routledge
711 Third Avenue, New York, NY 10017

and by Routledge
2 Park Square, Milton Park, Abingdon, Oxon, OX14 4RN

Routledge is an imprint of the Taylor & Francis Group, an informa business

© 2018 Taylor & Francis

The right of Elizabeth K. Markovits to be identified as author of this work has been asserted by her in accordance with sections 77 and 78 of the Copyright, Designs and Patents Act 1988.

All rights reserved. No part of this book may be reprinted or reproduced or utilised in any form or by any electronic, mechanical, or other means, now known or hereafter invented, including photocopying and recording, or in any information storage or retrieval system, without permission in writing from the publishers.

Trademark notice: Product or corporate names may be trademarks or registered trademarks, and are used only for identification and explanation without intent to infringe.

Library of Congress Cataloging-in-Publication Data
Names: Markovits, Elizabeth, 1975- author.
Title: Future freedoms : intergenerational justice, democratic theory, and ancient Greek tragedy & comedy / Elizabeth K. Markovits.
Description: New York, NY : Routledge is an imprint of the Taylor & Francis Group, an informa business, [2018] | Includes bibliographical references and index.
Identifiers: LCCN 2017022202 (print) | LCCN 2017034716 (ebook) | ISBN 9781315160337 (Master) | ISBN 9781351662192 (WebPDF) | ISBN 9781351662185 (ePub) | ISBN 9781351662178 (Mobipocket/Kindle) | ISBN 9781138064539 (hbk : alk. paper) | ISBN 9781138064584 (pbk : alk. paper) | ISBN 9781315160337 (ebk)
Subjects: LCSH: Greek drama—History and criticism. | Democracy in literature. | Justice in literature.
Classification: LCC PA3131 (ebook) | LCC PA3131 .M3415 2018 (print) | DDC 882/.01093581—dc23
LC record available at https://lccn.loc.gov/2017022202

ISBN: 978-1-138-06453-9 (hbk)
ISBN: 978-1-138-06458-4 (pbk)
ISBN: 978-1-315-16033-7 (ebk)

Typeset in Bembo
by Swales & Willis, Exeter, Devon, UK

For Joe and Ilona

CONTENTS

List of Figures   *x*
Acknowledgments   *xi*

    Introduction   1

1   Intergenerational Justice and Democratic Theory   9

2   A Narrative Turn   40

3   *Archê*, Finitude, and Community in Aristophanes   63

4   Mothers, Powerlessness, and Intergenerational Agency in Euripides   87

5   Freedom, Responsibility, and Transgenerational Orientation in Aeschylus   120

6   Art, Space, and Possibilities for Intergenerational Justice in Our Time   148

Bibliography   *168*
Index   *180*

FIGURES

6.1	*Stolpersteine* in Weichselstraße 52, Berlin	148
6.2	Coram's Fields, London	154
6.3	Haydel House, Whitney Plantation	158
6.4	Slave Quarters, Whitney Plantation	159
6.5	Utopia Fair, Somerset House Courtyard, London	159
6.6	Caer Heritage Project, Utopia Fair, London	160
6.7	Climate Change Elevator, *Doomocracy*, Brooklyn	161
6.8	*Hollow*, Exterior, Bristol	161
6.9	*Hollow*, Interior, Bristol	162

ACKNOWLEDGMENTS

I am very grateful to all the people who have helped bring this book into the world, especially Ali Aslam, Susan Bickford, Joan Cocks, Peter Euben, Dustin Ells Howes, Kristy King, Thornton Lockwood, Hollie Mann, Karen Remmler, Stephen Salkever, Arlene Saxonhouse, Erin Taylor, Christina Tarnopolsky, Liz Wingrove, and multiple anonymous reviewers. I was exceptionally fortunate to have benefitted from so many energizing discussions at the Association for Political Theory meetings over the last 10+ years and I owe a great deal to the wonderful community of political theorists there. The Yale Political Theory Workshop and the University of North Carolina Political Theory Workshop also provided important opportunities to test out arguments and hear new ideas. Special thanks also to Owen Kimm at *Situations* in Bristol for coffee and conversation, to Creative Time in Brooklyn for the use of *Doomocracy* materials, and to Viv Thomas from the Caer Heritage Project in Cardiff for his beautiful photographs from the Utopia Fair.

I want to thank my amazing colleagues at Mount Holyoke College for intellectual and financial support over the life of this project. I am also indebted to our students for their provocations, generosity, and inspiring faith in a better world. Finally, Abbey Clark-Moschella and Katie LaRoque were incredible research assistants here at Mount Holyoke—they will no doubt see their mark on these pages.

This book would never have happened without the kindness and support of friends and family. I want to especially acknowledge my sisters, Dianya, Lara, and Clare, and my parents, Michael and Andrew, for their laughter, love, and solidarity. To Amber, Joshua, Becky, Seamus, Eleanor, Allison, Gary, Chris, Tom, Khama, Melissa, Sarah, and Shelley: thank you for your inspiration and friendship over the years. Vielen Dank an Luisa und J für die schönen Zeiten, wunderbaren

Gespräche, und die Gastfreundschaft, sowohl in Berlin als auch in Amherst! And for unwavering encouragement, love, and partnership over more than a generation, thanks to Bennett Hazlip.

Another version of Chapter 2 appeared in *POLIS* ("As if we were codgers: Flattery, *Parrhesia*, and Old Man Demos in Aristophanes' *Knights*." *POLIS*, Vol. 29, No. 1 [2012]: 108–29), and another version of Chapter 5 appeared in the *American Political Science Review* ("Birthrights: Freedom, Responsibility, and Democratic Comportment in Aeschylus' *Oresteia*." *American Political Science Review* 103 [August 2009]: 427–41).

Thanks to Creative Time (Brooklyn, NY) for the use of the Climate Change Elevator script and photo from *Doomocracy*, to Museum Neukölln (Berlin) for use of the *Stolpersteine* photo, and to Viv Thomas for the use of his photo from the Utopia Fair (London).

"Oh, shit, the future, yes. I'd forgotten about that, old son. Um . . . I'll see what I can do. . ."

David Bowie, 1983 (*Rolling Stone*, Issue 395: May 12, 1983)

INTRODUCTION

> Freedom belongs to nobody but Zeus.
>
> —Aeschylus, *Prometheus Bound*

Imagine Rae, born two generations from now in the United States (around 2080). Although she expects to live past 100 thanks to previous medical advancements, she also grapples with a warmed climate, in which risen sea levels have left portions of the East Coast uninhabitable—a scenario that has required government leaders to divert both federal and state tax revenues from education into new infrastructure and recovery projects. Educational achievement has decreased relative to previous generations, as fewer students leave secondary programs with math and verbal skills equivalent to their grandparents, and fewer can afford to go on to higher education, with less access to loan and grant options. The new infrastructure projects provide decent jobs for skilled laborers and engineers, but national GDP declines, leading to lower overall tax revenues and calls to shrink state and federal budgets. Should Rae be angry that citizens in 2020 did very little to prevent climate change? Does she have similar opportunities to exercise agency and political voice—to experience democratic freedom—as her predecessors, given the constraints on her material world? Is the benefit of her longer life—thanks to earlier investments in medical research—worth increased vulnerability to severe weather events, or fewer opportunities for education? What is her own responsibility to the future, especially given the constraints she's facing as a result of the past?

This book is an effort to think through the political implications of living in an intergenerational world. What does democracy mean when citizens are in fact bound by the decisions of those who came before—so, in some important sense, living in an unfree condition? This arises in all sorts of ways. Right now, climate change is simply the most obvious—and existentially perilous—example of the danger of ignoring intergenerational concerns. The legacy of African-American slavery and the transatlantic slave trade reverberates over time, linking 15th-century papal proclamations with the contemporary Black Lives Matter movement. Choices made about the configuration of voting districts shape the contours of legislative politics for generations. War crimes committed by one generation create demands and obligations far into the future.

At the same time, Thomas Jefferson's rejection of a "perpetual constitution" reveals that a concern for generational sovereignty—an attempt to overcome the obligations of the past— has long animated the US political imagination. There is a deep-rooted liberal desire to shake free of the past and to live in a *self*-determined way. It is one of the basic features of American individualism, as Alexis de Tocqueville noted:

> [t]hus not only does democracy make every man forget his ancestors, but it hides his descendants and separates his contemporaries from him; it throws him back forever upon himself alone and threatens in the end to confine him entirely within the solitude of his own heart.[1]

This question of how generations relate to one another is not new or unique to contemporary US politics.[2] Ancient Athenian playwrights and philosophers also produced works focused on these questions—works I believe can enrich our own engagement with problems of intergenerational justice. Motivated by the contemporary political and theoretical landscape, this book examines the interconnected relationship between democratic citizenship (that is, our ability to exercise agency in the world) and human finitude (or the fact that time extends beyond our own lives) by engaging with ancient Greek tragedy and comedy. The material also extends beyond the particular case of intergenerational justice and enriches our understanding of democratic citizenship more generally, focusing on several key concepts in democratic theory—freedom, sovereignty, justice, responsibility. It reveals the ways in which democratic thought in the West has often depended upon ignoring intergenerational relationships and the obligations they create, in favor of an emphasis on freedom as sovereignty—individual, state, *and* generational. In contrast, as celebrations and critiques of Athens' political identity, the texts considered in Chapters 3–5 remind readers that intergenerational questions strike at the heart of the democratic sensibility. Because the deep intertwining of intergenerational concerns with democracy is revealed over and over again in ancient Greek theater, these texts deeply challenge our own contemporary faith in generational sovereignty—and call on us to rethink our own understanding of democracy (insofar as the animating ideas of democracy—freedom and agency—have become tied to notions of control). These are not simply problems to be addressed through social and economic policy, neither is ignoring them a justifiable exercise of the present generation's democratic power. Instead, intergenerational dynamics create productive tensions that inform conceptions of democratic citizenship at the most basic level. When amplified and engaged, these tensions can motivate a new democratic orientation toward taking responsibility for injustice across time by mobilizing a transgenerational orientation rooted in one's affective experience of membership in different assemblages over time.

A focus on *motivation* is key to this project. Intergenerational obligation may be a reasonable expectation for democratic citizens, but the more difficult question is how to inculcate an embrace of such an obligation, given the ease with which a generation can ignore the as-yet-nonexistent future. This problem—which is basically one of affect—is also addressed by recent work on environmental ethics. In *After Nature*, Jedidiah Purdy examines the American "environmental imagination," the history of practical and affective ideas that provide that "map of things worth saving, or of a future worth creating" that shape the world in which we live.[3] Technological and economic solutions alone will not suffice; we must have imaginative resources that motivate ways of seeing the world and sharing that vision with others. In a similar vein, Melissa Lane's work, *Eco-Republic: What the Ancients Can Teach Us about Ethics, Virtue, and Sustainable Living*, calls for reimagining "the social ethos" in the face of climate change, as our current motivations to address the problem have clearly been inadequate.[4] Technical solutions to intergenerational questions are always *part* of the solution. We cannot come up with a fair distribution of wealth across generations—for example, spending money on education or Medicare—without the work of economists. But whether or not we want to come up with a fair distribution (and what that might be) and whether or not we will move quickly enough to stop rising sea levels, requires attention to the psycho-social. It is true that many people *care* about intergenerational issues but feel helpless to do anything on their own—and for good reason, as the collective action problem surrounding something like climate change is indeed staggering. But assuming that we want to reject authoritarian impositions of change, the democratic way to enact collective solutions—on any scale—is to mobilize citizen support for new and, likely onerous, measures. This does not mean ignoring the structural and technical. Oftentimes, this internal desire can be cultivated by building structural pathways; the internal and external exist together in a sort of feedback loop—as Aristotle noted long ago.[5] For example, if you live in an area with curbside recycling, consider how odd it may now feel to toss a bottle into the regular trash bin (regardless of whether you wanted to recycle when the program began)? Many people want solar panels, but cannot afford them; in my own state of Massachusetts, the panels are now subsidized to the extent that an installation loan and operating costs are roughly equivalent to one's electricity bill. So the technical and structural are implicated in the formation of desires and attitudes, to be sure. But the question remains: why doesn't every community have such programs? Even if some large corporate or political power is blocking citizen action, how might we—citizens, elected officials, corporate members themselves—become motivated to overcome that seemingly insurmountable obstacle? This is where a radical revisioning of our shared political imagination comes in. As Jason Frank notes, "images of peoplehood mediate the people's relationship to their own political empowerment—how they understand themselves to be a part of and act *as* a people."[6] This requires changing the political landscape by first understanding how we came to our particular situation and then imagining new ways of acting and being in a community. In the following chapters, I elaborate on these claims and walk with readers through a series of narratives that can help spur our own thinking about intergenerational justice and its demands on democratic subjects. Because of the prominent place of theater in Athens and because of how often intergenerational themes appear across the extant plays, ancient Greek comedy and tragedy provide rich provocations for thinking about how to motivate the psycho-social change needed now. My hope is that by surveying these alternative imaginative resources from a relatively familiar yet untimely tradition, we might unsettle the current sensibility that renders the future invisible and privileges each contemporary generation's—or at least the most powerful voices within each generation—demand for sovereignty.

This book is not primarily about any single intergenerational issue—reparations, climate change, debt relief, memorialization. Although I will use those examples throughout, I am interested in intergenerational justice as a theoretical problem generally. The central focus is on the ancient material, as well as the usual suspects in contemporary democratic theory (John Rawls, Jürgen Habermas, Hannah Arendt, and so on). I also pick up a variety of other threads in contemporary thought: cosmopolitans who look at justice across spatial boundaries;[7] democratic theorists thinking through issues of agency and responsibility;[8] new materialists who focus on assemblages, affect, and distributed agency;[9] feminist theorists and critical race theorists working to interrogate the meanings of the self, embodiment, and community.[10] I gather together these various lines of thought to develop a map of current work on intergenerational justice, a better understanding of the tensions and problems left unexplored by that work, and an account of a way forward.

★★★

Chapter 1, "Intergenerational Justice and Democratic Theory," examines the place of intergenerational politics in modern and contemporary political thought. I argue that even as more attention has been given to intergenerational justice in philosophy and political theory of late, scholars have not found a sufficient solution to the problem of future generations for democratic theory. The chapter begins by reviewing three general approaches to the topic in the academic literature: generational sovereignty, generational representation, and generational distribution. I argue that although each provides important insight into the problem, none has been able to generate the sense of intergenerational responsibility necessary to address current challenges because they all rest on a problematic foundation of the aspiration to sovereign freedom. I also work through particular challenges posed by the structural nature of intergenerational injustice (that is, injustice without specific culpable individuals or victims, and which spring from everyday conditions of life). The chapter closes with an argument about the need to develop a set of self-directed practices that better acknowledge citizens' connections across time—that is, their temporal intersubjectivity—and which cultivate a particular orientation toward themselves and the future.

Chapter 2, "A Narrative Turn," moves to a discussion of the critical role of narrative in promoting a democratic orientation to intergenerational justice questions. Whereas reason and technical analysis can be great tools for working out justice claims, they cannot tell us how to move a citizen psychologically to action, especially action concerned with unknown, future individuals. Focusing on affective elements of untimely storytelling, the chapter argues that narrative is particularly important as a complement to judgment, helping citizens to cultivate an appreciation of intergenerational tensions and imaginative thinking about possible approaches to relieving those tensions. The next four chapters are an effort to demonstrate the value of that approach. The plays and playwrights are not treated chronologically, but rather the chapters are ordered in a way that develops my argument in logical sequence. I do that by first exploring the intergenerational tensions that accompany democratic life and which undermine claims to sovereign individualism (Chapter 3 on Aristophanes); then moving to a discussion of the difficulties of that lack of sovereign power and the alternative conceptions of agency that can better attend to temporal intersubjectivity (Chapter 4 on Euripides); and then finally looking for affective orientations and institutional arrangements that could open a path forward for us (Chapter 5 on Aeschylus).

Chapter 3, "*Archê*, Finitude, and Community in Aristophanes," begins the examination of the ancient material, with Aristophanes' comedic exploration of the tensions engendered by the passage of time and competing claims for sovereignty. The chapter focuses on two comedies, *Knights* and *Clouds*, and untangles the specific challenges posed by the procession of time: the need to confront human finitude—that is, the fact that lives end and that past decisions limit future ones—and the impossibility of sovereign power. Here we see the dangers posed by the "ontological narcissism" (to use William Connolly's wonderful phrase)[11] embedded in the notion of sovereignty and the inability of one generation to give way to the next (and that's not to say that the proceeding generation has much to recommend it either—after all, this is Aristophanes!). I examine what it means to share power with future citizens, especially when the future citizens seem intent on forging new paths of their own choosing, revealing the oft-neglected difficulties of calls for intergenerational justice. Thinking about intergenerational politics is not simply working out the details of future-oriented justice—it must address the profound losses that come with attending to those obligations. Aristophanes helps us better understand the challenges ahead—it's not a simple case of just telling citizens to accept intergenerational demands. Instead, the claim is fraught, tied up with risks to freedom, and a sense that our own ability to express our agency—affirm our own existence in the world—might be threatened. Aristophanes helps citizens to laugh at the failures of attempts at sovereign control, while also treating the desire seriously. I do not mean that Aristophanes (or later, Euripides or Aeschylus) was a self-conscious critic of liberal notions of sovereignty. If anything, Aristophanes counseled retreat from public life—because alone in the country, one could live as one desired, free from the hassle of the city and all its people. Hardly a celebration of human plurality. But he does give us a way to think about the animating tensions at play (and another challenge to the Arendtian claim that freedom-as-control is just a later idea of Plato's).[12] We see that freedom in this register is a constant risk that requires sustained, therapeutic discussion, and re-orientation. Thus, I focus *on* the tensions, rather than trying to resolve them. Recognizing the sacrifices of our own sense of agency is key to any attempt to better accommodate future worlds.

Chapter 4, "Mothers, Powerlessness, and Intergenerational Agency in Euripides," explores the themes of freedom, power, and powerlessness across generations through an examination of Euripides' tragedies. Here, we feel horror at both the absurdity of attempts to take control (*Medea*) and at the total lack of control (*Trojan Women*). Continuing the themes from Chapter 3, Chapter 4 reveals the sovereign self's very particular and ultimately destructive masculinist, bond-denying foundation—but here we also confront the tragedy of powerlessness. The chapter begins with a discussion of contemporary motherhood, before moving back to ancient Athens, where I focus on the ways in which the democratic ideology of the city excluded mothers. This exclusion helped to naturalize women's political powerlessness in Athens, a topic explored in Euripides' *Trojan Women*. I connect this socially constructed absence with women's roles as actual producers of the male citizens, focused on their incapacity to act as advocates or protectors of future generations. The powerlessness faced by women in Athens echoes the condition of the old man figure in Aristophanes—except that women never would have had such expectations of power and freedom. The chapter then moves to *Medea* to complicate this account of women's powerlessness. I examine the construction of mothers as creatures with terrible power, sacrificing their children in order to achieve the sovereign selfhood so prized by the men around them—but also suffering from that sacrifice because these individual humans actually form an assemblage from which the mother is unable to depart cleanly. Once again, the tensions arising from intersubjectivity, profound vulnerability (seen both in the Trojan royal women and in Medea's children), and a desire to act lead to the tragedy—but also help to generate a clearer understanding of the complexity with which we are confronted. Agency, seen in sovereign terms, is a source of unfreedom for others and self-destruction for the actor trying to achieve it. Yet the promises of agency remain a critical foundation for democratic community. How might we better conceive of agency in terms that get us to the notion of non-sovereign freedom and responsibility for others across time?

Chapter 5, "Freedom, Responsibility, and Transgenerational Orientation in Aeschylus," moves to a discussion of institutions and the attempt to cultivate a democratic orientation to intergenerational justice, built on distributed agency and an openness to the affective elements of our lives that can motivate the desire to attend to the future. I pay particular attention to the balance between freedom and responsibility—two concepts so far seen to be in tension with one another, but which turn out to require such tension to be meaningful. I argue that democracy requires a particular orientation to those tensions—and that this orientation needs an outlet in institutions that draw assemblages together. The chapter develops this claim by examining how each of the central figures in the *Oresteia* deals with their range of choices and then with the results of their actions. Only Orestes, the symbol of a new generation, is able to take responsibility for the actions of his family—an assemblage—and, thereby, provide the future Athenian citizens—another assemblage—freedom from the tragic history of cursed birthrights. The orientation toward intergenerational responsibility presented in the play serves to solicit a similar disposition in Athenian citizens, mobilizing a transgenerational orientation across a network of citizens. This is not just a commitment to willingly and individually consent to a loss of freedom, but an emergent property of a transgenerational assemblage. It is also not a settled or prescribed solution, but an iterative construction that requires continued engagement across spirals of time and experience. Moreover, Orestes—and the Athenian demos—is only able to do this with the help of democratic procedure, and while acknowledging mutual interdependence. Communal and institutional solutions, not just individual practices, move us from idiosyncratic and neoliberal/consumerist individual attempts to address intergenerational justice to a more robust and political effort, distributed across the actual political assemblage of which persons are part. In these ways, the Greek material serves as a resource for displacing the usual melodramatic "orgies of feeling" Elisabeth Anker argues we use to mediate our failures to achieve sovereignty ourselves.[13] Instead, we can face the tragi-comedy of these attempts and generate alternative ideas about the role of the self, community, and the future in democratic political life.

Chapter 6, "Art, Space, and Possibilities for Intergenerational Justice in Our Time," closes the book with a turn away from the ancient material and to a discussion of space and new public art movements, sounding out some further possibilities for disrupting the urge to generational sovereignty in our own time. Throughout the previous chapters, I highlighted the ways in which questions of intergenerational justice call out for a particular re-orientation to the self and others. The exploration of ancient Greek resources demonstrates one way of engaging narrative to help cultivate such an orientation. Because contemporary democracies lack such shared narrative experiences, I want to look for some analogous sites to generate the affective energy to reorient democratic citizenship. I explore contemporary urban landscapes as texts that offer further possibilities to cultivate particular citizen orientations—or to thwart such developments. In particular, I look at public art elements in a number of locations—Berlin, Bristol,

London, and New Orleans. Throughout, I am trying to understand how these sites commemorate a locale's history or draw attention to the future, and how they might inspire non-sovereignist thinking about the self and time.

Notes

1 Alexis de Tocqueville, *Democracy in America: Volume 2* (New York: Vintage Classics, 1990), 99.
2 This formulation often assumes generational homogeneity and distinctiveness. But neither quality accurately describes any grouping of citizens in time. Generations overlap and are continuously partially changing. Moreover, the cleavages *within* any generations are myriad—and more often the primary concern in studies of freedom or justice. But for the purposes of this book, I will reflect the standard usage that groups together citizens of particular time periods, taking their existence at a particular time as the relevant distinction.
3 Jedidiah Purdy, *After Nature: A Politics for the Anthropocene* (Cambridge, MA: Harvard University Press, 2015), 7.
4 Melissa Lane, *Eco-Republic: What the Ancients Can Teach Us about Ethics, Virtue, and Sustainable Living* (Princeton, NJ: Princeton University Press, 2012), 9.
5 For more on this, see Davina Cooper, "Against the Current: Social Pathways and the Pursuit of Enduring Change," *Feminist Legal Studies* 9, no. 2 (2001): 119–48; Nancy Hirschmann, *The Subject of Liberty: Toward a Feminist Theory of Freedom* (Princeton, NJ: Princeton University Press, 2003); Elizabeth Markovits and Susan Bickford, "Constructing Freedom: Institutional Pathways to Changing the Gender Division of Labor," *Perspectives on Politics* 12, no. 1 (March 2014): 81–99.
6 Jason Frank, "The Living Image of the People," *Theory & Event* 18, no. 1 (2015): 2.
7 See Seyla Benhabib, *Another Cosmopolitanism, with Commentaries by Jeremy Waldron, Bonnie Honig, Will Kymlicka,* ed. Robert Post (New York: Oxford University Press, 2006); James Bohman, *Democracy across Borders: From Dêmos to Dêmoi* (Cambridge, MA: MIT Press, 2004); Martha Nussbaum, *Frontiers of Justice: Disability, Nationality, Species Membership* (Cambridge, UK: Belknap Press, 2004); Peter Singer, *One World: The Ethics of Globalization* (New Haven, CT: Yale University Press, 2002).
8 See Sharon Krause, *Freedom beyond Sovereignty: Reconstructing Liberal Individualism* (Chicago, IL: University of Chicago Press, 2015); Patchen Markell, *Bound by Recognition* (Princeton, NJ: Princeton University Press, 2003); Iris Marion Young, *Responsibility for Justice* (New York: Oxford University Press, 2011).
9 See Jane Bennett, *Vibrant Matter: A Political Ecology of Things* (Durham, NC: Duke University Press, 2010); Timothy Morton, *Hyperobjects: Philosophy and Ecology after the End of the World* (Minneapolis, MN: University of Minnesota Press, 2013).
10 See endnote 5, as well as Susan Moller Okin, *Justice, Gender, and the Family* (New York: Basic Books, 1989); Sara Ruddick, *Maternal Thinking: Toward a Politics of Peace* (Boston, MA: Beacon Press, 1989); Alexander G. Weheliye, *Habeas Viscus: Racializing Assemblages, Biopolitics, and Black Feminist Theories of the Human* (Durham, NC: Duke University Press, 2014); Katherine McKittrick, "Unparalled Catastrophe for Our Species? Or, to Give Humanness a Different Future: Conversations," in *Sylvia Wynter: On Being Human as Praxis,* ed. Katherine McKittrick (Durham, NC: Duke University Press, 2015), 9–89.
11 William Connolly, *Identity/Difference* (Ithaca, NY: Cornell University Press, 1991), 30.
12 For more on Arendt's critique of sovereignty and the temporal "fiction" she employs, see James R. Martel, "Can There Be Politics Without Sovereignty? Arendt, Derrida, and the Question of Sovereign Inevitability," *Law, Culture and the Humanities* 6, no. 2 (2010): 153–66.
13 Elisabeth Anker, *Orgies of Feeling: Melodrama and the Politics of Freedom* (Durham, NC: Duke University Press, 2014).

1

INTERGENERATIONAL JUSTICE AND DEMOCRATIC THEORY

> To set the time aright means to renew the world,
> and this we can do because we all arrived at
> one time or another as newcomers in a world which was
> there before us and will still be there when we are gone,
> when we shall have left its burden to our successors.
> —Hannah Arendt, *Responsibility and Judgment*

Hannah Arendt consistently referenced the generational aspects of citizenship, often calling attention to our inheritance of a specific world with a definite history, one which we are not free to change at will, but must accept and work within. In the quote above, she pushes readers to see how each generation steps into prominence for just a bit of time, inheriting an already materialized world and passing it along to future citizens. During the time in which we are on the scene, we "renew it," taking up its materials, reworking them, and then bequeathing that new mixture to others. Yet continued inaction on an issue like climate change reveals that while this cycle of inheritance and bequeathing may be something people vaguely care about, it is simply not a compelling force within popular political discourse, even at a time when the current generation has the power to make the earth uninhabitable for all species and forms of life.[1]

Still, academic literature focused explicitly on notions of obligation and justice over time appears in various locations, especially within philosophy, environmental ethics, and the literature on welfare states, although it has yet to occupy a central place within democratic political theory more generally.[2] In the 1970s and 1980s, there was a wave of academic (and popular non-fiction) literature regarding responsibility to future generations. For the most part, this work was motivated by fears of nuclear annihilation and the dangers of environmental degradation.[3] As Jonathan Schell put it, "The possibility that the living can stop the future generations from entering into life compels us to ask basic new questions about our existence."[4] From the mid-1990s forward, discussions of intergenerational politics often focused on welfare state politics. According to much of this literature, there was a "coming generational storm," brought on by relatively generous welfare benefits that could not be sustained and by problematic accounting and taxation systems that have left governments broke and unable to fulfill their compact with future generations.[5] Other recent contributions in environmental ethics continue to highlight the relationship between environmental concerns and intergenerational obligations.[6] Current work in philosophy has taken up both threads (economic and environmental), trying to work out the general scope of intergenerational justice claims, what makes them special, how far they extend, and so on.[7] In most of this work, the emphasis is on questions of distributive justice. That is, what do current citizens owe members of future generations in terms of resources? Have past or current generations taken more than their fair share?[8]

In this chapter, I build on this work by reviewing this academic literature in an effort to explicate exactly why we should care about justice across generational time. From there, I consider exactly what sort of justice question this is—is it a matter of fair distribution? Of representation? Or freedom? Or recognition? In general, the argument rests on a couple of fairly simple premises. First, democracy is a good we want. Democracy is obviously related to legitimacy—consent and authority—and so a consequentialist might like democracy just because it can work pretty well to maintain stability. But it is also something others value because it is the only way of organizing power that allows for universal moral respect and the freedom for individuals to act in the world. Whether working with consent in a liberal theory of democracy or considering the force of rebellion against established powers in a Wolinian radical model, democracy depends upon and grounds notions of individual dignity and freedom. Second, as Dennis Thompson has clearly laid out, democracy has a distinct presentism for several reasons: the tendency to "prefer the immediate to the distant," the need for representatives to be responsive to constituents, the fact that democratic governments are time-limited and so tend to favor policies with immediate results (to increase potential for re-election), and the tendency of democratic government to put into place policies that favor older (voting) generations.[9] Yet—and third—there is no good moral justification for excluding future citizens from their own shot at democratic freedom. Just as theorists of cosmopolitan democracy have shown us this with respect to individuals outside our political borders, there is no valid reason why someone born into my political community in 100 years should not have access to the same universal moral respect as someone born this year. Yet the choices we make now may very well limit that possibility. Of course, there may be a tendency to favor those closer to oneself, but it is not morally justifiable.

This is a big claim, I realize—and the arguments will be further explicated in the following pages of this chapter as I review the various approaches to intergenerational justice claims. (Nevertheless, even as political theorists and philosophers have established the arguments *for* caring for future generations, many people will not care to attend to this obligation—which is one of the motivating factors behind the present volume.) Fourth, we live in an increasingly intergenerational polity. This is not because we somehow are more multi-generational than ever; in fact, the contemporary US is often individualist in the extreme and dismissive of both the very young and old, as if everyone were a healthy 30-year-old living alone with all their needs magically met. I only mean that our decisions have greater impact on the future. Of course, decisions made in 1930s about health care provision or transportation policy had path-dependent, long-term effects. But we now threaten the climate in such a way that the long-term future is no longer a given.

I begin by taking stock of the academic literature on intergenerational justice, which can be divided into a few general (and often overlapping) approaches:

1. Generational sovereignty. In this view, each generation is free to do as it pleases. However, this leads to an obligation for each generation to avoid indebting the future and impeding future citizens' ability to shape their own political life. The focus is on democratic freedom and the injustice of limiting that for future generations by committing them to policies or debts not of their own choosing. It's not so much that the present cares for future generations—but that the freedom of each present generation deserves as wide a scope as possible.
2. Generational distribution. This approach focuses on figuring out the basis of intergenerational obligation, with an emphasis on the just distribution of resources over time and a clear awareness of the special and often problematic position of future generations.
3. Generational representation. In these formulations, intergenerational dynamics are accounted for by figuring out a way to represent the future in democratic decision-making. It's a difficult group to incorporate, obviously, but those working within this area generally take theories of democracy and figure out a way to add in future voices.

Although the generational sovereignty approach taps into a powerful impulse—and connects with a broader tradition of thinking about sovereign power—our aspiration to democratic freedom cannot negate the fact that we live in a temporal continuum, inheriting and bequeathing particular historical contexts that demand attention.[10] However, the impossibility of knowing future individuals also creates specific problems for any attempt to incorporate future concerns. My concern is that all three approaches tend to reinscribe the liberal aspiration to a sovereign self that lies at the root of our inability to actually attend to that obligation.

The final section of this chapter works through the connection between these three approaches and a problematic understanding of freedom-as-sovereignty. I go on in the remainder of the book to argue we should instead focus on a set of self-directed practices that better acknowledge temporal intersubjective vulnerability and cultivate a particular orientation toward ourselves and the future that can combat the sovereign individualism that bombards us today. At the same time, this set of self-directed practices is not meant individualistically. They are self-directed in an instrumental way, meant to encourage a sense of intersubjective connection and appreciation for the unpredictability of the world, as well as concrete political action, which would in turn enhance democratic freedom for all, whether living in 2018 or 2118.

★★★

Generational Sovereignty. Sovereignty refers to the quality of being self-sufficiently self-determining. *Generational sovereignty* here applies the same aspiration to a generational cohort—each group is meant to be independent of others and able to determine their own aspirations and actions. Of course, generations are never so distinct; they overlap and members may or may not share much sense of identity. In fact, generational claims too often dismiss critical disagreement and plurality *within* a generation, instead representing the dominant group's interest to the exclusion of others (as any engagement with Thomas Jefferson's work must remind us—the forced silences are deafening). Regardless, thinkers in this group tried to work out whether or not future generations can be bound by the decisions made by members of previous generations. The most prominent of these perspectives belongs to Thomas Jefferson (working in a similar register as Thomas Paine, and as opposed to Edmund Burke). In a 1789 letter to James Madison, Jefferson declared that "the earth belongs in usufruct to the living."[11] For Jefferson, the idea that current citizens could be bound by the decisions of previous generations was unacceptable: "we seem not to have perceived that, by the law of nature, one generation is to another as one independent nation to another."[12] Each generation may enter into agreements—such as taking on debt from France—but such obligations would only last 19 years, ensuring that "succeeding generations are not responsible for the preceding."[13] Like John Locke and others, Jefferson is clear about the importance of maintaining adequate resources for the future, although that is not Jefferson's primary focus. Current generations have an obligation to not use everything up: "for if he could, he might during his own life, eat up the usufruct of the lands for several generations to come, and then the lands would belong to the dead and not to the living."[14] The current generation should enjoy the world free and clear of the debts of the deceased. The corollary of this is that the current generation also has an obligation not to indenture future generations, with an implication—by the word "usufruct"—to also *not* leave the earth in disarray or completely spent.

Although sustainability is at least a tangential concern for Jefferson, the central emphasis is on freedom and generational sovereignty. The future citizen should not be bound or obligated by the decisions of the previous generation. The concern to maintain adequate resources is relevant because to not do so would be to unjustly limit the freedom of future generations. Each generation is free to master its own world, and not be yoked by its predecessors. Jefferson consistently emphasizes the individual's natural right to work with other individuals to direct his own will toward some project. This is a self-directed choice, not a burden imposed by the past. Powers reside in the individual and "expire with his life, by nature's law."[15] Jefferson's critique of "perpetual constitution" also makes this clear.[16] He writes:

> [t]hey are masters too of their own persons, and consequently may govern them as they please. But persons and property make the sum of the objects of government. The constitution and the laws of their predecessor extinguished them, in their natural course, with those whose will gave them being. This could preserve that being till it ceased to be itself, and no longer. Every constitution, then, and every law, naturally expires at the end of 19 years. If it be enforced longer, it is an act of force and not of right.[17]

It is not enough to make laws subject to repeal, because democratic politics is fraught with difficulty and the future would be bound by those previous decisions as the system worked itself out. Thus, the obligation to preserve future freedom remains with those making the laws in the first place, not with their descendants. Jefferson provides a powerful articulation of the relationship between freedom, temporality, and responsibility in democratic life—we are free to do what we want, insofar as future citizens may also enjoy that same freedom.

Yet Jefferson's elegant call to stick to our own time poses obvious problems, including the reality of overlapping generations. The practical issues with these limits on democratic power have been ably discussed by Víctor Muñiz-Fraticelli. According to Muñiz-Fraticelli, the "leg up" provided by an established (yet alterable) constitutional arrangement is an important component of a "prosperous and stable society."[18] Likewise, permanent safeguards for civil and political rights and the principles of contract and property are features that require transgenerational stability to generate their most beneficial aspects. Muñiz-Fraticelli is less worried than Jefferson about "the decadence of self-indulgent generations," pointing out that it is "by no means the general case."[19] Although I agree with many of his practical critiques of Jefferson, I do not find this latter point convincing—or at least not convincing enough in the face of the kind of existential threat we now face with climate change. Still, the importance of the potential for some transgenerational projects is clear, *especially* in light of the fact that current generations often make choices with lasting impact on the future.

Yet for Jefferson, each generation is its own sovereign nation, not obliged to others, and free to act according to the wills of the individuals present—not the deceased. Moreover, each generation must refrain from doing *anything*—good or bad—to bind the future.[20] Janna Thompson characterizes Jefferson's perspective as "synchronic" (as opposed to "diachronic"): "citizens have political obligations to each other that arise from their endorsement of a social contract and their participation in democratic decision-making. The relationship that gives them these obligations does not hold between them and non-existent generations."[21] However, this is not quite right. Jefferson sees that current generations *do* have an obligation to the future—an obligation to refrain from affecting them. Because of his particular formulation, this also means that the future has no obligation to the past; it's a one-way street. And it is limited—it is not that current generations are tightly bound by the imagined needs of the future. This is a negative obligation to *not* pass on a depleted world and a tangle of legal and financial obligations. The current generation simply has no right at all to interfere in any way with the decisions of future generations. The future citizenry has to be able to make their own choices (even as they remain a heterogeneous group—what decision-making process they use must be one for members of that future time). This requires freedom from old contracts, as well as a world that has not been eaten up by greedy predecessors.

One doesn't have to agree with Edmund Burke that society is "a partnership not only between those who are living, but between those who are living, those who are dead, and those who are to be born," to remain troubled by the Jeffersonian disregard for past or lifetime-transcending obligations.[22] Cleaning waterways, building major infrastructure, mining a resource, or establishing public education programs would often—and legitimately—last longer than 20 years. Why should we care about the future? Because our actions are *not* bounded by discrete units of time that conveniently correspond to our own life span. Moreover, intergenerational justice particularly calls for thinking about what Timothy Morton terms "hyperobjects"—"things massively distributed across time and space relative to humans," like nuclear radiation or global warming—or even just the Styrofoam cup we casually use and throw away.[23] Such hyperobjects are inherently transgenerational. For example, and contra Burke, I do not have to see myself in some sort of partnership (whether based upon familial ties or shared culture) with antebellum slaves or slave-owners in the Deep South to think that contemporary US citizens have a legitimate obligation to address the enduring legacy of African-American slavery in this country. It is a legacy that persists into the present and that is quite enough to ground obligation (at the same time, understanding the history is critical for addressing the present injustice).[24] That is, these obligations need not be rooted in a shared sense of historical identity. The past is with us *in the present*. The obligations are the result of the fact that we live in a historical continuum. We presently receive various benefits, but also debts, from this fact.

Although Jefferson taps into a critically important democratic ethos—one of freedom—and helpfully reminds us of the potential tyranny of obligating the future in order to fulfill our own desires, he ignores the fact that we simply can't get away from the past. Trying to do so is a fantasy—perhaps *the* democratic fantasy, in which each person (and nation-state, and generation) is a sovereign master. But, as Janna Thompson notes, individuals themselves have transgenerational concerns. That is, their wills are directed toward projects that inevitably take at least part of their value from their connection to either a heritage (so, for example, collecting fine art) or to the future (having children, building a business).[25] Even without buying into her communitarian critique of the Jeffersonian approach, we can see that even as the promise of freedom on a clean political slate is deeply appealing, it just does not exist. If we abolished the US Constitution tomorrow and canceled the national debt, the current generation would still have to contend with a history of racism, income inequality, environmental damage, etc.—and still benefit from the investments made by previous generations. That is, they have a "birthright," as Wolin puts it: a set of "ambiguous historical moments" to be interpreted and carried forward by citizens.[26] We cannot escape the past, neither is it clear that we should want to.

★★★

Generational Distribution. In the second approach, theorists are less concerned with questions of freedom and sovereignty and instead are focused on an explicit orientation toward distributional questions of intergenerational justice. It is an approach with roots in John Locke: "since there was still enough, and as good left; and more than the yet unprovided could use."[27] Many environmental ethicists have taken this as a problematic justification for the exploitation of natural resources. Meanwhile, Susan Liebell points out the ways in which the Lockean proviso actually sets bounds on the accumulation of property.[28] Moreover, Locke's claim that "nothing was made by God for man to spoil or destroy" provides an injunction to conserve resources for future generations.[29] In any case, while Locke was primarily concerned here with a defense of private property, many contemporary theorists take up the concern to leave "enough, and as good" in some way, but couch their work within theories of justice, developing accounts of the fair division of resources across generations, whether those resources are clean air, water, welfare state services, etc.

The most influential efforts along these lines spring from John Rawls' work. Rawls argues for the inclusion of an intergenerational perspective by imagining those in the original position as heads of families, who would "care about the well-being of some of those in the next generation."[30] Meanwhile, those heads of families would not know to which generation they belonged. Thus, the "present generation cannot do as it pleases but is bound by the principles that would be chosen in the original position to define justice between persons at different moments in time," motivated by "ties of sentiment between successive generations."[31] This mechanism was seen as sufficient to ensure fairness across generations, but in time, Rawls modifies his arguments. In *Political Liberalism*, he relies solely on inclusion of generational position in the "veil of ignorance," removing sentiment as the motivation for intergenerational cooperation:

> Consider the case of just savings: since society is a system of cooperation between generations over time, a principle for savings is required . . . the correct principle is that which the members of any generation (and so all generations) would adopt as the one their generation is to follow and as the principle they would want preceding generations to have followed.[32]

Instead of paternal affection for one's descendants, intergenerational justice comes to depend on contract and consent, just as other aspects of Rawls' distributive justice.[33]

Some scholars, like Martha Nussbaum, argue that Rawls' treatment of intergenerational justice suffices and move on.[34] Others argue that his framework is not robust enough to prevent exploitation by earlier generations and that the lack of enforceability for future people renders the theory insufficient to account for intergenerational obligations.[35] In any case, Rawls' opening into the subject of justice over time has developed into something of a subfield within philosophy.[36] Peter Laslett and James Fishkin, editors of a 1992 volume exploring the topic, offer a useful definition of intergenerational justice, which indicates the scope of the inquiry:

> It consists in an obligation on all present persons to conduct themselves in recognition of the rights of all future persons, regardless of geographical location and temporal position. No generation is at liberty to ransack the environment, or to overload the earth with more people than can be supported, or even, though this is more debatable, to act in such a way as to ensure that the human race will disappear. This duty goes beyond beneficence, the idea that it would be better to act in this way and be magnanimous to our successors. Rather, we are required so to conduct ourselves because of the rights of future persons.[37]

Thus, coming out of Rawls, there have been attempts to finish working out the details of the precise scope of such claims and how exactly justice over time could be achieved. Many authors have worked with questions of overlapping generations (that is, generations present in society at the same time but in different age cohorts) and such work has tended to focus on distribution of social welfare benefits. Other work is more concerned with distant future generations, people who do not exist when decisions that may affect them are made.[38] In the second group, many of the contributing authors to Alex Gosseries and Lukas Meyer's 2009 volume, *Intergenerational Justice*, work with or against Rawls' setup, explicitly addressing the subject of obligations between generations. These essays attempt to work out solutions to a number of familiar problems in the philosophical debates on the subject, such as the non-identity problem, appropriate discount rates, the problems of generational free-riders, or whether the issue can be seen along the lines of Marxist theories of exploitation. These theorists are not generally concerned with bringing definitive representation of future persons to existing democratic institutions, neither do they accept the possibility of just refraining from affecting the future, as Jefferson would demand. Instead, the idea here is that we can work out the justification for and scope of our obligations to the future, developing detailed frameworks that, for example, "can guide our decision-making with respect to decisions that will have an impact on both the well-being of future people as well as the composition of future people."[39] These guidelines are practical philosophy, meant to provide ways to gauge actual decision-making about spending and savings across time.[40] They acknowledge one generation's ability to shape the future and develop an account of the obligations incurred because of that ability, without necessarily trying to speak *for* the future.

This generational distribution approach has much to recommend it. Since it is where the majority of work appears these days, there is a great deal of diversity within it and a number of fruitful avenues for thinking about how to justly distribute resources across time and to reduce the *short-termism* of current institutions.[41] But questions of democratic freedom and problems of sovereignty are not generally a central focus in this literature.[42] The effort here is to work out what is *just* and with whom obligations lie, not to consider the social relations that drive conflict arising between a future-orientation, historical obligation, and democratic decision-making or rights. In this way, the just distribution approach to intergenerational dynamics often suffers from the same problems Iris Marion Young first identified with distribution approaches more generally:

> [t]he distributive paradigm tends to conceive of individuals as social atoms, logically prior to social relations and institutions . . . [and] fails to appreciate that individual identities and capacities are in many respects themselves the products of social processes and relations. Societies do not simply distribute goods to persons who are what they are apart from society, rather constitute individuals in their identities and capacities.[43]

What then happens is that even amid their own disagreements, these frameworks are able to resolve the problems rather neatly and abstractly—the present generation is obligated to consider the welfare of future generations in this or that way, for this or that reason, and to this or that extent. They offer particular solutions for distributing resources, but we hear little of what this means for the creation of democratic subjectivities, democratic processes more generally, neither do we consider the possibility that intergenerational justice could pose legitimate and irresolvable conflicts between groups, leaving us ill-prepared to deal with actual challenges posed. There is a sense that this is more of a technical question, and less a political one, waiting to be figured out by the right econometric model.

It is an aggregation of individuals at time X who owe a certain amount of resources to the group of individuals at time X+1. The lack of attention to this relationship between intergenerational justice and the desire for freedom (as sovereignty) seems to me part of the reason we have done so little to address intergenerational concerns in our contemporary political life. Because this work does not resonate in a fundamental way with our worries about our own freedom or with our aspirations to self-rule, it has not been able to inspire and motivate the sort of radical change in attitude that is required to address the existential threats our descendants now face. Ignoring both conflict and affect, the technocratic generational distribution approach yields many coherent arguments about future-oriented justice, but it does little to address the challenges that render those arguments inaudible to too many democratic citizens.

★★★

Generational Representation. With the generational sovereignty approach, we clearly see a democratic impulse at play—but we can also see how impossible this fantasy of sovereignty is. Meanwhile, the generational distribution approach underplays the tensions that the sovereignty approach captured. To account for both the conflict and the need to engage in transgenerational projects, the obvious solution is to represent future perspectives in our own democratic processes. This might be done through a number of frameworks. Consider Jürgen Habermas' work on deliberative democratic theory, in which he aimed to demonstrate the link between the formal institutions of the democratic state and the informal processes of opinion and will formation in civil society.[44] Here, democracies achieve consensus through an intersubjective discussion of experience that allows people to "harmonize" worldviews and actions. Working in this same approach, Seyla Benhabib notes:

> [d]emocracy . . . is best understood as a model for organizing the collective and public exercise of power . . . on the basis of the principle that decisions affecting the well-being of a collectivity can be viewed as the outcome of a procedure of free and reasoned deliberation among individuals considered as moral and political equals.[45]

Democracy is legitimate because it strives not just for majority rule, but for openness and rationality. All those affected by political decisions should be included in the process and given equal political rights to communicate their ideas. In this way, polities can come to valid political decisions. Intergenerational dynamics could theoretically be incorporated but pose a challenge to deliberative theories then because of the fact that not all potentially affected by the decision could possibly be included in the discussion. Some are too young, others are not yet born. While deliberative theory provides a window into how actual deliberation works and should work in democratic society, it, quite understandably, remains focused on present individuals who deliberate together, making it difficult to imagine how exactly the particular perspectives of yet-unborn groups of people might find their way into the conversation.[46]

The central problem here is one of non-existence. For philosophers, the "non-identity" problem has been discussed for years, but I'm referring to something slightly different. Generally, "non-identity" refers to the problems described by Derek Parfit—a harm must be directed toward a specific, unique person (or persons).[47] Here, the question of whether we should exploit or conserve a resource runs into the problem that the result of our choice will lead to particular individuals being born or not born—and thus render it, at least in this formulation, nonsensical to speak of harming those particular persons since their very existence is dependent on that choice. So choosing to exploit resources leads to a different set of individuals being born—individuals who would not have been born under the conservation regime and who therefore cannot be said to be harmed by the choice to exploit rather than conserve. I am not convinced that we need to spend a lot of time on this problem. Like others, I'm not persuaded that we bear no responsibility for an increase in future famine simply because particular Person C endures it (but the unique Person C would not have even been born had a famine-alleviating policy been instituted).[48] Meanwhile, non-existence does pose real, practical obstacles for democratic theorists hoping to incorporate future perspectives—and has no obvious solution. We might agree that future generations would have particular perspectives on our present deliberations, but their non-existence makes it impossible to ensure accountability for claims about their likely view of things. Various theories of democracy—not just deliberative theory, but also liberal, pluralist, republican, agonal, participatory, radical—all depend upon individuals using their power or expressing their preferences. But what of specific individuals who are unable to express preferences through voting? Or transform their own or others' opinions through deliberation? Looking to provisions for severely disabled individuals provides some possibilities.[49] Yet this assumes a level of understanding and communication from the definite existing individual. The difficulty there lies in discerning an uncommunicative individual's desire and expressing it as best one can. This cannot be the case for future individuals or cohorts—because they do not exist and no one even knows for sure that they will exist. There are no formed preferences to discern or voice, no unique who to reveal, no demotic power to claim yet. It is only a potential.

Several scholars—notably Andrew Dobson, Robyn Eckersly, Kristian Ekeli, and Robert Goodin—have begun the work of more explicitly incorporating future concerns into deliberative models.[50] Proposals by Dobson and Ekeli, for instance, call for proxy representatives to bring the perspectives of future generations to bear on deliberations within legislative bodies. While Ekeli's model differs from Dobson's in that she does not pre-emptively decide *who* gets to represent the future (Dobson suggests the representatives come from environmental sustainability advocates), both proposals remain limited by the impossibility of knowing future interests in any authoritative way. Ekeli acknowledges this issue, but holds out a few important benefits, nevertheless. Most compellingly, this new arrangement might help to make the future more "imaginatively present" in the minds of current citizens and "improve the future orientation of political institutions."[51] The problems of legitimacy—the absence of *accountability* and *authorization* (essential components of representation)—remain. As Dennis Thompson argues, however:

> [t]hey assume that to be legitimate the representatives of the future must be as much like ordinary representatives. But the attempt to make the role of the future representatives replicate as far as possible the role of the ordinary representative is bound to fall short, and consequently destined to undermine the legitimacy of the future representatives.[52]

His own idea of *democratic trusteeship* would involve a commission modeled on the ancient Roman Tribune of the Plebs, with powerful trustees, chosen from among ordinary citizens, without possibility of re-election (to make each trustee less likely to be bound to particular present interests), with a specific charge to protect the democratic *process* for future generations (rather than a particular set of specific policy goals). This would likely entail safeguarding some sort of minimum environmental, educational, and welfare standards, but it would focus primarily on checking the presentist tendencies in current democratic forms.[53]

Even if we adopt an alternative vision of representation—such as surrogate representation, which requires that we be able to justify our decisions to future citizens *as if* they were actually present,[54] or discursive representation, in which discourses—"a shared way of comprehending the world embedded in language"—are represented, rather than definite individuals or groups[55]—two closely related problems remain. First, the language of legitimacy makes it too easy to congratulate ourselves with claims that, yes, indeed, future generations would be ok with this or that policy. If we claim to *represent* the aggregated interests of future individuals *without* definite and particular voices to hold actors to account, accountability and epistemic challenges arise. We run the risk of grossly misunderstanding the future landscape and the desires of the individuals who will inhabit it, coming up with self-serving claims to know what is best for posterity. Of course, we run the risk of misunderstanding ourselves (and what is best for us) all the time too. But to *speak for* a population poses particular dangers, even when that population is alive and present. To do so when they do not yet even exist—and we cannot we know their particular set of problems, resources, and needs—further reduces our ability to speak on their behalf.[56] There also seems to be an assumption here that the interests are relatively stable and discernible—but of course interests are created, transformed, or discarded during deliberations. Moreover, future generations are not some homogenous group, marked by consensus. Instead, they are likely to disagree themselves about the best paths forward. Thus, it is not at all clear that we could just add them like any other group that needs better inclusion, since there is no possibility of actual dialogue, accountability, or enforcement.[57] On the other hand, this problem of non-existence does not remove the obligation for thinking about the welfare of future generations. The obvious solution, at least in terms of democratic theory, would be to come up with some way to incorporate the perspective or interests of future persons, as generational representational theorists do. This approach may indeed by the best way forward at this moment, when the existential threat is becoming so dire. The question then becomes: how do we come to *want* to even include the future in our representative and deliberative institutions? Before we can agree on how to do this—charging surrogates and particular institutions with representing the future or enlarging our own perspectives to include future perspectives in mainstream discussion—we have to become motivated to make the change. Second, the focus on finding individual representatives of future interests or ombudspersons reaffirms a problematic vision of the self, which is the deeper problem here. The idea of the sovereign self (which also leads to a desire for generational sovereignty) undergirds the very idea of future citizens as a distinct group who must claim particular rights and shares of resources against current citizens (and which they obviously cannot actually do because of their non-existence). Although more open to tension and social relations than most distributive approaches, the representational approach reaffirms individualist visions of subjectivity, which do little to deconstruct the ideal of sovereign mastery and atomism. The future is a competing interest group, subject to better or worse representation. "They" are separate, and therefore a potential rival. Ultimately, this approach to politics is part of the problem, as it posits a view of political life where we see ourselves as individual actors vying to achieve sovereign freedom, who must be persuaded to invite competing interests into the conversation.

★★★

While the generational sovereignty approach focuses in an almost pathological way on the freedom of generations—recognizing but largely rejecting the relationships and conflict between social groups across time—the distributional and representational views then pull back from those tensions to see generations composed of individuals who rightfully possess certain rights (to representation, to material goods). What is needed in that case is the just allocation of those resources. But what falls out is the power, processes, motivations, and tensions that mark the creation of both democratic citizens and larger society. In contrast, I argue that focusing on what type of creatures we really are, how power flows between individuals across both space and time, and how temporal position and time in turn shape the potential for both justice and democratic freedom, are critical for understanding these problems. At the most basic level, attending to intergenerational justice requires acknowledging future generations as worthy fellows. But we cannot do so because we do not see it for what it is—and we then ignore the power relations generated by that blindness. That is, we *misrecognize* the future. Charles Taylor's language provides the entry here:

> [t]he thesis is that our identity is partly shaped by recognition or its absence, often by the *mis*recognition of others, and so a person or a group of people can suffer real damage, real distortion, if the people or society around them mirror back to them a confining or demeaning or contemptible picture of themselves. Nonrecognition or misrecognition can inflict harm, can be a form of oppression, imprisoning someone in a false, distorted, and reduced mode of being.[58]

The injustice here is not just unequal distribution of wealth or other resources in society, but also in the marginalization of one's identity, or "a person's understanding of who they are, of their fundamental defining characteristics as a human being."[59] In Taylor's framework, then, the injustice of misrecognition would involve not seeing people as they really are because their membership in a particular group causes others to see them in a distorted way. In the case of future citizens, this distortion rest on invisibility—that is, in terms of not recognizing them as future fellow citizens, whose interests and needs are worthy of consideration and respect. Our view of political life focuses on the present and injustices committed against contemporaneous fellows. Of course, the current non-existence of future individuals means it seems entirely sensible that this group would remain invisible. It is not that there is some identity out there just waiting to be recognized if we could just stop making the default identity a present one. And the practical problems are obvious. But, on the flip side, is it really defensible to not grant future citizens a place at the table—any more than we can really justify the inequalities and injustices that spring from geographical accidents of birth? We *should* have a deep sense of unease about the lack of participatory parity when it comes to, say, undocumented workers in the United States *and* Generation X+60 years (or animals or other nationalities or the severely disabled).[60] So even if we can admit that the practical problems are huge and possibly unworkable, we can use this mapping to see where the injustice lies. It's not simply a matter of the fair distribution of resources or more clearly recognizing future perspectives, but also a matter of their advantageous invisibility, which can then lead to a too-radical reduction in future citizens' space for decision-making (in that we might choose to use up all the resources for ourselves, leaving them with a much more constrained array of options, not thinking they matter, or thinking that perhaps they will solve the problems we could not—a self-serving passing-the-buck that masquerades as a positive recognition).

This issue of invisibility plays out in critical ways for discussion of intergenerational justice and helps shape the seeming impossibility of addressing it. Young argues that conventional discussions of justice generally rely upon a notion of "responsibility as liability" (she proposes instead a "social connection model of responsibility").[61] That is, to be viewed as injustice, there must be a responsible agent who violates a norm or law, resulting in specific harm to an identifiable victim. Yet many harms we have an interest in mitigating are instead "structural," as Young argues:

> Structural injustice exists when social processes put large categories of persons under a systematic threat of domination or deprivation of the means to develop and exercise their capacities, at the same time as these processes enable others to dominate or have a wide range of opportunities for developing and exercising their capacities. Structural injustice is a kind of moral wrong distinct from the wrongful action of an individual agent or the willfully repressive policies of a state. Structural injustice occurs as a consequence of many individuals and institutions acting in pursuit of their particular goals and interests, within given institutional rules and accepted norms. All the persons who participate by their actions in the ongoing schemes of cooperation that constitute these structures are responsible for them, in the sense that they are part of the process that causes them. They are not responsible, however, in the sense of having directed the process or intended its outcomes.[62]

Questions of intergenerational dynamics fit well with Young's vision of structural injustice. Too much remains invisible if we are focused on identifying individual agents and victims. Moreover, intergenerational injustice often springs from the very background conditions of our lives. As in Young's account, there is often no direct relationship between the actions of a specific responsible party and the harm. Moreover, actions producing the harm are not necessarily deviations from acceptable norms. For example, our aggregated, everyday actions—driving our gasoline-powered cars to Town Meetings, school pickups, our jobs—help produce a harm—climate change—that will significantly impact the abilities of future generations to exercise their capacities, whether considered in terms of their enhanced vulnerability to severe weather events (and therefore their physical survival) or their need to focus political energies on addressing this issue, rather than others. These are daily activities that fall within the range of accepted norms.[63] But over time, they will lead to the "deprivation of the means to develop and exercise their capacities." And, as Jade Schiff argues, drawing on Young's work, these qualities of structural injustice render it invisible to most people.[64] Philosophers might figure out the most just discount rate or lay out what we need to do to represent future citizens (or the need to address both recognition and distribution), but how do we motivate contemporary citizens to see the injustice and to change their everyday practices? Why would a person come to see that connection, when the relations are so distant and one's own role in the harm so seemingly indirect—and the solutions require one to change otherwise acceptable modes of daily life?

Patchen Markell's critique of the politics of recognition offers a stepping stone to an alternative.[65] The problem is that the way we have gone about demands for justice springs from a fundamental misunderstanding about the nature of political life and our relationship to one another. Markell notes that:

> [e]very attempt to specify the set of agents to whom an issue of justice pertains will itself, as an act of identification and recognition, be a potential site of injustice . . . and, second, even among agents who already have standing within a jurisdiction, every appeal to the identity as a settled criterion of distribution will likewise be a potential site of (nondistributive) injustices, both because existing patterns of identity and difference may bear the traces of past wrongs, and even more fundamentally because those people for whom justice is a live issue are not done becoming who they are; or, better, who they will turn out to have been.[66]

To distribute or identify *definitively* is to risk further injustice. This in no way absolves us from addressing obligations and questions of harm. But it does redirect our focus:

> [t]he pursuit of recognition involves "misrecognition" of a different and deeper kind: not the misrecognition of an identity, either one's own or someone else's, but the misrecognition of one's own fundamental situation or circumstances . . . I offer an alternative diagnosis of relations of social and political subordination, which sees them not [as] failures by some people to recognize others' identities, but . . . ways of patterning and arranging the world that allow some people and groups to enjoy a semblance of sovereign agency at others' expense.[67]

This sovereign agency at another's expense is the same sovereignty Jefferson tries to demand for each generation, yet which remains impossible. Our desire to control our lives and create a life invulnerable to forces outside of ourselves leads us to close ourselves off from the unpredictability of others and maintain a fiction of invulnerability. Markell does not speak of the future, concerned only with intersubjectivity in the present. But his particular approach is well-suited to the problem at hand. In terms of future generations, we might begin to note how—similar to the ways in which we are politically dependent upon the plurality that exists here and now—we are also deeply affected by the past and always re-enacting those dynamics of inheritance for the future. The invisibility of the future might instead be seen as a privilege the present maintains—a "psychological wage" in W.E.B. DuBois' terms—that helps maintain the fiction of generational sovereignty Jefferson craved. The invisibility of the future perhaps also tempers our own frustration at inheriting a deeply flawed world that demands our focus, limiting our freedom by imposing unchosen burdens and obligations, specific (even if interpretable, as in Wolin's telling) birthrights and sometimes dubious benefits. We take what we inherit because we must, but we erase that fact, denying its power over us, and proceeding in our pursuits as if the present citizens were the only ones who matter (or as if they are sufficient trustees of an inevitably better future). This stance toward our own condition as members of both spatial and temporal communities helps to sustain the structural injustices that future generations will experience. Thus, instead of looking at the issue of intergenerational justice as practically impossible because of the non-existence of future individuals, we should instead look at what advantage and privilege this erasure serves. We subordinate the future to the present, not simply because it is the correct thing to do given their non-existence, but because the benefits are so desirable. It allows us some sense of freedom and mastery we would otherwise have to relinquish. In Markell's terms, it is "social subordination [that] . . . involves closing off some people's practical possibilities for the sake of other people's sense of mastery or invulnerability; and it is the exploitative character of this relationship . . . that makes it unjust."[68] Thus, that frustration with the intersubjective nature of political life, which helps to sustain the invisibility of the future and the structural harms they will face, extends across the democratic landscape. Consider the great frustration induced by the fact that democracy promises freedom, yet citizens are not only constrained by the choices of contemporaneous others, but also by the choices made generations before their own time. As Danielle Allen notes:

> [d]emocracies inspire in citizens an aspiration to rule and yet require citizens constantly to live with the fact that they do not. Democracies must find methods to help citizens deal with the conflict between their politically inspired desires for total agency and the frustrating reality of their experience.[69]

The problem is not just about the future, but about all democratic citizens and the desire to get a semblance of sovereign freedom.

Thus, intergenerational politics is not simply a matter of understanding more clearly the identity of the future generations or figuring out what they are fairly owed in terms of distribution of resources. It is fundamentally a matter of coming to terms with our own situation, with respect to our own past and our own desires for the future (or, at least, our belief in our ability to shape the future). This means being more comfortable with our own vulnerability. Markell argues:

> [d]emocratic justice does not require that all people be known and respected as who they really are. It requires, instead, that no one be reduced to any characterization of his or her identity for the sake of someone else's achievement of a sense of sovereignty or invulnerability, regardless of whether that characterization is negative or positive, hateful or friendly . . .

> It demands that each of us bear our share of the burden and risk involved in the uncertain, open-ended, sometimes maddeningly and sometimes joyously surprising activity of living and interacting with other people.[70]

To live with the reality of temporal intersubjectivity means we must come to terms with conflict, unpredictability, and alienation in our own political life—both with present others and with our inherited world, as well as our own frustration with our own vulnerability and the radical unpredictability and boundlessness of the future. It is a function of each generation opening itself to the presence of others, which means understanding ourselves, our limits, and the ramifications of Jefferson's aspiration to sovereign freedom. And throughout his critique of the politics of recognition, Markell suggests an alternative to recognition—acknowledgment:

> Acknowledgement is in the first instance self- rather than other-directed; its object is not one's own identity but one's own basic ontological condition or circumstances, particularly one's own finitude; this finitude is to be understood as a matter of one's practical limits in the face of an unpredictable and contingent future, not as a matter of the impossibility or injustice of knowing others; and, finally, acknowledgement involves coming to terms with, rather than vainly attempting to overcome, the risk of conflict, hostility, misunderstanding, opacity, and alienation that characterizes life among others.[71]

In this formulation, then, accepting temporal intersubjectivity would not just require an extension of more recognition, representation, or resources. Instead, it begins with an attempt to dismantle our own generational privilege and to come to terms with our own actual vulnerability to others—both in the present and across time. What, then, is it that maintains the present's privilege and the future's subordination?

★★★

My central claim is that the inability to seriously confront questions of intergenerational justice, especially as they pertain to as-yet-nonexistent future generations, springs from our own misunderstanding of both the individual and of democratic action. Attending to future generations implies responsibility and limits on what we may do—on our freedom. But the foundational promise of democracy in the contemporary era is one of (a particular kind of) freedom. That is, democracy is worth having because it provides individuals with the freedom to chart the course of their own lives—and that freedom is conceived of in sovereign terms. Although it is most obvious in the Jeffersonian approach, all three modes of attending to intergenerational justice I have reviewed reinforce a sovereigntist view (of the individual and of each generation). Future-oriented justice remains only a willingly donned yoke, an optional addition to the array of perspectives to include in deliberations and resource calculations. Perhaps even more troubling, in the generational sovereignty approach, current generations are actually absolved from taking responsibility to bequeath anything better to future generations (just as they are prohibited from worsening conditions—as if inaction did neither). Instead, the individual retains his freedom, conceived of as the right to control the world around him or her (even if only during his particular and finite time on earth).

Before critiquing this idea of freedom, I also want to note the implicit claims about time that serve to shore up our comfort with these perspectives on intergenerational relations. In all these modes, there is a particular temporal regime, one based on notions of linear time and inevitable progress. Choices made now are often justified by the future benefits that the passage of time will surely bring about. That is, we can feel pretty good about our political decisions and their effect on future generations because we operate within a mental frame of expected progress. According to Smita Rahman:

> "Our time" is a progressive and sequential time, linear in form, where the past is succeeded by a present, which is then enveloped by the future. It draws on Christian traditions from which it adopts its metaphorical linearity, a straight line from Genesis to the Day of Judgment. It is in some ways the legacy of the modern—our contemporary understanding of it having less to do with an awareness of the Christian tradition that gave rise to it, than with familiar notions of historical development, inexorable progress, technological advancement, and forward motion generally. It is a concept of time that orders the messy events of our lives into a straight line—an irreversible current, always moving us toward the promise of an end of history, or a more enlightened age, or some sundry teleological end.[72]

For example, when we operate within progressivist frames, we miss the contingency and the struggle that marks democratic political life. Instead, Rahman encourages an appreciation of the "out of joint-ness" of time and an awareness of how past, present, and future "rub up against each other." In this view, "the present moment is therefore not simply one more point along the vector of time; it is also a moment that is pregnant with the past and that anticipates and therefore contains the future."[73] But it is not a preconceived or assured future. This is a matter of political choices and power—and can lead to any number of formations, progressive or not. The democratic use of freedom does not guarantee any political outcome, but instead only an array of possible achievements, dependent upon "contingent arrangements of relations that occur over time."[74] By disrupting this particular understanding of time—and the background assumption of inevitable progress that it sneaks in—we will be better able to move beyond the current perspectives on intergenerational justice, and the foundation of sovereignty underlying them.

I should also make clear that "freedom" as used here is that it is a multifaceted concept, centered around a person's ability to make choices and to recognize those choices in the world. That is, "agency thus has both an efficacy side and an identity side. The efficacy side distinguishes agency from mere willing—or dreaming."[75] Freedom so conceived has an inherently public quality, but remains rooted in the desiring individual. Both sides get complicated quickly: Where does desire come from? How efficacious must one be for it to count as free action—full control over the world outside of an individual's mental arena? An ability to act without interference, domination, or oppression by others? Equal opportunity to participate in the creation of the world?

But this is to get somewhat ahead of the argument—we must first make clear the dangers dominant understandings of freedom pose to attempts to think through intergenerational justice. Hannah Arendt's genealogy of freedom is especially useful here, and will no doubt be familiar to many readers.[76] According to her, freedom began for the ancient Greeks as an outwardly focused exercise—a performance akin to that of dancers or singers, who rely on their audience for reception—and becomes inwardly focused in terms of free will, as the Western tradition moves out of the polis and into a Christian and then modern Europe. Arendt wants to salvage this earlier notion, arguing, "without [freedom], political life as such would be meaningless. The *raison d'être* of politics is freedom."[77] Arendt here means that politics is "the realm where freedom is a worldly reality," as opposed to the freedom of the philosopher's mind or the Christian's inner dialogue with himself.[78] In order to be free, a person needs a community in which to act, to make an impression upon the world outside herself and begin new things. The sense of freedom in our contemporary era, however, has moved to this inner freedom—and it has become so completely naturalized that "we find it difficult to realize that there may exist a freedom which is not an attribute of the will but an accessory of doing and acting."[79] This seemingly necessary understanding of freedom as a lack of constraint on one's inner self then sets the foundation for our current vision of freedom-as-sovereignty:

> Freedom was no longer experienced in acting and in associating with others but in willing and in the intercourse with one's self, when, briefly, freedom had become free will . . . the ideal of freedom ceased to be virtuosity . . . and became sovereignty, the idea of a free will, independent from others and eventually prevailing against them.[80]

Sovereignty here means "uncompromising self-sufficiency and mastership" and, for Arendt, "is contradictory to the very condition of plurality."[81] This contradiction is not because we are weak and therefore cannot achieve what we want on our own—that's another myth of the ideal of sovereignty—but because freedom-as-mastery requires vanquishing all other wills that have not fully aligned with one's own. Thus, not only is it practically impossible (for all but a very few exceptionally powerful individuals) to carry through one's intentions with absolutely no help from others, but it's also an assault on the very idea of freedom, because doing so requires forcing others to cease being spontaneous and unpredictable themselves. For Arendt (and others):[82]

> [t]his identification of freedom with sovereignty is perhaps the most pernicious and dangerous consequence of the philosophical equation of freedom and free will. For it leads either to a denial of human freedom—namely, if it is realized that whatever men may be, they are never sovereign—or to the insight that the freedom of one man, or a group, or a body politic can be purchased only at the price of the freedom, i.e., the sovereignty, of all others.[83]

One word of caution here: it is not the case that the idea of freedom as control over others is absent from the earlier ancient Greek material, as many others have noted and as Chapter 3 will make clear. Indeed, freedom often meant ruling over others—non-Greek, slaves, women, children.[84] Acting in concert with others is a view of freedom that Arendt wants to recover. But it is not one which was simply replaced by freedom-as-sovereignty with the rise of Christianity. It had already co-existed with other views, just as in our own time. Moreover, to valorize the ancient Athenians as having a "better" sort of freedom seems to me hopelessly nostalgic—and nothing blinds to the future quite like an overblown affection for the past. What is attractive in Arendt's story, however, is its *story*; she offers a different vision of what freedom might mean. In that case, recourse to Greek texts here is sort of incidental—I am not reading them because they offer some sort of salvation from liberal individualism, although they can illuminate alternatives at times. I will also read the Greek plays to illustrate the dangers of freedom-as-control (especially control over the future), so obviously I see the works as containing something at least analogous to our contemporary notions of freedom-as-sovereignty. Regardless, many commentators have picked up on Arendt's critique of freedom-as-sovereignty, especially in recent years. With this book, I join this chorus, bringing an intergenerational, temporal perspective to the critique.

The term "sovereignty" itself has deep roots within the Western tradition and was first explicitly articulated by Jean Bodin. Like "freedom," the term is complex and debated, containing multiple meanings. It circulates within International Relations to refer to state control over territory, but has also surged forward more recently as an object of critique for those working on democratic theory, specifically problems of individual agency and political responsibility. The basic idea is that the sovereign—whether the self, the demos, or the state—acts with final and irresistible authority. The sovereign is *free* to act and is released from accountability to others. As Joan Cocks writes:

> To command instead of being commanded, to possess an effectual will instead of meekly bowing to a master, to control the conditions of one's existence instead of being at the mercy of alien forces, to shine with the dignity of a sovereign self instead of living in shadow of another's grandeur, to corral the state to serve one's own needs and interests instead of being exploited or neglected by those who monopolize state power: these desires have proved so compelling that, except for a few intellectual skeptics, sovereignty today is widely seen as the prerequisite and inner substance of a freely lived life.[85]

Over time, sovereignty has come to define and subsume our vision of freedom on almost every level—individual, demotic, state, and generational. Just as the concept has animated political theory for many years, the critique of sovereignty is not new.[86] The death of sovereignty has been upon us for so long, one wonders why it retains such a tenacious and problematic hold on our democratic imagination. Is it built into us as humans? Or, do we live in a context that shapes us into thinking this is the only way to be? Joan Cock's position is that "such a will is a highly mediated form of an elemental desire of [the] human being to survive and thrive in an environment not initially made *by* them, but waiting *for* them."[87] That is, there is a human desire to interact with the world, but its character has not been pre-determined. Meanwhile, Anker argues that post-9/11 political discourse—a distinctly melodramatic genre—in the US (re)produces this desire for sovereign freedom, linking the aspiration to individual sovereignty with claims to sovereign state power. In her view:

> The norm of freedom that circulates in melodramatic political discourse is rooted in particularly liberal and Americanized interpretations of freedom as self-reliance, as unconstrained agency, and as unbound subjectivity. It combines these interpretations together as normative expressions of a sovereign subject, one who obeys no other authority but one's own, who can determine the future and control the vagaries of contingency through sheer strength of will . . . This version of sovereignty implies that the state—and by extension the individual citizen—should not be free *from* the coercions of others but also free *over* others. This latter freedom, though seldom explicitly acknowledged, is what ensures the possibility of the former.[88]

A particular constellation of factors produces this desire for freedom *as sovereignty*, and paradoxically links that individual aspiration with a willingness to empower state authority over individuals. Although he prefers to salvage the idea of sovereignty, Ali Aslam also makes this connection, noting how the reduction of space for collective-worldmaking has left us with an impoverished, state-centered notion of sovereignty that estranges the citizen from political life. "The experience of political freedom that democratic citizens found in popular sovereignty has been sacrificed to safeguard what remains of state sovereignty . . . devitalized forms of sovereignty cleave connotations of self-authorization from the concept, leaving only the idea of sovereignty as autonomy."[89] Thus, the desire for freedom ends up with a narrow range of expression—here, individualist—which only serves to exacerbate a "deep sense of impasse and devitalized agency."[90] The will to freedom can find no collective, solidaristic expression and so focuses on freedom as self-legislation—which is then thwarted by the massive forces of contemporary governance and neoliberalism that currently value domination and control over fluid, unpredictable interaction.

Becoming aware of this as a *story*, rather than a founding reality, is key. Expanding on the idea of the self as a historically specific construction, Sylvia Wynter's critical race theory work on "genres of humanity" further helps us to appreciate the ways in which humanity is a "hybrid-auto-instituting language-storytelling species" that remains unaware of its own hybrid *bios/mythos* origin (and which has historically celebrated the domination of others).[91] In this view, the seemingly irrepressible drive for sovereignty can more clearly be seen as a *genre* of being human—a particularly Western *performance* that is embodied, gendered, classed, raced, and sexualized. This is a *story*—a *mythos*—we have been told and which we re-tell about the types of beings we are—and which then shapes the genre of human we praise and become. As Anker shows, it is repeated in our civic discourse through melodrama. We also see it in our popular culture—from social media (celebrity Instagram accounts curated with filtered images of bodily perfection) to film (*Castaway*, *Gravity*, *The Revenant*) to music lyrics (Beyoncé's "Formation"). It is, in Wynter's terms, a *praxis*, rather than a descriptive noun. In other words, there is no ontological human drive to sovereign power; it's simply a story we have told over and over again until it seems like *the* natural and normal way to be a human. The question then becomes: How to radically transform this *praxis*? Could we look to other embodiments for alternatives? Looking around the politico-aesthetic landscape, there do not seem to be many alternative stories about the types of people we are or how the practice of freedom is actually not reducible to the free imposition of one's unfettered will. Of course—and as Chapters 3 to 5 will show—the actual material conditions of many people's lives belie this story. Once we look to the dependency and care relations that mark human lives, the reality of distributed agency—as opposed to sovereign power—is clear. Indeed, the sovereignty claim is a "degeneration of self–other relations" that only *appears* unassailable or natural.[92]

This critique of sovereignty in Anker and Cocks focuses on contemporaneous self-other relations. Bringing a temporal perspective to the problem here helps expand our understanding of the dangers of sovereignty and, I hope, directs us to alternative imaginaries. Just as the sovereign individual identifies only with itself, the sovereign generation does the same, ignoring the claims of the past, and attempting to control the future. Only then can the sovereignty-obsessed present experience this version of freedom. And once that self-identification (and other-abnegation) occurs, then sovereignty over children and future generations is understood to be a given.[93] Our patriarchal notions of generational rights over the future foreclose the possibility of recognizing the interdependence among generations—between the past, present, and future—just as it limits our ability to see interdependence among humans (and between humans and nature—another compounding problem for any attempt to address the most pressing intergenerational challenge now, climate change).

At what cost to the future do we hold on to this notion of sovereign freedom? How else might we chip away at its seeming power? The presentist aspects of the sovereignty ideal mean that we are making choices in the present with little care for the potential limits on future generations imposed by those choices. In fact, our effort to command the present often seems like a desire to control the future. But both the command and control functions here are myths, borne of a particular and problematic understanding of self and community. Our belief in the legitimacy of our own generational sovereignty, itself a sedimented by-product of individualist and state sovereignty ideals—cuts us off from the possibility of engaging with the reality of finitude and time. We see the present moment as a bounded whole, imposing order on a chaotic march of time, overlapping generations, distant futures, and receding pasts.

Instead of holding fast to a notion of masterful control as a necessary condition for freedom, we must move to an attention to plurality as the fundamental condition of our political lives—which means accepting the unpredictability of our action in the world. In this way, freedom becomes the result of doing things in the world—a world populated by other, unique, uncontrolled, and unknown individuals over time, meaning that our action is only a continuously unfolding and potentially boundless contribution to larger processes. An individual is not powerful because he or she is able to undertake projects alone, willing the world to exist as he or she wants it to exist. A generation is not powerful because it can ignore the past, discard historical legacies, and fashion whatever it cares to fashion, without regard for the obligations it thereby imposes on future generations. That delusion—built upon the domination and misrecognition of others—leads to both micro- and macro-scale destruction.

Excepting the temporal aspects, these critiques of sovereignty are fairly well-known at this point, if not widely accepted in the popular democratic imagination. Both Markell and Sharon Krause, among others, have persuasively taken apart this ideal of sovereignty and offered compelling alternatives. For Markell, the key is beginning—not self-sufficiency and mastership or command and control.[94] Freedom is recognizable as a moment that calls for responsiveness from others, not control over results and other individuals. For Krause, agency is detached from sovereignty and is the "affirmation of one's subjective existence or personal identity through concrete action in the world. To be an agent is to have an impact on the world that one can recognize as one's own."[95] That is, a person recognizes their own part in the world, seeing their action as an expression of their individuality, but without a presumption of control. Although I'm largely persuaded by their arguments (and I do not mean to suggest that Markell and Krause agree), this question of individual agency needs revisiting—and temporal expansion. That is, this is a particular genre of human that engages only our presentist and sovereign notions of time and power. Critiquing this view does not mean we are never individual selves or cannot claim responsibility for any actions or are somehow guilty of actions that predate us. Agency becomes a sense of involvement (instead of control), offering us a more apt description of our actual relationship to the future and a way to critique highly individualistic notions of freedom (that too easily slide into presentist, sovereigntist positions). Our agency is distributed over time and across individuals and collectives, which both expands our range of responsibilities and places individuals into larger networks with greater potentials for political action. Of course, my approach remains an individualist one in many respects. Actually, I want it both ways—breaking down the lone, atomistic individual that undergirds notions of sovereign power but also retaining a commitment to individual agency and responsibility. I think that rather than being contradictory, my middle ground only seems untenable if you haven't noticed something different. And the fact is, our imagination is taken from a very specific ableist, masculine experience or genre of human. Like Athena in the *Eumenides*, we often side with the (idealized) male in all things, even when all of our actual lived experience tells us we are not sovereign, atomized individuals. What if we identify with the child, the mother, the dependent?

In the end, what I want to move forward is an understanding of plurality as extending not only across space but also across time—and push contemporaneous citizens to consider the possibility of freedom-enhancing practices for future generations. The insistence on control in order to claim responsibility is precisely one of the ways in which we are able to avoid the most pressing intergenerational crisis we now face: climate change is too often seen to be out of our control. To be free means to be in control, to be able to assert one's will in the actual world, to make things happen in some permanent way. And the freest is the one able to make all this happen on his own—the lone cowboy, the action movie hero, the independent self-made titan. Western ideas about the individual tend to deny our embodiment, our placement in time, our interdependence, and the normative goodness of our vulnerability. Our aspiration to this particular sort of freedom leads us to idealize a problematic sense of self—an individual sovereign (although this, of course, depends on one's status—generally white, male, and able-bodied; otherwise, one is assumed to be self-abnegating to the point of erasure). This individual aspiration is mapped onto our understanding of time and generations. That is, the legitimacy of one generation's authority over their own time is rarely questioned. The potential infinitude of action is not viewed as cause for alarm, transformation, or responsibility. Our particular intellectual inheritance has led to a conflation of freedom—the promise of democracy—with sovereign power that brooks no intergenerational linkage that it does not itself desire. And this problematic vision of freedom pretty much dominates the entire landscape—as Anker argues, "the language of individualism often exhausts contemporary American understandings of power, freedom, and agency, and thus dedifferentiates all other ways that power functions to shape individuals."[96] In the case here, freedom-as-sovereignty for one generation will mean denying past and future generations their freedom, because it will drive that one generation to a desire to prevail over others, fully controlling their own generation's circumstances (impossible because we inherit the very conditions of our present from the past) and masterfully commanding future outcomes (impossible because we will die and must pass on the world to the future). Indeed, that victory can feel quite real—but that is only temporal illusion since we are only briefly in the company of past and future, and then with only those nearest to us temporally. And even when we try to do better—to fairly distribute resources over time or to represent future perspectives, our alternatives rely on the bedrock of sovereign individuals, which leaves us only with those present now, who must be reasonably persuaded to consent to limits on their freedom. As long as we remain committed to the idea of freedom as *control*, as sovereignty, rather than the more democratic opportunity for response or participation in collective world-making, then we can never open ourselves to the future. Because that is precisely what the future must be—a (relatively) free opportunity to take up the givenness of the world and respond to it in unique, unpredictable ways.

Notes

1 Regardless, there is a significant body of popular work devoted to the general idea of the future. This includes not just science fiction authors such as Octavia Butler, *Kindred* (Boston, MA: Beacon Press, 1979) and *Lillith's Brood* (New York: Aspect, 2000) and Kim Stanley Robinson, *Green Earth: The Science in the Capital* (New York: Del Rey, 2015), but also non-fiction work of futurists like Alvin Toffler, *Future Shock* (New York: Bantam, 1984) and Jaron Lanier, *Who Owns the Future* (New York: Simon & Schuster, 2013). Whereas the science fiction tends to treat issues of power, sacrifice, and community in explicit ways, the non-fiction futurist work tends to focus on technological change and economic trends. Of course, there are political implications to that, but I have found these works focus mostly on how those reading the book can weather coming transformations and find economic security in a new type of economy. The future is less about other generations and what might be owed by one generation to another, and more about prescient individuals adapting to new circumstances.

2 Whereas I'm focused here on the case of intergenerational dynamics as it pertains to the future, work focused on the past has been concerned with working out how to best address historical injustice, the role of collective memory, the possibilities of reparations, and so on. See, for example, Lukas H. Meyer, ed. *Justice in Time: Responding to Historical Injustice* (Baden-Baden, Germany: Nomos, 2004); Jon Miller and Rahul Kumar, eds. *Reparations: Interdisciplinary Inquiries* (Oxford, UK: Oxford University Press, 2007); Jeff Spinner-Halev, *Enduring Injustice* (New York: Cambridge University Press, 2012). Spinner-Halev's work helpfully bridges this distinction, connecting the past with the present and future by arguing that it is the *enduring* quality of the injustices that merit attention. Also, feminist theorists, especially Mary O'Brien, *The Politics of Reproduction*

(Boston, MA: Routledge and Kegan Paul, 1981), as well as those concerned with care ethics, have long attended to intergenerational themes and a concern for future individuals (see, for example, Joan Tronto, *Caring Democracy*, New York: NYU Press, 2013).
3 Ernest Partridge, ed. *Responsibilities to Future Generations: Environmental Ethics* (Buffalo, NY: Prometheus Books, 1981); Jonathan Schell. *The Fate of the Earth and the Abolition* (Stanford, CA: Stanford University Press, 2000/1982); R. I. Sikora and Brian Barry, eds. *Obligations to Future Generations* (Philadelphia, PA: Temple University Press, 1978).
4 Schell, *The Fate of the Earth and the Abolition*, 17.
5 Claudine Attius-Donfut and Sara Arber, eds. *The Myth of Generational Conflict: The Family and State in Ageing Societies* (New York: Routledge, 2000); Paul Johnson, Christoph Conrad, and David Thomson, eds. *Workers Versus Pensioners* (New York: St. Martin's Press, 1989); Lawrence Kotlikoff and Scott Burns. *The Coming Generational Storm: What You Need to Know about America's Economic Future* (Cambridge, MA: MIT Press, 2005); Peter Laslett and James S. Fishkin, eds. *Justice between Age Groups and Generations* (New Haven, CT: Yale University Press, 1992); Thomas Lindh, Bo Malmberg, and Joakim Palme, "Generations at War or Sustainable Social Policy in Ageing Societies?" *The Journal of Political Philosophy* 13, no. 4 (2005): 470–89; David Thomson, *Selfish Generations? How Welfare States Grow Old* (Wellington, New Zealand: White Horse Press, 1996).
6 See, for example, Brian Barry, *Justice as Impartiality* (New York: Oxford University Press, 1995); Andrew Dobson, ed. *Fairness and Futurity: Essays on Environmental Sustainability and Social Justice* (New York: Oxford University Press, 1999); John Barry and Marcel Wissenburg, *Sustaining Liberal Democracy* (New York: Palgrave, 2001); Robyn Eckersley and Andrew Dobson, eds. *Political Theory and the Environmental Challenge* (Cambridge, UK: Cambridge University Press, 2006).
7 See, for example, Iñigo González-Ricoy and Axel Gosseries, eds. *Institutions for Future Generations* (New York: Oxford University Press, 2016) or Alex Gosseries and Lukas H. Meyer, eds. *Intergenerational Justice* (New York: Oxford University Press, 2009). See also Simon Caney, "Two Kinds of Climate Justice: Avoiding Harm and Sharing Burdens," *Journal of Political Philosophy* 22, no. 2 (June 2014): 125–49.
8 Some may argue that the present has no obligation whatsoever to the future. Yet the academic literature on these questions is fairly unified—because of our inability to neatly demarcate either generations themselves or the issues that span generations, most scholars considering such questions argue that the present generation does in fact hold some obligation to the future. The underlying logic, the scope, and the means of addressing it are what vary in the three approaches I discuss here. At the same time, in fact, the logic of generational sovereignty approach will turn out to be dangerously close to the no-obligation position after all.
9 Dennis F. Thompson, "Representing Future Generations: Political Presentism and Democratic Trusteeship," *Critical Review of International and Political Philosophy* 13, no. 1 (2010): 17–37.
10 The question of "time" brought up by my use of "temporal continuum" is an important one. Is there in fact a continuum? Is it linear? Or just experienced as linear? As Smita Rahman argues, there are particular and culturally specific regimes of time—that is, the "rhythms of lived experience." Her critique of these regimes and effort to recover a space for an "out of joint" experience of time is one to which I will return in later chapters. See Smita A. Rahman, *Time, Memory, and the Politics of Contingency* (New York: Routledge, 2014).
11 Thomas Jefferson, *Political Writings* (New York: Cambridge University Press, 1999), 593.
12 Ibid., 596.
13 Ibid.
14 Ibid., 593.
15 Ibid., 599.

16 See Victor M. Muñiz-Fraticelli, "The Problem of Perpetual Constitution," in *Intergenerational Justice*, eds. Axel Gosseries and Lukas Meyer, 377–410.
17 Jefferson, *Political Writings*, 596.
18 Muñiz-Fraticelli, "The Problem of Perpetual Constitution," 386.
19 Ibid., 387.
20 Thomas Jefferson's 1814 Letter to Edward Coles illustrates the tragedy of this position. When pressed by Coles to support emancipation, Jefferson includes this note: "No, I have overlived the generation with which mutual labors & perils begat mutual confidence and influence. This enterprise is for the young; for those who can follow it up, and bear it through to its consummation. It shall have all my prayers, & these are the only weapons of an old man" (August 25, 1814).
21 Janna Thompson, *Intergenerational Justice: Rights and Responsibilities in an Intergenerational Polity* (New York: Routledge Press, 2009), 7.
22 Edmund Burke, *Reflections on the Revolution in France* (London: Penguin, 2004), 194–5.
23 Timothy Morton, *Hyperobjects: Philosophy and Ecology after the End of the World* (Minneapolis, MN: University of Minnesota, 2013), 1.
24 See Jeff Spinner-Halev, *Enduring Injustice*.
25 See Janna Thompson, "Identity and Obligation in a Transgenerational Polity," in *Intergenerational Justice*, eds. Axel Gosseries and Lukas H. Meyer, 33–8.
26 Sheldon Wolin, *The Presence of the Past: Essays on the State and the Constitution* (Baltimore, MD: The Johns Hopkins University Press, 1989), 141.
27 John Locke, *Second Treatise of Government* (Indianapolis, IN: Hackett, 1980), Chapter V, Paragraph 33.
28 Susan Liebell, "The Text and Context of 'Enough and as Good': John Locke as the Foundation of an Environmental Liberalism," *Polity* 43, no. 2 (April 2011): 210–41.
29 Locke, *Second Treatise of Government*, Chapter V, Paragraph 31.
30 John Rawls, *A Theory of Justice* (Cambridge, MA: The Belknap Press of Harvard University Press, 1971), 128. According to Rawls, people would be assumed to be in the same generation as it stretches "fantasy too far" to imagine all possible persons across time (139).
31 Ibid., 293, 292.
32 John Rawls, *Political Liberalism* (New York: Columbia University Press, 1993), 274.
33 Ibid., 273–4. For more, see Bryan Norton, "Intergenerational Equity and Environmental Decisions: A Model Using Rawls' Veil of Ignorance," *Ecological Economics* 1, no. 2 (May 1989): 137–59.
34 Martha C. Nussbaum, *Frontiers of Justice: Disability, Nationality, Species Membership* (Cambridge, MA: The Belknap Press of Harvard University Press, 2006), 23.
35 David Heyd, "A Value or an Obligation? Rawls on Justice to Future Generations," in *Intergenerational Justice*, eds. Axel Gosseries and Lukas H. Meyer, 167–88.
36 That is, discussions of justice (rather than the more specific "intergenerational justice" work) often lack what James Fishkin and Peter Laslett refer to as a "processional" perspective or what Janna Thompson refers to as a "diachronic" perspective (Peter Laslett and James S. Fishkin, "Introduction: Processional Justice," *Justice between Age Groups and Generations*, eds. Peter Laslett and James S. Fishkin, 1–23).
37 Ibid., 15.
38 See for example, Peter Laslett and James Fishkin, eds. *Justice between Age Groups and Generations*; Derek Parfit, *Reasons and Persons* (Oxford, UK: Clarendon Press, 1987); Brian Barry, *Theories of Justice* (Berkeley, CA: University of California Press, 1989); R. I. Sikora and Brian Barry, eds. *Obligations to Future Generations* (Philadelphia, PA: Temple University Press, 1978).
39 Lukas H. Meyer and Dominic Roser, "Enough for the Future," *Intergenerational Justice*, eds. Axel Gosseries and Lukas H. Meyer, 219.

40 See, for example, the Intergenerational Foundation's York Conference in September 2013, where "The main goal of the conference is to discuss different conceptions of intergenerational justice and their concrete implications for policy-oriented issues" www.if.org.uk/york-conference-2013 (last accessed January 28, 2017).
41 See Ricoy and Gosseries, eds., *Institutions for Future Generations*. This volume includes pieces across the distributional and representational approaches to intergenerational justice.
42 The exception to this, at least in the Gosseries and Meyer volume, is the essay by Victor Muñiz-Fraticelli, which works more explicitly as a response to the Jeffersonian claims of generational sovereignty.
43 Iris Marion Young, *Justice and the Politics of Difference* (Princeton, NJ: Princeton University Press, 1990): 27.
44 Jürgen Habermas, *On the Pragmatics of Social Interaction: Preliminary Studies in the Theory of Communicative Action* (Cambridge, MA: MIT Press, 2001); *Between Facts and Norms: Contributions to a Discourse Theory of Law and Democracy* (Cambridge, MA: MIT Press, 1996); *A Theory of Communicative Action, Vol. 2, Lifeworld and System: A Critique of Functionalist Reason* (Boston, MA: Beacon Press, 1987); *A Theory of Communicative Action, Vol. 1, Reason and the Rationalization of Society* (Boston, MA: Beacon Press, 1984).
45 Seyla Benhabib, "Toward a Deliberative Model of Democratic Legitimacy," in *Democracy and Difference: Contesting the Boundaries of the Political*, ed. Seyla Benhabib (Princeton, NJ: Princeton University Press, 1996), 68.
46 At the same time, Habermas has devoted a great deal of thought to considering the meaning of historical legacies. See, for example, his engagement in the *Historikerstreit*, his work on the "postnational constellation" (*The Postnational Constellation*, Cambridge, MA: MIT Press, 2001), or his reflections on the role of religion in public life (with Joseph Ratzinger, *On the Dialectics of Secularization*, San Francisco, CA: Ignatius Press, 2006), as well as the complications of genetic intervention for future generations (*The Future of Human Nature*, New York: Polity, 2003). I limit my critique here to the general presentism of deliberative democratic theory. For a discussion of the "unresolved tensions" between "universal-democratic norms and atoning remembrance . . . of the past" in Habermas, see W. James Booth, "Communities of Memory: On Identity, Memory, and Debt," *American Political Science Review* 93, no. 2 (June 1999): 249–63.
47 Derek Parfit, *Reasons and Persons*. See also Gregory Kavka, "The Paradox of Future Individuals," *Philosophy and Public Affairs* 11, no. 2 (Spring 1982): 93–112.
48 See also Kristian Skagen Ekeli, "Giving a Voice to Posterity: Deliberative Democracy and Representation of Future People," *Journal of Agricultural and Environmental Ethics* 18 (2005): 444.
49 Stacy Clifford, "Making Disability Public in Deliberative Democracy," *Contemporary Political Theory* 11 (2012): 211–28.
50 Andrew Dobson, "Representative Democracy and the Environment," *Democracy and the Environment*, ed. W. Lafferty and J. Meadowcroft (Cheltenham, UK: Edward Elgar, 1996), 124–39; Robyn Eckersley, "Deliberative Democracy, Ecological Representation, and Risk: Towards A Democracy of the Affected," *Democratic Innovation: Deliberation, Representation and Association*, ed. Michael Saward (New York: Routledge, 2000), 117–32; Kristian Skagen Ekeli, "Green Constitutionalism: The Constitutional Protection of Future Generations," *Ratio Juris* 20, no. 3 (September 2007): 378–401; Kristian Skagen Ekeli, "Giving a Voice to Posterity: Deliberative Democracy and Representation of Future People," *Journal of Agricultural and Environmental Ethics* 18 (2005): 429–50; Robert E. Goodin, *Reflective Democracy* (Oxford, UK: Oxford University Press, 2003); Robert E. Goodin, "Democratic Deliberation Within," *Philosophy and Public Affairs* 29, no. 1 (Winter 2000): 81–109. Relatedly, John S. Dryzek's "ecological communication" and James Bohman's emphasis of "capability equality" also offer interesting resources for thinking about the relation of future generations to contemporary deliberative politics

(Robert E. Goodin, "Political and Ecological Communication," *Environmental Politics* 4, no. 4, 1995: 13–30 and James Bohman, "Deliberative Democracy and Effective Social Freedom," *Deliberative Democracy: Essays on Reason and Politics*, eds. James Bohman and William Rehg, Cambridge, MA: MIT Press, 1997, 321–48). See also contributions in Iñigo González-Ricoy and Axel Gosseries, ed. *Institutions for Future Generations* (New York: Oxford University Press, 2016).
51 Ekeli, "Giving a Voice to Posterity: Deliberative Democracy and Representation of Future People," 440, 441.
52 Thompson, "Representing Future Generations," 20.
53 Ibid., 22. Thompson lays out specific guidelines and powers for the trustee group. First, "an office of trusteeship could be established not only at the national but also at the international level. Because . . . national boundaries are less significant as we look into the future, an international trustee would be eventually necessary, even if currently difficult to implement." Second, he offers a list of possible powers (rather than concrete proposals): suspensive powers (to stop actions that would limit democratic processes in the future); posterity impact statements (along the lines of environmental impact statements currently required); democratic balance sheets (annual reporting of gains and losses in the democracy to see "whether the government is improving the capacity of the people in the future to control their own destiny"); contingency trust funds (money put aside for future grants to improve voting systems or other democratic procedures in the future); international collaboration (entering into agreements with trustees in other states); age-differentiated political rights (trustees might propose legislation to require an upper age limit on voting or to provide parents with more votes); and constitutional conventions (limited to provisions related to democratic processes like voting).
54 Iñigo González Ricoy and Axel Gosseries, eds., *Institutions for Future Generations* (New York: Oxford University Press, 2017), chapter 2.
55 John S. Dryzek, *Foundations and Frontiers of Deliberative Governance* (New York: Oxford University Press, 2012).
56 For example, see Linda Alcoff's "The Problem of Speaking for Others," *Cultural Critique* 20 (Winter 1991–2): 5–32. She offers a set of practices for anyone trying to represent the interests of another marginalized group. Whereas it is possible to examine one's own urge to speak, as Alcoff recommends, it is impossible to examine the impact of one's words on the status of the represented group, for example.
57 See Axel Gosseries and Lukas H. Meyer, "Introduction: Intergenerational Justice and Its Challenges" in *Intergenerational Justice*, eds. Axel Gosseries and Lukas H. Meyer, 1–22, for a review of the special case of futurity.
58 Charles Taylor, "The Politics of Recognition," in *Multiculturalism: Examining the Politics of Recognition*, ed. Amy Guttman (Princeton, NJ: Princeton University Press, 1994), 25.
59 Ibid.
60 See Nussbaum, *Frontiers of Justice*, 2006.
61 See Young, *Responsibility for Justice*.
62 Iris Marion Young, "Responsibility and Global Justice: A Social Connection Model," *Social Philosophy and Policy* 23, no. 1 (January 2006): 114.
63 For related discussion, see Dale Jamieson, *Reason in a Dark Time: Why the Struggle against Climate Change Failed and What It Means for the Future* (New York: Oxford University Press, 2014), 160.
64 Jade Schiff, *Burdens of Political Responsibility: Narrative and the Cultivation of Responsiveness* (New York: Cambridge University Press, 2014).
65 Markel, *Bound by Recognition*.
66 Ibid., 179.
67 Ibid., 5.
68 Ibid., 23.

69 Danielle Allen, *Talking to Strangers: Anxieties of Citizenship since Brown V. Board of Education* (Chicago, IL: University of Chicago Press, 2004), 22–3.
70 Markell, *Bound by Recognition*, 7.
71 Ibid., 38.
72 Rahman, *Time, Memory and the Politics of Contingency*, 11.
73 Ibid., 51.
74 Paulina Ochoa Espejo, *The Time of Popular Sovereignty: Process and the Democratic State* (University Park, PA: Penn State University Press, 2011), 199.
75 Krause, *Freedom beyond Sovereignty*, 4.
76 For more on Arendt's reading as genealogy, see James R. Martel, "Can There Be Politics Without Sovereignty? Arendt, Derrida, and the Question of Sovereign Inevitability," *Law, Culture, and the Humanities* 6, no. 2 (2010): 153–66.
77 Hannah Arendt, "Freedom and Politics," *Chicago Review* 14, no. 1 (Spring 1960): 28.
78 Hannah Arendt, *Between Past and Future: Eight Exercises in Political Thought* (New York: Penguin, 1993), 154.
79 Ibid., 165.
80 Ibid., 163.
81 Hannah Arendt, *The Human Condition* (Chicago, IL: University of Chicago Press, 1998), 234.
82 According to Krause: "On this view, evident in one way or another in thinkers from Locke to Kant to John Stuart Mill, the individual is likewise understood, at last in principle, to be the master of her domain. The presence of a rational will gives her the capacity to control her action, it is thought, and the equal moral status of persons means that she is entitled to do so, or at least that she has no natural obligation to obey anyone else" (*Freedom beyond Sovereignty*, 2).
83 Arendt, *Between Past and Future*, 164.
84 See, for example, Kurt Raaflaub, *The Discovery of Freedom in Ancient Greece* (Chicago, IL: University of Chicago Press, 2004), as well as Dustin Ells Howes, *Freedom Without Violence: Resisting the Western Political Tradition* (New York: Oxford University Press, 2016) and Arlene Saxonhouse, "The Tyranny of Reason in the World of the Polis," *American Political Science Review* 82, no. 4 (December 1988): 1261–75.
85 Joan Cocks, *On Sovereignty and other Political Delusions* (London: Bloomsbury, 2014), 36.
86 Jonathan Havercroft points out that these lines of thinking have arrived in waves over the last 130 years, most recently in their Arendtian (what Havercroft terms the *normative critique of sovereignty*) and Foucauldian forms (the *architectonic critique*). Jonathan Havercroft, *Captives of Sovereignty* (New York: Cambridge University Press 2011), 15.
87 Cocks, *On Sovereignty and Other Political Delusions*, 4.
88 Elisabeth Anker, *Orgies of Feeling*, 9.
89 Ali Aslam, *Ordinary Democracy: Sovereignty & Citizenship beyond the Neoliberal Impasse* (New York: Oxford University Press, 2016).
90 Ibid., 7.
91 Katherine McKittrick, "Unparalled Catastrophe for Our Species?", 28–9.
92 Cocks, *On Sovereignty and Other Political Delusions*, 45.
93 The coupling here is worth emphasizing—my hunch is that one way we legitimate power over future generations is by imagining them as perpetual children, compared to our adult present.
94 Patchen Markell, "The Rule of the People: Arendt, Archê, and Democracy," *American Political Science Review* 100, no. 1 (February 2006): 1–14.
95 Krause, *Freedom beyond Sovereignty*.
96 Anker, *Orgies of Feeling*, 169.

2
A NARRATIVE TURN

> In those years, people will say, we lost track
> of the meaning of we, of you
> we found ourselves
> reduced to I
> and the whole thing became
> silly, ironic, terrible
>
> —Adrienne Rich, "In Those Years"

The key question for now becomes: How can we open ourselves to the demands of future freedom, given the particular qualities of this sort of structural injustice? In this chapter, I turn to a discussion of the ways in which narrative can redirect our energies to the type of thinking adequate to the particular challenge of intergenerational justice, connecting narrative's possibilities with the institution of the theater in ancient Athens. With the entry into comedy and tragedy, we can begin the task of reimagining the self, temporally unbounded, situated within a larger assemblage, navigating the tension between freedom and responsibility over generations, without the sovereign presentism that marks our current democratic imagination and politico-aesthetic landscape.

A major difficulty arises here because this a "problem of the new," using Hannah Arendt's language. It is not that intergenerational justice is a *novel* problem that just arrived on the scene because of anthropogenic climate change (although this has certainly heightened academic attention on the issue). Rather, intergenerational justice is a problem of the new because it always involves the unknown, the invisible. These questions cannot be fully incorporated into our abstract analytical categories and familiar procedures for political resolution. Intergenerational politics deals, at least in part, with the unknowable and contingent future, and so the exact contours and eventual realities of intergenerational justice must necessarily and always constitute an ever-receding horizon. Thus, intergenerational justice calls for *reflective judgment*—a constant process of making meaning of our complexity and accepting uncertainty while still acting (rather than aiming for a settled resolution with specific positive claims before moving forward). Moreover, we must find ways to encourage democratic citizens to *want* to engage in that process of reflective judgment. And, for this task, narrative—rather than abstract, analytical theory—will be our best guide. Of course, I am not unaware of the irony of writing analytically about this. My promotion of narrative is not an argument that narrative is the *only* means to understanding, but rather a reflection of my own experience of coming to better understand intergenerational justice through narrative—and an attempt to invite discussion about the particular texts that helped me on my way.

★★★

What is a "problem of the new"? Discussed by Linda Zerilli in a commentary on Hannah Arendt, it refers to things "the nature of which we are not yet able confidently and coherently to state, let alone to propose the solution it demands."[1] Instead of justification and validity, the point is to open up new possibilities for thinking, to begin the process of coming to even see what seems extraordinary and unfamiliar. The future poses this sort of problem—and this helps to explain why none of the three approaches discussed earlier fully captured the complexity of intergenerational justice. For example, in his 2014 book, *Reason in a Dark Time*, Dale Jamieson discusses the unique challenges posed by climate change, arguing "climate change is not a problem that conforms to our traditional models of individual morality and global justice."[2] He notes how:

> [i]ts causes and effects are geographically and temporally unbounded . . . [and] there are other psychological mechanisms at work that inhibit action. The scale of a problem like climate change can be crippling. When we do not feel efficacious with respect to a problem, we often deny that it exists.[3]

Moreover, economic analyses of the problem of climate change—akin to what we most often saw in the distributional perspective on intergenerational justice— do not satisfy because "there is more at stake than what numbers reveal . . . even if climate change were economically neutral, many people would still find something deeply wrong with humans changing the global climate."[4] Jamieson goes on to examine other ways of viewing climate change's effects on the future, considering whether it is a human rights violation or a case of domination. In the end, however, he decides against those options, arguing that climate change "poses a unique challenge to our commonsense moral notions" and calling for a new "ethics for the anthropocene."[5]

The "problem of the new" is on full display here; climate change does not fit well into the usual categories and "commonsense moral notions." Likewise, how do we take unknowable future interests into account? How do we represent the future in our democratic deliberations when there is no possibility of authorization or accountability? How do we determine the value of fresh water in the future? How do we account for potential losses of freedom engendered by a radical transformation of coastlines? Moreover, how can we come to care about a problem that is seemingly so outside our ability to affect it? Jamieson argues that, so far at least, such questions have led to our collective inability to do much of anything to prevent climate change and that we must now radically rethink our notions of justice and morality in order to begin to adapt to our changed reality.

As our inaction regarding climate change helps to highlight, we generally neglect the future, not taking seriously the ways in which our own decision-making structures future potentials and binds future citizens to paths not of their own choosing. Of course, in many ways, this is simply our existential condition—an artifact of temporal relations that *just is*. All of us inherit a past and bequeath a future; there is a rather democratic equality about our temporal relations. But that does not mean that these relations do not have particular consequences for how we experience democratic citizenship and freedom—consequences that are largely unseen and ignored, yet which shape our own responses to the past and our disregard for the future—and our own relationship to the idea of sovereignty and democratic freedom in the here and now.

Facing those consequences begins with recognizing intergenerational justice as a problem of the new—as something that does not fit our usual categories and which cannot be held as an object of knowledge. Linda Zerilli argues that:

> [t]he problem of the new is a political question about how we, members of democratic communities, can affirm human freedom as a political reality in a world of objects and events whose causes and effects we can neither control nor predict with certainty.[6]

Instead of knowledge and intersubjective validity, what is required is *judgment*—"the faculty that allows us to order or make sense of our experience."[7] While tackling the critique that Arendt problematically neglects the necessary cognitive dimensions of politics, Zerilli argues that Arendt's:

> [p]oint is not to exclude arguments from the practice of aesthetic or political judgment . . . but to press us to think about what we are doing when we reduce the practice of politics to the context of better arguments. Arendt disputes . . . the assumption that agreement in procedures for making arguments ought to produce agreement in conclusions, hence agreement in the political realm cannot be reached in the manner of giving proofs.[8]

Thus, Zerilli focuses on Arendt's use of judgment as more than mere perception, as it refers to our ability to make meaning out of what we perceive. But this is not a meaning that everyone must agree upon because there is an impartial correct view, just waiting for deliberation to achieve consensus. Rather, it is a matter of *sensus communis*. As Arendt explains:

> This *sensus communis* is what judgment appeals to in everyone, and it is this possible appeal that gives judgments their special validity. The it-pleases-or-displeases me, which as a feeling seems so utterly private and noncommunicative, is actually rooted in this community sense and is therefore open to communication once it has been transformed by reflection, which takes all others and their feelings into account.[9]

Judgment takes place in the world, among community—and creates community. Because it is so open to contingency and conflict, yet focused nonetheless on the creation of community, this vision of politics seems especially helpful when thinking of how to move to incorporate intergenerational concerns into everyday politics. Instead of a single individual or group placed in a specific time, we would instead need to view political questions from a number of standpoints across time—and, as we do so, we create community across time and improve our political judgment. As Zerilli points out, "the worldly relations that judging creates turn crucially on the ability to see the same thing from multiple points of view, an ability that, in Arendt's telling, is identical with what it means to see politically."[10] Moreover, it is an iterative practice: "Arendt emphasizes thinking and judging as activities, not judgments as the result of an activity, judgments that, being valid for all, could be extended beyond the activity of judging subjects and applied in rule-like fashion over other subjects."[11] That is, judgment is a process that continually reshapes the world, disclosing it in new ways to our fellow citizens, and calling for new responses from others. This process may find us returning to the same questions and issues over and over again, giving them new meaning each time.

So the question is not how do we have knowledge of what future generations will need or want in order to better represent them or to develop a fair accounting practice that takes no more than a fair share for each preceding generation. Instead, we aim for judgment—the ability to consider something in light of a complex, uncertain world in which we must make decisions whose effects we can never fully predict. This happens through *representative thinking*:

> Political thought is representative. I form an opinion by considering a given issue from different viewpoints, by making present to my mind the standpoints of those who are absent . . . This process of representation does not blindly adopt the actual views of those who stand somewhere else . . . this is a question neither of empathy . . . nor of counting noses and joining

a majority but of being and thinking in my own identity where actually I am not. The more people's standpoints I have present in my mind while I am pondering a given issue, and the better I can imagine how I would feel and think if I were in their place, the stronger will be my capacity for representative thinking and the more valid my final conclusions, my opinion.[12]

Thus, each current citizen might engage in representative thinking herself, re-presenting to her mind the standpoint of a future person, as she herself judges a particular political question. This is not trying to nail down the needs or imagined desires of the future; to do so would raise threat of misrecognition. Instead, representative thinking here might require considering an issue as if one were living in the future. The point is not axioms or directives. We are working through our contemporary presuppositions and blind spots, examining what we think we know, refusing to go along with convention, and instead considering how our decisions could be accounted for 20, 50, 200 years on. It is *not* knowledge which is certain, verifiable, and concrete. Here, we are in the world of the invisible. "An object of thought is always a re-presentation, that is, something or somebody that is actually absent and present only to the mind which, by virtue of imagination can make it present in the form of an image."[13] There are no proofs or designated representatives; instead, "to think with an enlarged mentality means that one trains one's imagination to go visiting."[14] Arendt goes on to point out that this does not mean that one could claim to know what is going on in another's mind. And, as Lisa Disch elaborates, one must avoid:

> [a]n assimilationist fantasy by which I make myself so at home in your position that I erase the differences between us. As a visitor, I think my own thought but from the place of somebody else, permitting myself to experience the disorientation necessary for understanding how the world looks different to that person.[15]

In other work, I have been critical of representative thinking in terms of contemporaneous citizens, believing that imaginative visiting is not enough and instead argued that citizens must actually get out there and listen to others.[16] As Bickford warns:

> Representing to myself other opinions is tricky, for I cannot attribute opinions to specific others without knowing—without *hearing*—that they in fact hold that opinion. That is, we cannot confuse a possible judgment from a particular perspective with a specific person's actual judgment. By ourselves, we can never really know the innumerable perspectives in the world. The unpredictability of action and speech, the ability of humans to begin and give voice to something new, means that the opinions we hear may be—or perhaps even tend to be—surprising.[17]

Yet the situation with the future can only rest upon imagination by necessity. We cannot ever find out how surprising those opinions may be or how radically different from our expectations the actual physical and historical contexts may turn out. Still, the best option we have may be trying to cultivate an enlarged mentality through representative thinking, using imaginative visiting to rethink our politics. But how do we get there? How do we visit the future? How do we imagine those perspectives in ways that do not claim to *know* them but which nonetheless propel our own thinking outside of our provincial temporal place? And how might we come to want to do this work?

★★★

As I've been tracking Arendtian lines here, an obvious candidate is storytelling, or narrative.[18] Disch argues "storytelling invites critical engagement between a reader and a text and, more important, among the various readers of a work in a way that the impersonal, authoritative, social science 'voice from nowhere' cannot."[19] Disch goes on to argue that Hannah Arendt's effort in *The Origins of Totalitarianism* was "to craft the story of totalitarianism in a way that does not compel assent but, rather, stirs people to think about what they are doing" and that the "task of political theorist is not to report objectively but to tell a story that engages the critical faculties of the audience."[20] In this mode, readers are called to judgment, rather than informed of the correct path forward (because there is likely no clear correct path). María Pía Lara likewise argues that narrative is particularly critical in "disclos[ing] something that we were incapable of seeing without having them brought to life. These dramatic expressions are disclosive because they trigger our capacity for judgments."[21] She argues that this happens because "language can be disclosive by shocking us with new meaning and stimulate us to reorient our moral thinking."[22] Thus:

> [j]udgment and imagination allow us to express the unimaginable [in Lara's work, genocide] by creating linguistic terminologies that can convey the means to express what is unsayable. Indeed, it is the privilege of the well-told story to be able to disclose aspects of the human condition that would seem impossible to translate into pure philosophical concepts.[23]

As with Arendtian judgment, this is a continuous process of "reconstructed representations," an effort to create meaning that is never settled and always calls forward new claims, contestations, and understandings.[24] Likewise, if future oriented justice is so difficult because it's a problem of the new—full of unknowns and potentially threatening to our understandings of our own everyday practices, it requires discourses that will continuously highlight the contingency of meaning in the world and which have the potential to shock citizens out of their complacency.

Along the same lines, Markell argues that his politics of acknowledgment, discussed earlier, requires a reconsideration of identity, action, and temporality in *retrospective accounts*.[25] This doesn't work for the future in any obvious way; they do not yet exist so cannot possibly have their real stories told and interpreted. But Markell's suggestion does lead us again to storytelling and literature as ways of understanding our identity, both in terms of understanding our own vulnerability to the procession of time and inheritance, as well as in terms of science fiction or other imagined accounts of the future. Jade Schiff likewise emphasizes the importance of narrative in motivating moves toward greater political responsibility. She agrees that Markell's acknowledgment is one component of a better approach to politics, but argues that it does not get us very far in considering what we ought to do in terms of others once we have reoriented ourselves to better understand our intersubjective vulnerability and the unpredictability of political life. Meanwhile, a more just orientation to intergenerational matters requires both a reorientation to ourselves and a responsiveness to others. According to Schiff, appreciation of intersubjective vulnerability in politics lays a foundation for other actions, but does not help make explicit those links between our political decisions and the terms of freedoms for, and the concrete harms endured by, others. She therefore pushes for "a different object of acknowledgement: Not our ontological condition, but our concrete, practical condition . . . the relevant objects of acknowledgement are the connections between our everyday experiences, and the often distant experiences of others."[26]

Schiff argues that narrative can help transform three "dispositions that problematize our acknowledgment of structural injustice and social connection, and thus threaten our ability to confront our political responsibility: thoughtlessness, bad faith, and misrecognition."[27] In the first case, Schiff draws upon Arendt's analysis of the Eichmann trial to argue that "institutional arrangements can insulate us from the harms to which we contribute . . . such thoughtlessness can hinder severely our capacity to confront our implication in, and therefore our responsibility for, structural injustice."[28] That is, we simply don't see the harms for which we share responsibility. Thoughtlessness has another side though: we simply cannot be responsive to all claims upon our thought because of the infinite number of such potential claims. Thus, thoughtlessness can be a part of a normal and unproblematic way of being; it's rather that we must choose the right things to direct our thinking toward (and in Eichmann's case, he chose nothing but bureaucratic ambition). In the case of bad faith, individuals simply lie to themselves about their role in those harms; they see them, but downplay their part. Like thoughtlessness, bad faith can be essential to living in the world as it can also "provide necessary insulation against the overwhelming burdens of existence."[29] In the final disposition, ideological misrecognition (from Bourdieu), Schiff argues that:

[t]he thing about which we would need to think or to be honest with ourselves—the actual contingency of the social and political arrangements that sustain structural injustice and that are susceptible to transformation—*simply disappears into the self-evidence of the natural order.*[30]

That we might live another way, or that our ordinary, daily lives have devastating consequences for others simply falls away under the guise of "that's just the way things are." The problem of intergenerational justice fits well with all three accounts here—we pay the future no mind and fail to see the damage being called forth; when we do, we fail to see our own role in the harms; or, lastly, we think this is just the way things have to be. The way out is narrative—"telling stories about the concrete, lived experience of human beings contributing to and suffering injustice—might be a fruitful way to promote acknowledgement."[31]

For Schiff, and for me, narrative provides the possibility of overcoming our problematic dispositions and recognizing connection across great distance—whether geographical or, as in my case, temporal. Concrete details about the effect that Jane's decisions have on Li's ability to live and make meaningful choices, about the ways in which Li's and Jane's lives are intertwined, and how that intertwining itself becomes a thing that shapes the world—these are always going to be more compelling than abstract analysis (even when they are also delusional or misleading—nothing here assures us of factually correct or normatively appropriate narratives). Meanwhile, philosophy and its emphasis on the abstract and on systematization can obscure our attention to the particular, rendering invisible the dimensions of reality that we need to imagine in order to come to terms with the democratic potentials of the future and our role in them. Instead of a theory or a set of rules we can apply to current decision-making, we more urgently need to cultivate acknowledgment of connections across time (that is, our temporal intersubjectivity) and the potential infinitude of our action, despite the finitude of our life.

★★★

In terms of intergenerational justice specifically, narrative has several very specific advantages over other forms of discourse. As a "problem of the new," a situation full of unknowns and indeterminate elements, the way forward is not readily clear. Instead of valid arguments that will compel assent, we need judgment. For Arendt, Disch, Schiff, and others, narrative is particularly well-suited to help cultivate that judgment and orient us to a problem that has otherwise remained invisible to many citizens. Oftentimes, though, narrative seems to work because it provides more information to the rational thinker. Once armed with the concrete details of others' lives, our perspective expands and we form better opinions. Here I want to dive more deeply into why narrative is particularly well-suited to the problem of future-oriented justice—and this is not only because stories give us more information. Because narratives are *indeterminate* yet *concrete*, because they offer *emotional motivation*, moving us affectively as well, because they explicitly deal with the *temporal*, and because they are part of *everyday life*, they can offer unique possibilities for cultivating in citizens an openness to questions of intergenerational justice.

Part of the challenge is that it's just so fashionable to discuss the value of narrative and of literature for political thinking; the entire endeavor becomes nearly meaningless as we repeat the same platitudes and assumptions. Although focused on reading (as opposed to other ways of connecting with narrative, such as storytelling or performance), Simon Stowe's *Republic of Readers* addresses this 'literary turn in political thought" head on. There are two cautions I take from his book: (1) the dangers of claiming determinate meanings for particular texts (as he claims Nussbaum and Rorty do) and (2) the danger of believing that literature written by "a special genius" *proves* something about the *unwritten* world. Stowe argues for a weaker sense of the verb "show," in which the term indicates not demonstration or proof but "display." So literature can be "a source of insight" "raising a possibility or option," and "it can even call its own perspective into question in a way that the more formal methods of social science cannot."[32] But literature cannot demonstrate a particular claim about an empirical reality. In order to remain in that first category, readings must highlight the contingency of the reader's perspective:

> If we are used to approaching texts with sensitivity and humility, exploring them as another world, different from our own, accepting the possibility that they might show us something unexpected, new, or surprising, then such an endeavor might well produce a civil and constructive engagement, one that is possibly beneficial to both parties as well as the broader democratic polity.[33]

The difference here between determined readings by privileged critics and more open, democratic engagement is key for Stowe:

> [t]he suggestion that particular books will have definite and predictable impacts upon their readers is an impossible one to maintain . . . that both Nussbaum and Rorty feel the need to champion their own readings of the texts that they recommend—rather than simply assigning texts and sitting back to watch as liberal democracy flourishes—suggests that they too have less than complete faith in this aspect of their claims.[34]

As an academic, part of what I do is offer readings of texts, in the hopes that my view of the text resonates with others and helps to spur thinking about some political dilemma. Yet in our writing and in the classroom, the difference between "championing" a particular reading and offering one as a defensible and compelling possibility can be difficult to discern, especially given power relations (in that students might defer too much to the professor's reading—or other academics might defer to Nussbaum or Rorty). Yet I do not need to believe that George Shulman's view of *Beloved* is the only way to view Toni Morrison's novel to nonetheless find it *a* compelling interpretation that leads me to understand the world differently.[35] Moreover, a text doesn't need a definitive meaning to nonetheless have particular, more-likely-than-others meanings—as well as indefensible readings. Here, Stephen Salkever puts it most succinctly—and solves the problem by drawing on Harry Berger's work:

> The great pedagogical problem we all need to address is this: How can the activity of text interpretation be characterized in a way that will give students a sense of rigor and discipline without supplying them a misleadingly precise algorithm? I know of no better guide to how to achieve this purpose than a lightly but essentially ironic piece of advice from Harry Berger, a master of literary and philosophical interpretation, about how to "induct" students into the community of interpreters we wish to construct in the classroom:
>
>> The first and most important move every young citizen of the interpretive community should make is to perform the pledge of allegiance to interpretation, and I don't think it's a bad idea for students to learn a little piety along with the move. So I urge all teachers everywhere to insist that their students begin every class by murmuring in unison, and with expression, dutifully and even prayerfully, the two parts of the primal invocation that will prepare all American children to question both church and state:
>>
>> 1. Let there be at least one unacceptable interpretation of any text.
>> 2. Let there be at least two acceptable interpretations of any text.
>
> This little pair of exhortations seems innocuous, but taken together and perused more closely they open up a space between dogmatism and indeterminacy; they establish textual boundaries that can be policed.[36]

Thus, we have a field of discussion where it's not "anything goes," yet which allows for multiple interpretive positions and which calls on readers to offer reasons for why a particular text might be read in this or that way. These exhortations are also especially important if we are to avoid simply choosing stories and readings that just reassure us into complacency or lead us into delusion. Readings must be contested, challenged, and refined—and this is the role of the academic, the student, and the citizen. Narratives—when they are focused on showing (rather than proving)—can be an invitation to a larger conversation that one did not know one even needed to have. As part of a *conversation*, no reading can claim to definitively explain a text but may instead offer a new way of viewing the world, highlighting relations or conditions which had previously remained invisible to readers.

It should be clear why this methodological approach is well-suited to intergenerational justice. In the realm of future politics, there is no way to know exactly what will happen, what future individuals will want, or how to best respond to those desires. Yet we do know that some things are very likely off the table—future generations will likely want access to life-sustaining environments, an ability to make decisions about their own welfare, and so on. Thus, the indeterminacy of narrative mirrors that of intergenerational politics, cultivating in citizens a comfort with ambiguity and contingency, yet refusing relativism. Arguing about meaning can help remind us of this, and—provided we don't slip into the ever-present danger of misology—give us tools for negotiating the lack of certainty in our political life. Moreover, narrative's relative openness and indeterminacy is particularly well-suited for problems of structural injustice, where direct causation and explicit intent are hard to come by. As Caroline Levine argues, narratives "tend to present causality metonymically, through sequences of events, rather than by positing some originary cause. They afford 'conjoining,' to use David Hume's words, rather than 'necessary connexion'."[37] These are not just bits of concrete detail that will amplify understanding, but stories that can radically expand our sense of what is possible, interconnected, and timely. Finally, some narratives do a better job of encouraging this type of reflection than others. As a widely touted study demonstrated, readers of literary fiction had a marked improvement in their capacity for empathy, as compared to readers of non-fiction or popular fiction.[38] According to the study's authors, popular fiction tends to reaffirm readers' expectations in terms of plot and character psychology, while literary fiction tends to explore character's inner lives and in ways which often confound expectations and open space for interpretation. Thus, readers of literary fiction are more accustomed to inferring motivations and thus might be more likely (in the real world) to understand what others are thinking and feeling, to empathize with them, and to appreciate complexity.

At the same time, and as discussed earlier, narrative offers *concreteness* that can help us move beyond the cold abstractions that often allow us to ignore the potential suffering of future others. All sorts of communicative forms can provide concrete details, of course, but narratives in this mode create an entire world and pull the reader/viewer/listener into a new vision of reality. By confronting thick descriptions of others' lives or situations, narratives, according to Young, "can also serve to explain meanings and experiences when groups do not share premises sufficiently to proceed with an argument."[39] Young continues: "A norm of political communication under these conditions is that everyone should aim to enlarge their social understanding by learning about the specific experience and meanings attending other social locations. Narrative makes this easier and sometimes an adventure."[40] With those concrete details about the lived reality of others, our own thoughtlessness, bad faith, and misrecognition became harder to sustain. Of course, with the future, this can never be a known reality for us. But that does not preclude us from considering relatively plausible accounts presented by novelists, filmmakers, or others, that call on us to dwell on the concrete reality of life in a future marked by climate change, sustained warfare, or persistent racial injustice.

Moreover, this concreteness has a particular effect in terms of motivation. Offering an image of the palpable harms versus concrete but bloodless facts has an affective advantage—compare a tearful parent describing the kidney problems and impulsive behaviors in his daughter to a state report about lead levels reaching 10ppb (parts per billion) in some Flint, MI neighborhoods.[41] The affective pull of the concrete calls us to judgment in ways that rational argument that purports to cast emotion aside simply cannot. Bickford argues that "we should recognize that emotion talk is both a constituent of our judgments and also gives us the materials to remake those judgments, and thus ourselves, and thus the world."[42] By "affect," however, I mean more than the emotions; in line with the "affective turn," I use the term in an encompassing way to refer to sensations—both emotional and bodily—that *move* us "in excess of consciousness."[43] Think of the physical sensations of nursing an infant, as well as the love and sorrow that marks parent–child relationships; of being bathed by another person; of joy while ocean swimming; of hunger; of knitting a sweater; of using a wheelchair; of sexual desire. These affects can be experienced first hand, they can be remembered, and they can be related through narrative, calling on our imagination or memory in order to share in that moment, to be moved "in excess of consciousness." Whereas reason will take us a long way in recognizing injustice in thick descriptions of the concrete conditions of people's lives (or help us arrive at the just discount rate or the legislative arrangements leading to the greatest levels of democratic legitimacy), it tells us less about why we ought to value particular reasons above others, or why we should be reasonable in the first place, or how to move us psychologically to action. Sensation, emotion, exhortation, inspiration—these things play a critical role in moving us to understanding and action. Without this affective element, our work on justice distribution or future discount rates goes nowhere.

As Schiff further explains:

> Our theories about politics, for instance, are stories that deploy implicit and explicit assumptions, logics, and arguments to weave an account of how some aspect of political life unfolds. Their characters are often bloodless, lifeless, abstract; their settings relatively static; their plots only thinly contextualized. But others, such as literary stories and the stories we tell about our own lives and the lives of others, often deploy concrete characters that may be real or imagined, alien or familiar. They use shifting settings, moods, and themes to organize dynamic plots that connect (or disconnect) events across diverse times, spaces, and places. They are richly contextual. Both kinds of stories illuminate some features of our condition and obscure others.

> But they do not invite the same sorts of emotional investments and disinvestments, the same sort of receptivity or repulsion; and they do not pose the same risks of frustration, disappointment, even betrayal, or of being emotionally swept away or left cold.[44]

Moreover, narrative puts the *temporal* landscape front and center. Susan Sontag points to the ways in which narrative is especially well-suited to helping to cultivate an appreciation of time in particular:

> In other words, a novel is the creation not simply of a voice but of a world. It mimics the essential structures by which we experience ourselves as living in time, and inhabiting a world, and attempting to make sense of our experience. But it does what lives . . . *cannot* offer, except after they are over. It confers—and withdraws—meaning or sense upon a life . . . A conviction of the potential richness of our existence *in time* is also characteristic of the imagination that is distinctively novelistic, even when the novelist's point . . . is to illustrate the futility and repetitiousness of action in time . . . The understanding of the novelist is temporal, rather than spatial or pictural. Its medium is a rendered sense of time—time experienced as an arena of struggle or conflict or choice.[45]

As opposed to philosophical argument, the conventions of literature activate a sense of temporal flow, allowing readers to enter into a world where the unpredictability of action in the present merges into a future right there within the narrative. As decision-making and action unfold across time, readers might gain a better understanding of the ways membership in a particular generation shapes the potential for agency or the ways in which one's actions can reverberate infinitely across time. Thus (and as I will explore in subsequent chapters) some narratives could be especially provocative in terms of cultivating a future orientation among democratic citizens. In a similar vein, Levine's work focuses on rhythm as a central form organizing narratives, noting that an attentiveness of the "patternings of time" is critical because "we find a social world where temporal structures often thwart or compete with one another."[46] That is, standard expectations about time, duration, and progression, organize life in particular ways—ways that can render some things invisible, unthinkable, or unmanageable (think here of geologic time as a hyperobject, poorly suited to our current sense of scale). In Levine's view, though, the alternative rhythms embedded in some narratives might be taken as their own "organizing principle, one that competes, struggles, and sometimes even interferes with other organizations of social time."[47] That is, by bringing our focus to these alternative patternings, perhaps we can disrupt the presentism that renders future generations invisible, amplifying our own temporal bounds beyond a single lifespan.

Moreover, those alternative patternings might not just be revealed in the quirky temporal disruptions and out-of-jointness we see in some Greek plays, but some narratives may be especially key here because of their *untimeliness*. Peter Euben has explored the Nietzschean notion of "untimeliness" in political theory and pointed to the ways in which it may expand our temporal horizons. This is the idea of acting counter to the fashions of one's time, of choosing another epoch from which to approach political life (yet without falling into nostalgia):

> Nietzsche's notion of untimeliness undermines the metaphysics or theology of birth origins and beginnings. He does not so much directly deny them as remove the privileged status that accrues to them from their being regarded as natural or first. Living in two times means that, at the very least, we have dual allegiances and a distance from any single incarnation of our world and ourselves in it. No one time is originary beyond being a starting (but not ending) point to be refurbished, renewed, refashioned, or reinvented.[48]

In this way, Nietzschean untimeliness might be especially useful for moving us to consider generations aside from our own immediate ones, to think beyond the perceived linearity and presentism of our own temporal position, and to go "visiting" in Arendtian terms. Moreover, certain texts also have more of a capacity to do this for us because of their settings' temporal distance from the audience's own temporal realities. As Euben explains in regard to ancient tragedy, its "distance from the urgency of daily decisions . . . allowed it to develop a uniquely 'theoretical' perspective."[49] Athenian theater was not about the particulars facing the spectators, neither was there any policy prescription to be gleaned from the playwright. In this forum, spectators developed the habits of mind necessary for citizenship. Untimely narratives can disorient us and push us to appreciate that out-of-jointness of time. We see things that should not make sense or speak to our experience jump into focus as the present bumps into different pasts. Of course, we do not have to travel back to the Greek sources ourselves (although I do that here); there are plenty of texts that approach political questions that remain painfully relevant for us, but which come to us from another period or play with time and setting in non-linear ways. In the case of Black Lives Matter, James Baldwin's much older essays on racial injustice in the US come quickly to mind here as untimely in this sense. Literary science fiction like Octavia Butler's *Kindred* or Kiese Laymon's *Long Division* would be particularly relevant as well, as they manipulate temporal settings.

Finally, the everyday accessibility of narrative has great potential for spurring a reorientation toward the future. All people have access to narratives in some form—whether the stories are told among friends, novels, plays, movies, television, and so on. The point of orienting citizens toward the claims of intergenerational justice is not simply to develop better expert knowledge about what that type of justice might entail. Instead, we need a broadly based understanding of responsibility to the future and the nature of the individual within time. Thus, we need to think about forms of discourse that are likely to be compelling to large groups of citizens. This was the role of ancient theater in Athens—a widely shared, civic experience that brought forward particular problems of citizenship and asked regular citizens to consider and judge. Today, the stories we share about our past, present, and possible futures have great potential to reach a wide audience and inspire collective judgment, even if digital media has fragmented audiences in myriad ways. The challenge is to offer new, intergenerationally oriented readings of widely shared narratives.

★★★

Whereas philosophical and economic analysis may help a decision-maker arrive at proper distributions or representation schemas, it does not move us beyond abstract categories that help inure us to the harms our actions may cause, neither does it tell us much about how to move a citizen psychologically to action. Narrative, however, provides the possibility of overcoming the reluctance to even see intergenerational aspects of politics and can help citizens recognize agency across great temporal distance. Through an engagement with stories that focus on these issues, democracies may be able to cultivate an acknowledgment of both temporal intersubjectivity and a desire to attend to the democratic responsibility created by that condition. Thus, intergenerational justice calls for affective engagement and reflective judgment—a constant process of making meaning of our own interdependence and accepting uncertainty. This requires a more robust acknowledgment of both our own relationship to time and a responsiveness to others across time, even others we cannot know in detail. This chapter has argued that narrative—with an attendant appreciation of its own indeterminacy—is a critical tool in this effort.

The next three chapters are an attempt to demonstrate the utility of this approach. I am not claiming these are *the* only interpretations of these ancient Greek works and that by reading them, citizens will somehow find themselves transformed into actors who care deeply about the temporal dimensions of political life and the implications of that for democracy. Indeed, for most of these works, the interpretation I offer is at odds with standard readings—readings with which I often agree and which have enriched my understanding of the plays and ancient Greek political life. We tend not to focus on themes of time and futurity in these texts—and I think that is an interpretive loss, especially given the intergenerational themes that were part of Athenian civic life and theater rituals (discussed later in this chapter). To be sure, these themes are not *only* present in the texts I discuss here. As Karmola Cateri has shown, Plato picks up on the intergenerational tensions between fathers and sons, relaying Cephalus' desire to retire in ease and his son's own eagerness to begin an agentic life in *Republic*.[50] Likewise, Demetra Kasimis also highlights intergenerational tensions in her work on citizenship in *Ion*.[51] But I do believe the plays offer a unique opportunity to dwell on these questions—both for us and for ancient Athenians.

As I move to a focus on the plays of Aristophanes, Euripides, and Aeschylus, I also want to make clear that I am interested in the texts from ancient Greece not because they reflect timeless wisdom or provide models for contemporary democracy. I am not interested in forcing them to speak to our particular problems (what would Aeschylus think of Black Lives Matter?). Instead, through a contextualized study of this material, it is possible to dwell in that untimely narrative landscape, which can aid in the development of new approaches to political problems that have been rendered invisible by the seeming naturalness of our current practices. As Salkever describes engagements with the Greeks as a comparative exercise, this effort "provides a constructive escape from the powerful presuppositions or 'endoxa,' Aristotle's very useful term for the prevailing opinions within a particular community that provide an indispensible point of departure for the practice of both liberal education and political philosophy."[52]

This mode of untimely political theorizing focused on Greek theater is particularly rich because it gets right at questions of everyday accessibility and social imaginaries. That is, Athenian theater helps us see the central role for narrative and public art in shaping political subjectivity and the possibilities for reclaiming such a role today. Ancient tragedy was a public institution, shared in by the citizens of Athens and cultivating a particular democratic orientation among those citizens. As a reflection of then-contemporary democratic sensibilities, 5th-century tragedy was both a product of the democratic environment and helped constitute the political understandings of citizens.[53] By taking up the heroic myths and recasting them in light of the new ways of thinking that marked the young democracy, tragedy was both a link with the aristocratic past and a rejection of it. It was:

> [o]ne of the forms through which the new democratic city established its identity: Setting the actor in opposition to the chorus . . . it took its prince-turned-tyrant from distant myth, set him on stage and assessed him, presenting his errors and the mistaken choices that led him to catastrophe.[54]

This was public and democratic work. It was not limited to a literate elite; instead, these plays were presented as part of city-wide festivals. Indeed, in the absence of formal schooling, the theater was a critical educational force in democratic Athens:

> [i]n the first instance participation in the democratic process, including being present to hear such a public civic oration, was conceived primarily as an education for Athenian citizens . . . For such average citizens, tragic theatre was an important part of their learning to be active participants in self-government by mass meeting and open debate between peers.[55]

The plays opened a space for citizen judgment in multiple ways. Most obviously, the plays can model individual citizen judgment and the difficulties it entails in the story itself, presenting individuals in a variety of scenarios, actively judging and acting in different ways. This emphasis on judgment is also reflected in the chorus, "the collective and anonymous presence embodied by an official college of citizens . . . [whose] role is to express through its fears, hopes, and questions, and judgment the feelings of the spectators who make up the civic community."[56] Alongside the stories of judging that the plays presented, the theater also involved a call on the spectators to judge for themselves. It was not that tragedy dictated to the citizens how to think about and solve particular problems; instead, it provided Athenians with a "space for questioning and reflection."[57] For example, *Trojan Women* is not simply a story about the final annihilation of the Trojan royal family, but is part of a larger story in which relatively privileged women face enslavement and complete powerlessness, offering the spectators a space where they might consider the gendered meaning and limits of their radical democratic experiment. Additionally, plays appeared at a competitive theater festival that required audience judgment to produce a winner. Sara Monoson describes the connections between theater, judgment, and citizenship:

> The practice of judging the productions and awarding prizes—that is, of issuing a decision—not only fits with the competitive ethos of the society but also stresses the Athenian patriotic claim that, for them, action issues from mental work. By being theatai and meeting the challenge of the plays, especially in passing judgment on their merits, Athenian citizens enacted a claim to be intellectually capable folk.[58]

She argues that theater was an important element of Greek democracy: a political act that enacted political norms and negotiated political tensions.[59] Meanwhile, Paul Cartledge argues that tragedy was "an education for Athenian citizens . . . an important part of their learning to be active participants in self-government by mass meeting and open debate between peers."[60] The theater festivals in Athens were not merely for individual consumption and entertainment. This was not *reading*, but *performance*. Because of that, the affective roles I have been claiming for narrative were likely amplified (although the distinction between these forms of circulation of narratives is not my primary concern here. Instead, I focus on the content of the narratives themselves). This was a shared experience, with a civic purpose. In this way, ancient tragedy and the festivals at which it appeared had a profound effect on actual practices of democratic citizenship in Athens. It did so not only by providing space to engage in practices like deliberation, argument, and judgment. The particular themes and level of affective intensity of the Greek theater were critical as well. David McIvor elaborates:

> The Great Dionysia provided a space within which the members of the polis could work through public trauma and intense anxieties by facing down the ambivalence of self and other and by advancing simultaneous

moral and tragic narratives about the political project in which they were engaged—including an awareness of this project's fragility, contingency, contestability, and susceptibility to radical rupture.[61]

Coupled with its appearance as part of the city's Great Dionysia festival, with its patriotic pageantry, tragedy allowed the city as a whole (a partial whole, clearly) to reflect on itself and consider the conflicts characterizing political life in a democracy. Thus, ancient theater had protreptic effects that are not often replicated elsewhere in the canon. Theater was public art, not an event or literature reserved for the connoisseur or specialist. In a radical democracy, with posts largely filled by lottery, this inclusivity takes on critical importance—the health of the polis depends on every citizen developing good judgment.

Moreover, the civic *paideia* of the theater was not limited to tragedies. In fact, it is now no great insight to speak of the political nature of ancient comedy, and the political relevance of Aristophanes' work is well-established in the literature (although the same cannot be said for his particular positions on the issues of the day nor even the question of whether he held such positions).[62] Jeffrey Henderson points to a vision of ancient comedy "as essentially democratic and politically engaged, as against the modern tendency to see comedy as detached, innocuous, and essentially apolitical."[63] Whereas many commentators have read Aristophanes as a conservative or reactionary voice,[64] and although Stephen Halliwell points out that Aristophanic comedy was "no more respectful of democratic authority than of any other kind,"[65] it is also true that comedy in Athens developed alongside democracy and was considered a central forum for *parrhesia*—the frank speech that was supposed to characterize democratic discourse in Athens.[66] On the comedic stage, poets criticized and mocked the powerful, reflecting and shaping Athenian attitudes about such figures. Individuals like Cleon or Socrates found themselves the butt of Aristophanic jokes. The comedian was in turn called to account for his attacks (Plato has Socrates refer to the portrayal in *Apology*, while Cleon sued Aristophanes). Comedy also provided a forum for reflecting on more general, thematic issues in Athenian politics. Education, war, wealth, the status of women, democratic rhetoric—all find a place in Aristophanes' plays, as they did in tragedy. In comedy, we find another source of commentary on the relevant issues in Athens and an opportunity for his Athenian audience to focus their attention on these issues.[67] Comedy's laughter could forge community and release anxieties through its playfulness; at the same time, it could be used "consequentially," running the gamut from mild shaming to the destruction of one's reputation.[68] Thus comedic *parrhesia* deepened the Athenian culture of accountability, both recognizing citizens' social embeddedness, as well as providing an outlet for dealing with this interdependence and the tensions generated by it. Moreover, there is still another effect of the work, relevant for both ancients and us. It is not simply that Aristophanes contributes to particular understandings of Socrates, or Cleon, or the war with Sparta, or the denial of political rights to women, although he certainly does that. He also uses particular figures to do this, which then help construct views of those types of figures. For example, when Aristophanes uses sex-desperate old hags to reflect on women's political status, there is a message about that status, as well as a message about older women that comes across. This will be especially pertinent in Chapter 3, when we see Aristophanes construct, and then rely upon, a vision of old men as ineffectual fools, unable to manage their own households.

The larger theatrical context of both tragedy and comedy is also important here. For one, the theater festival explicitly emphasized intergenerational themes. One of the ceremonial events preceding the tragedies consisted of a parade of war orphans, young men whose fathers had died in battle for the polis. These future (although already existing) citizens were raised and educated at the state's expense and would later receive hoplite armor from the city, taking part in another parade before promising to defend the city as their fathers had.[69] Here the city could see the procession of the next generation of soldiers and the special intergenerational needs created by their political judgments. The parade also strengthened the city's claim to those young people—about to be citizens of the polis:

> The fact that the festival of the Great Dionysia, a major civic occasion, is chosen for the moment of this expression of the city's relation to its young men endows it with considerable force. Children, the moment of leaving childhood and becoming a man, what it means to be a man, are all influenced by democratic polis ideology. The city's claim on the citizen as man affects the status of the child.[70]

More generally, "Greek tragedy shows a serious preoccupation with family concerns," a theme with obvious intergenerational aspects.[71] Throughout tragedy, and Aristophanes as well, families are put through the most trying circumstances as they negotiate impossible conflicts and hopeless circumstances. And quite often, it's the children who face the worst fates in the tragedies—dismembered, throats cut, haunted, hung by their own hands. Meanwhile, comedy's blundering fathers and ungrateful sons reveal fundamental generational divisions within families. What is it about this relationship that drives the action to such utter and final negativity—the abandonment of the future of the house, a refusal to see the world from the perspective of those to whom one is most close?

Intergenerational issues were also a part of regular civic life in Athens. Upon becoming citizens, young men swore the ephebic oath, by which they promised, among other things, to hand over not only as good a city as they received, but one in even better condition.[72] Intergenerational concerns also arise in the *dokimasia*, or scrutiny, that preceded *deme* acceptance upon one's 18th birthday. While this first *dokimasia* examined a citizen's birthright—that is, were they descended from an Athenian father?—a later *dokimasia* also inquired as to whether he had treated his parents respectfully, among other things. (If the candidate was up for the office of *strategos*, he was also asked if he had legitimate Athenian children.) If one had honored his connection to both past and future, one might be seen as more likely to value community norms, democratic decision-making, and the future of the polis. We also know that participation in the polis was relatively circumscribed in one's youth. Not only did a young citizen face the informal limits imposed by a relative lack of experience, the emphasis placed on respect for one's elders, and the nostalgic attitude Athenians tended to hold toward the past, one was not allowed to participate in the Council until 30 years old. We can imagine the frustration felt by new citizens as they realized the limits placed on their freedoms.

Thus, the works of ancient comedy and tragedy examined here were presented in a political and artistic context that primed intergenerational concerns and invited citizen judgment. I do not mean to draw some sort of causal relationship between the readings of the plays I offer here and the existence of these intergenerational artifacts. But I do want to emphasize the ways in which Athenian attention to generations—and the decentering the present as *the* arbiter of good judgment—differs from our own. Questions of intergenerational justice are deeply rooted in the democratic sensibility. Even if—or especially since—contemporary liberals don't generally see that, the Athenians provide a critical counterpoint. Moreover, given the distance between the polis and the 21st-century political landscape, the extant works of the ancient Greek theater may also offer us the opportunity to put aside our immediate political commitments and look at the problems of intergenerational justice with new, untimely eyes.

Notes

1 Nikolas Kompridis, "Turning and Returning: The Aesthetic Turn in Political Thought" in *The Aesthetic Turn in Political Thought*, ed. Nikolas Kompridis (New York: Bloomsbury, 2014), xxii.
2 Jamieson, *Reason in a Dark Time*, 8.
3 Ibid., 102–3.
4 Ibid., 143.
5 Ibid., 161.
6 Linda Zerilli, "'We Feel Our Freedom': Imagination and Judgement in the Thought of Hannah Arendt," in *The Aesthetic Turn in Political Thought*, ed. Nikolas Kompridis, 34.
7 Ibid., 33.
8 Ibid., 31.
9 *Lectures on Kant's Philosophy*, 72
10 Ibid., 39.
11 Ibid., 59.
12 Arendt, *Between Past and Future*, 241.
13 Ibid., 165.
14 Hannah Arendt, *Lectures on Kant's Political Philosophy* (Chicago, IL: University of Chicago Press, 1992), 43.
15 Lisa Disch, "Please Sit Down, But Don't Make Yourself at Home: 'Visiting' and the Prefigurative Politics of Consciousness-Raising," in *Hannah Arendt and the Meaning of Politics*, ed. Craig Calhoun and John McGowan (Minneapolis, MN: Minnesota University Press, 1997), 136.

60 A Narrative Turn

16 Elizabeth Markovits, *The Politics of Sincerity* (University Park, PA: Penn State University Press, 2008), ch. 5.
17 Susan Bickford, *The Dissonance of Democracy: Listening, Conflict, and Citizenship* (Ithaca, NY: Cornell University Press, 1996), 86.
18 I mean these terms in their everyday usage as an account of events. To be clear, story and narrative are separate concepts—the story being the plot or action and the narration/story*telling* being the discursive representation of that sequence of events.
19 Lisa Disch, "More Truth Than Fact: Storytelling as Critical Understanding in the Writings of Hannah Arendt," *Political Theory* 21, no. 4 (1993): 665.
20 Ibid., 671, 681.
21 María Pía Lara, *Narrating Evil: A Postmetaphysical Theory of Reflective Judgment* (New York: Columbia University Press, 2007), 2.
22 Ibid., 10.
23 Ibid., 14.
24 Ibid., 169.
25 Markell, *Bound by Recognition*, 24.
26 J. Schiff, "Inclusion and the Cultivation of Responsiveness," *The Good Society* 18, no. 1 (2009): 65.
27 J. Schiff, "Confronting Political Responsibility: The Problem of Acknowledgement," *Hypatia* 23, no. 3 (2008): 103.
28 Ibid., 104.
29 Ibid., 108.
30 Ibid., 111.
31 Ibid., 112.
32 Simon Stowe, *Republic of Readers? The Literary Turn in Political Thought and Analysis* (Albany, NY: SUNY Press, 2007), 142, 148–9.
33 Ibid., 153.
34 Ibid., 121.
35 George Shulman, "American Political Culture, Prophetic Narration, and Toni Morrison's Beloved," *Political Theory* 24, no. 2 (May 1996): 295–314.
36 Stephen Salkever, "Teaching Comparative Political Thought: Joys, Pitfalls, Strategies, Significance," *Political Science Faculty Research and Scholarship.* Paper 26, 14–15; Harry Berger, *Situated Utterances: Texts, Bodies, and Cultural Representations* (New York: Fordham University Press, 2005), 494–5.
37 Caroline Levine, *Forms: Whole, Rhythm, Hierarchy, Network* (Princeton, NJ: Princeton University Press, 2015), 19.
38 Julianne Chiaet, "Novel Finding: Reading Literary Fiction Improves Empathy," *Scientific American.* October 4, 2013.
39 Iris Marion Young, *Inclusion and Democracy* (New York: Oxford University Press), 7.
40 Ibid., 77.
41 One could also argue those *hearing or seeing* this parent speak would have a greater impact than *reading* their words. In this way, the move between reading and performance that I keep unproblematically making *is* problematic. But I would suggest readers see this as a continuum, with ancient Greek theatrical performance on one side, for example, followed by reading such texts, and then graphs of just discount rates to the far other side.
42 Susan Bickford, "Emotion Talk and Political Judgment," *Journal of Politics* 73, no. 4 (2011), 1036.
43 Patricia Ticento Clough, "Introduction," in *The Affective Turn: Theorizing the Social*, eds. Patricia Ticento Clough and Jean Halley (Durham, NC: Duke University Press, 2007), 2. Affect here is seen as a "a substrate of potential bodily responses, often automatic responses, in excess of consciousness … bodily capacities to affect and be affected or the augmentation or diminution of a body's capacity to act, to engage, and to connect, such that autoaffection is linked to the self-feeling of being alive—that is, aliveness or vitality."

44 Schiff (2014), 3–4.
45 Susan Sontag, "At the Same Time: The Novelist and Moral Reasoning," in *At the Same Time: Essays and Speeches*, eds. Paolo Dilonardo and Anne Jump (New York: Picador, 2007), 215–17.
46 Levine, *Forms*, 51.
47 Ibid., 53.
48 Peter Euben, *Platonic Noise* (Princeton, NJ: Princeton University Press, 2003), 17.
49 Peter Euben, *The Tragedy of Political Theory: The Road Not Taken* (Princeton, NJ: Princeton University Press, 1990), 56.
50 Kateri Carmola, "Noble Lying: Justice and Intergenerational Tension in Plato's *Republic*," *Political Theory* 31, no. 1 (February 2003): 39–62.
51 Demetra Kasimis, "The Tragedy of Blood-Based Membership: Secrecy and the Politics of Immigration in Euripides' *Ion*," *Political Theory* 41, no. 2 (2013): 231–56.
52 Stephen Salkever, "Teaching Comparative Political Thought," 4.
53 An alternative view may be found in P. J. Rhodes' work ("Nothing to Do with Democracy: Athenian Drama and the Polis," *Journal of Hellenic Studies* 123 (2003): 104–19) in which the author takes on claims that Athenian tragedy was a specifically democratic institution. Even if one is more sympathetic to his view than the present work, Rhodes' claims do not pose an insurmountable problem here. First, Rhodes acknowledges the democratic themes contained in particular plays, especially his arguments regarding *Eumenides*. Second, I am less concerned with whether the institution itself was a specifically democratic development and more interested in the democratic effects of the plays. Moreover, while accountability and responsibility may be concerns for a variety of polis-dwelling Greeks (and not only democrats), the appearance of these themes in a tragedy presented to a *democratic* audience reaffirms the democratic importance of the trilogy.
54 Jean-Pierre Vernant and Pierre Vidal-Naquet, *Myth and Tragedy in Ancient Greece* (New York: Zone Books, 1990), 257.
55 Paul Cartledge, "'Deep Plays': Theatre as Process in Greek Civic Life," in *The Cambridge Companion to Greek Tragedy*, ed. P. E. Easterling (Cambridge, UK: Cambridge University Press, 1997), 19.
56 Vernant and Vidal-Naquet, *Myth and Tragedy in Ancient Greece*, 33–4.
57 Euben, *The Tragedy of Political Theory*, 30, 52.
58 S. Sara Monoson, *Plato's Democratic Entanglements: Athenian Politics and the Practice of Philosophy* (Princeton, NJ: Princeton University Press, 2000), 105.
59 Ibid., 89.
60 Cartledge, "Deep Plays," 19.
61 David McIvor, *Mourning in America: Race and the Politics of Loss* (Ithaca, NY: Cornell University Press, 2016), 130.
62 See, for example Lowell Edmunds, *Cleon, Knights, and Aristophanes' Politics* (Washington, DC: University Press of America, 1987); Peter Euben, *Corrupting Youth: Political Education, Democratic Culture, and Political Theory* (Princeton, NJ: Princeton University Press, 1997); Jeffrey Henderson, "Attic Old Comedy, Frank Speech, and Democracy," in *Democracy, Empire, and the Arts in Fifth-Century Athens*, ed. Deborah Boedeker and Kurt A. Raaflaub (Cambridge, MA: Harvard University Press, 1998), 255–73; Rosanna Lauriola, "Aristophanes' Criticism: Some Lexical Considerations," *AION* 32 (2010): 25–61, especially 25–32; Niall W. Slater, *Spectator Politics: Metatheatre and Performance in Aristophanes* (Philadelphia, PA: University of Pennsylvania Press, 2002); John Zumbrunnen, *Aristophanic Comedy and the Challenge of Democratic Citizenship* (Rochester, NY: University of Rochester Press, 2012). For an alternate take that acknowledges politics as a "kind of pretext or precondition," but which refuses questions of Aristophanic intent, see M. S. Silk, *Aristophanes and the Definition of Comedy* (New York: Oxford University Press, 2000), ch. 7.

63 Henderson, "Attic Old Comedy, Frank Speech, and Democracy," 255.
64 For further discussion, see Zumbrunnen, *Aristophanic Comedy and the Challenge of Democratic Citizenship*, Introduction or Slater, *Spectator Politics*, chapter 1, especially 5–7.
65 Stephen Halliwell, *Greek Laughter: A Study of Cultural Psychology from Homer to Early Christianity* (New York: Cambridge University Press, 2008), 250. A commentator like Sheldon Wolin would point out, however, that such refusal of authority and limits is the very essence of democracy; see Sheldon S. Wolin, "Norm and Form: The Constitutionalizing of Democracy," *Athenian Political Thought and the Reconstruction of American Democracy*, eds. Peter Euben, John Wallach, and Josiah Ober (Ithaca, NY: Cornell University Press, 1994), 29–58.
66 See Stephen Halliwell, "Comic Satire and Freedom of Speech in Classical Athens," *The Journal of Hellenic Studies* 111 (1991): 48–70; and Henderson, "Attic Old Comedy, Frank Speech, and Democracy." At the same time, comedic *parrhesia* was a complicated practice, as Halliwell notes; the city "was caught between a democratic impulse towards freedom of speech and, on the other hand, an inclination . . . to provide protection and redress against abusiveness." As he goes on to ask, "can one, in short, have freedom of speech without tolerance of aischrology?" Halliwell, *Greek Laughter*, 218, 235. For an alternate view of comedy as nonpolitical in intent and noncritical in the face of the power of the *demos*, see Malcolm Heath, *Political Comedy in Aristophanes* (Göttingen, Germany: Vandenhoeck & Ruprecht, 1987).
67 Euben, *Corrupting Youth*, 110.
68 Stephen Halliwell, "The Uses of Laughter in Greek Culture," *The Classical Quarterly* 41, no. 2 (1991): 279–96.
69 Simon Goldhill, "Civic Ideology and the Problem of Difference: The Politics of Aeschylean Tragedy, Once Again," *The Journal of Hellenic Studies* 120 (2000): 34–56.
70 Simon Goldhill, "The Dionysia and Civic Ideology" *Nothing to Do with Dionysos? Athenian Drama in Its Social Context*, eds. John J. Winkler and Froma I. Zeitlin (Princeton, NJ: Princeton University Press, 1990), 113–14.
71 Judith Maitland, "Dynasty and Family in the Athenian City State: A View from Attic Tragedy," *The Classical Quarterly* 42, no. 1 (1992): 26.
72 "I will never bring reproach upon my hallowed arms nor will I desert the comrade at whose side I stand, but I will defend our altars and our hearths, single-handed or supported by many. My native land I will not leave a diminished heritage but greater and better than when I received it. I will obey whoever is in authority and submit to the established laws and all others which the people shall harmoniously enact. If anyone tries to overthrow the constitution or disobeys it, I will not permit him, but will come to its defense single-handed or with the support of all. I will honor the religion of my fathers. Let the gods be my witnesses, Agraulus, Enyalius, Ares, Zeus, Thallo, Auxo, Hegemone." John Wilson Taylor, "The Athenian Ephebic Oath," *The Classical Journal* 13, no. 7 (April 1918): 499.

3
ARCHÊ, FINITUDE, AND COMMUNITY IN ARISTOPHANES[1]

> O sir, you are old.
> Nature in you stands on the very verge
> Of his confine. You should be ruled and led
> By some discretion that discerns your state
> Better than you yourself.
>
> —*King Lear*, Act II, Scene 4

> Most admirable Polus, it's not for nothing that we get ourselves companions and sons. It's so that, when we ourselves have grown older and stumble, you younger men might be on hand to straighten our lives up again, both in what we do and what we say.
>
> —*Gorgias*, 461c

The foray into the ancient Greeks begins with Aristophanes, who shows readers the comically pathetic struggles of old men trying to control the actions of others around them, particularly the actions of their offspring. Aristophanes' solution is to retreat from political life—an option I cannot advocate, and so I do not offer his vision up as a good alternative to our own. But Aristophanes' *Knights* and *Clouds*, with their emphasis on the inability of elderly men to get what they want, illustrate both the allures and failures of the aspiration to sovereign freedom. According to this reading, then, the plays can help to render our current imaginary as the absurdist fantasy it is—in part by recognizing and processing the desire for such freedom.

Both plays show desperate old men who try to control their households, yet who find themselves thwarted either by those who would flatter them (into thinking they are in control when they are not) or else by their own offspring.

The readings offered here explore the argument that intergenerational justice will always involve tension and conflict, and must therefore be grounded in an awareness of the social and temporal relations springing from human finitude. When we do not recognize the challenge posed by our attachment to sovereign freedom—even as that attachment helps to destroy the world across both time and place—we become more and more like the pathetic case of Strepsiades, burning down Socrates' Thinkery in a fit of cathartic but ultimately pointless violence. I will probe—and dwell upon—those tensions so that we can more fully appreciate what deep attachments stand between our current thinking and a different approach. This is what the plays offer: a chance to be moved out of our own presentism by the comic-tragedy of the challenges awaiting at the intersection of the individual self, community, and time.

I begin here with Aristophanes' use of the old man (*gerontas*) figure in *Knights*. In this work, Aristophanes presents a particular notion of old age, one that highlights its difficulties in a polity that demands youthful vigor. We see here both the allure and failures of conceiving of sovereign individual action as the fulfillment of the promise of democratic freedom, as well as the challenges posed by the assumed, particular embodiment of sovereign actors (as young men). I then move to Aristophanes' portrayal of intergenerational dynamics in *Clouds* to probe the nature of these difficulties and what meaning they hold for democracy more generally. Because he so consistently draws upon the elderly figure, and because his work directly engages with the democratic life of Athens, Aristophanes' work offers us an opportunity for "comedic voyaging,"[2] a chance for readers and audiences to spectate, to theorize themselves by inviting them into a story, and leaving open interpretive space for this activity. This work fits into the description of narrative outlined in the last chapter; the plays hold out indeterminate meanings for the audience/reader to explore, rooted in concrete details about the course of human lives. In Aristophanes' case, affective engagement is a key part of this voyaging, as audience members (and readers) are moved emotionally through laughter in the everyday experience of Greek theater.

★★★

In *Knights*, Aristophanes represents the decay in Athenian politics with the near-destruction of an elderly man's Athenian household by the Paphlagonian slave (representing Cleon, the name a way to highlight both his servility and his obnoxious rhetoric, since the word is similar to the Greek word for "bluster"). The household here is headed by Demos Pyknites, a cynical old man who believes he is getting what he wants from Paphlagon, but is instead being used by him. Athens, in this characterization, has become a diminished place, represented by the figure of Demos—an old, relatively incapable fellow, long past his prime. Like the city, Demos is enthralled with flattering demagogues—all the more powerful because of their insistence to be the truth-telling, anti-demagogues needed by the decaying city that nostalgically looks to its past, a golden age marked by the military achievements of Marathon and Salamis and before the rise of the sophists and their rhetorical tricks. Throughout the play, we hear of Demos's old age and its attendant losses time and again. Although rarely commented upon in the literature on the play, Aristophanes consistently focuses audience attention on Demos's elderly status in *Knights*, inviting us to ask what that status might mean for the larger themes in the play.

Whereas Aristophanes' particular construction of old age is the theme I want to most deeply explore, the central concern throughout the text is the problem of flattery (Aristophanes then ties this problem to generational change and aging). This begins with the opening description of the household (40–72; all citations taken from Loeb editions), when the two slaves discuss all the ways in which Paphlagon panders to Demos, giving him treats and taking credit for the work of others. As Andrew Scholtz notes:

> [n]o single term quite does justice to the constellation of behaviors that the speaker attributes to Paphlagon. Our sources do suggest, though, that just such groveling, gratifying, and gulling converge in the figure of the *kolax*, whose *kolakeia* [flattery] would seem to supply the model for persuasive strategies to which one or another "flattery" label is affixed at various points in Aristophanes' play.[3]

In this setting, Paphlagon's invocations of love for the master, as well as his ability to pander to Demos's desires, becomes destructive *kolakeia*, causing chaos in the household. Over and over again, Paphlagon is a shameless promiser of whatever he thinks will get him the advantage, all the while telling Demos it's all in his (Demos's) interest. According to Rosanna Lauriola, such antics fit under the wider critique of Cleon/Paphlagon as the *bomolochos*, full of buffooneries with which "he tries to fool the Athenians and distract them with trivial devices that are intended to please them."[4] When Paphlagon is first attacked, he immediately calls the people to defend him: "Elders of the jury courts, brethren of the three obols, whom I cater to by loud denunciations fair and foul, reinforce me: I'm being roughed up by enemy conspirators" (255–7). The chorus leader responds that this is deserved, as Paphlagon is greedy, opportunistic, and slanderous. Meanwhile, Paphlagon promises that he was just about to do something nice for the knights! It's a deep shamelessness, one that the knights are able to see through, realizing that this slave will try to treat them like old men as well—that is, like the dim-witted, elderly Demos (270).

Of course, the themes of old age and flattery are related—such shameless flattery in the context of democratic politics is precisely the mechanism leading to that dim-wittedness on Demos's part. Later in the play, when we finally see Paphlagon address Demos directly, he quickly invokes his love for Demos: "Because I adore you, Mr. Demos, and because I'm your lover!" (730). He brings him all sorts of goodies and constantly reminds Demos of his past offerings (even those that involve the work of others). This profession of love continues throughout the last sections of the play, as Paphlagon and the Sausage Seller debate who loves Demos best. Of course:

> Aristophanes' specific intent is to make his audience aware of Cleon's popularity-seeking maneuvers among which are actions apparently consisting of assuring and giving wealth and well-being generously to the Athenian *demos*. What Cleon usually does is to "take and snatch," thinking only of himself.[5]

Demos is only convinced of Paphlagon's falsity when the Sausage Seller reveals that Paphlagon's basket is still full of treats, while the Sausage Seller had brought everything in his basket to Demos. But those professions of *demophilia* took their toll: the Sausage Seller explains to Demos his problem: "whenever somebody said in the Assembly, 'Demos, I'm your lover and I cherish you, and I alone care for you and think for you,' whenever anybody started a speech with that stuff, you'd flap your wings and toss your horns" (1340–5). Flattery has destroyed the old man's good sense, rendering him incapable of keeping his own house in order. Aristophanes here caricatures the professed *demophilia* of Athenian politicians, stretching the claim to absurdity, showing the difficulty of democratic dynamics.[6]

Flattery is also related to the larger problem of clever, non-stop chatter in Athens. Much like Thucydides' Cleon, Aristophanes criticizes the Athenian fascination with speeches more generally. When they move the rhetorical battle to the Pynx, the Sausage Seller laments, "when he's at home the old fellow's the shrewdest of men, but when he's sitting on that rock, he gapes like a chewer of dried figs!" (752–5) It is the noise and bluster of all the debate that helps to erase any possibility of thoughtful speech and consideration. When the Sausage Seller begins his direct engagement with Paphlagon (around line 275), it is a shouting match from the start. They trade insults, threatening to outdo each other with their bellowing, slanders, and promises of physical violence; this continues throughout the entire play. The knights most succinctly summarize the problem with this type of rhetor:

> You filthy disgusting shout-downer, your brazenness fills the whole land, the whole Assembly, the taxes, the indictments and lawcourts, you muckraker, you who have thrown our whole city into a sea of troubles, who have deafened our Athens with your bellowing, watching from the rocks like a tuna fisher for shoals of tribute.[7]
>
> (303–12)

In this case, it is Paphlagon's endless and shameless shouting that has set the city upon "a sea of troubles." The city's problems are deeper than just having a single trouble-making politician, however; otherwise, the *demos* could just toss him aside for better leadership.[8] It is the particular way in which Cleon makes trouble—through his flattering and overpowering rhetoric, he panders to people, corrupting them, rendering them dependent on demagogic flattery, and making it impossible for them to tell friend from foe.

Ultimately, it takes a physical demonstration of Paphlagon's dishonesty toward Demos to break his spell over Demos. The elderly Demos himself cannot at first summon the intellectual strength to recognize Paphlagon for what he is, given that he's been made decrepit by flattery. The danger of flattery is not simply that it is a single offense against reality or the individual, but its corrupting effects on the object of flattery, stoking vanity in order to manipulate that person into doing what the speaker wishes them to do.[9] This stoking only works when the desire to see oneself as in control helps insulate the object of flattery from the (pandering) claims. As this happens repeatedly, the object of flattery becomes less and less likely to detect flattery and more reliant upon the affirmation of the flatterer for his sense of self—even though he thinks he is immune to such things (because he believes he is above flattery and smart enough to see through it); the intellectual strength and vigor of the listener is sucked away by the shameless flatterer, who is willing to say anything to maintain his position of favor.

In the end, the blame not only lies with the politicians. Demos has been lazy, greedy, and stupid. Paphlagon just took advantage and deepened that already pathetic state. Demos simply isn't interested in exposing bad leadership, so long as he thinks it is serving his material interests. Paphlagon is able to wreak his havoc because he had earlier "sized up the old man's character" (46). Likewise, when the Sausage Seller recounts the verbal battle with Paphlagon in front of the Council, he notes "the ears of the whole Council were as quickly overgrown by his lies as by weeds, their eyes looked mustard, and their brows were knitted together . . . I saw that they were swallowing his story and being fooled by his flimflam" (629–32). Interest in exposing the politicians for the frauds they are is simply missing in Demos (and the *demos*). The Sausage Seller is able to distract the Council with a speech about sprats and anchovies; they are easily led away from what really matters. As Paphlagon argues, "I can make a fool of him [Demos] as much as I want . . . I know the sort of tidbits he likes" (712–15).

As Henderson notes:

> The villains and their dupes are not the people whom the *demos* has in fact recently voted against but the ones they voted *for*, not the social failures but the successful. And the *demos* is not the all-sovereign *demos* that chooses as leaders those best able to serve its interests, but a poor mob whose role models and heroes are bad people and which is eager to carry out the policies of self-serving con men to its own disadvantage. The more we enjoy this debunking of our leaders which draws on their acknowledged shortcomings, evokes our own worst suspicions, and plays on the antiauthoritarian invidiousness that festivals only intensify—the more persuasive our own negative caricature becomes.[10]

It is not clear that the *demos* wants a fundamentally different sort of leadership. The problem, according to the Sausage Seller, is that Paphlagon first takes the best pieces for himself (716). When they battle on the Pynx, the question is who can get the best pieces of food and clothing for Demos. "Which of us is the better man for you and your stomach?" (1208). The answer is whichever person has been willing to serve Demos most fully—Paphlagon loses because he left his basket full of treats for himself. It is not that Demos or his servants should be noble or fine, but that the servants must work on Demos's behalf and never for their own enrichment. For the corrupted *demos*, the "great" leader is "loudmouthed, low class, and down market" (180–1). Each one is more disgusting and low class than previous leaders, willing to do whatever it takes to convince the *demos* of his affections. "Political leadership's no longer a job for a man of education and good character, but for the ignorant and disgusting" (191–3). This all has been enabled by the *demos*'s susceptibility to and corruption by flattery: the point is to "make a hash of their affairs and turn it into baloney, and always keep the people by your side by sweetening them with gourmet bon mots" (213–16). The *demos* has become dependent on the pandering politicians, unable to summon the vigor necessary to cast them aside and return to its earlier golden age.

One particularly difficult problem is that the *demos*, in its corrupted state, believes it is in control of these leaders—that it is indeed sovereign. Instead, it has been carried away by the rhetoric and pandering. Leaders like Cleon pander and grovel; they are slaves to the *demos*, to be sure, but they are also deceitful and harm the people. In the long choral speech near the end of the play, we hear:

> Demos, you have a fine sway, since all mankind fears you like a man with tyrannical power. But you're easily led astray; you enjoy being flattered, and thoroughly deceived, and every speechmaker has you gaping. You've a mind, but it's out to lunch.
>
> (1115)

Of course, Demos claims he's going to get what he wants out of these leaders and then toss them aside. "I raise him up, and when he's full, I swat him down" (1129–30). He goes on later: "My lovers are certainly going to make me blissfully happy today, if I play hard to get" (1163).

Yet the final scene clarifies the struggle: Demos finally recognizes his senility and powerlessness. The Sausage Seller explains how foolish Demos has been since he was enthralled by all the speeches in the Assembly—"your ears would open up like a parasol and flap shut again" (1347). But the truth-demonstrating Sausage Seller has finally broken through. Demos is ashamed of his actions once they are explained—"was I that mindless and senile?" (1349). The Sausage Seller puts the blame squarely on the leadership—"the blame's with those who deceived you in this way" (1356–7). The Sausage Seller then runs through a bribery scenario and helps Demos figure out the proper way to act, reinvigorated again and able to take control of his future. Demos will no longer be fooled by the young folk with all their chatter (1378), but will stop them and force them back into a more rustic lifestyle, one worthy of the Marathon victors.

The use of the elderly figure to signal decline, powerlessness, and dependency depends on the idea that the earlier self—the younger man—was in fact able to fully exercise his democratic freedom. In that effort, he would be able to kick out the demagogues and live simply and as master of his home (given the ways Aristophanes valorized the Marathon generation, the individual master is clearly a worthy one because of his successful victory over invading Persian forces). In this case, Aristophanes uses this idea as a metaphor for the overall decline of the polity, not some direct critique of the elderly. But the point is clear. Here we see the ideal democratic self as particularly embodied: vigorous, simple, and strong. Other embodiments—here, old age—indicate an inability to be real democratic citizens, worthy of sovereign authority. Fortunately for Aristophanes, the plot of the play reveals a solution—reinvigoration and a return to the simple rustic lifestyle outside of the city.

Thus, *Knights* can be read as Aristophanes' effort to get the *demos* to recognize their errors. At the same time, the playwright also engages in flattery, pointing out how "clever" the audience is (225–34). Indeed, one must retain the favor of the audience if one is to stand any chance of being heard, but the audience may be so accustomed to flattery that it is no longer able to make good judgments about who to favor and for what reason. Therefore, a straightforward critique is unlikely to persuade the *demos* to see their faults and we have a hazier boundary between flattery and truth-telling than we would prefer. Mixing flattery with condemnation of the overall situation, the Sausage Seller tells Demos, "You aren't to blame for them, never think it!" (1356–7). In this way, the poet signals that he recognizes the problem of clever speakers—they *are* tricky! Fortunately, the Sausage Seller (Aristophanes?) is here to help lead Demos out of the confusion created by the corrupting influence of the likes of Paphlagon. Aristophanes' moves between flattery and critique keep questions about truth and authority at the heart of play. Given this, how can citizens know whom to trust? Adding to this difficulty, the Sausage Seller—and Aristophanes—engages in the sort of rhetorical fireworks and cleverness with words that most speakers—including Aristophanes within *Knights*—point to as so inimical to truth-telling. Of course, Aristophanes also harangues the audience throughout the play, even alongside his flattery and wordplay; his portrait of Demos is ugly and insulting, much more so than any of the relatively tepid critiques served up by Thucydides' Cleon. Yet, Aristophanes is able to signal his trustworthiness over rival speakers in another critical way.

★★★

Aristophanes establishes his authority with his audience not by promising them rewards or simply flattering their sense of self, but by drawing parallels between the literally decrepit Demos, the playwright's own anxieties about the potential weakening of his own intellectual powers over time, and the flattery-loving, figuratively senile *demos*. Thus, as Hubbard argues more generally, "the parabasis . . . serves as a crucial nexus-point for the multiplication of spectator-spectacle relationships among poet, audience, chorus, and (indirectly) comic characters."[11] In the play, Demos is corrupted and aged. All the rhetorical manipulations—of which Demos seems to have been an accessory—have taken their toll and literally aged him. The negative characterizations of the city are exemplified by the elderly Demos: "a cranky, half-deaf little codger" (43–4), "made blind to [Paphlagon's] crimes" (803). Here, old age is an obvious time of decline and diminished intellectual powers, not up to the challenges of democratic politics. This is a clear inversion of the usual association of old age with wisdom—an association other commentators often see in Aristophanes. Indeed, Cartledge argues that Aristophanes' use of the old man figure was "a way of celebrating the virtue of political wisdom that came with age, experience, and adherence to traditional values," noting the visual representation of an old man on a carved relief on an inscription of a law against tyranny.[12] As in our own day, age was often associated with authority and wisdom. Certainly, youth was not looked upon as a time of great knowledge; "forty was the most *sophron* age and the canonical end of youth."[13] Similarly, Henderson argues for a positive view of Aristophanes' elderly:

> Unlike later comedy, Old Comedy seems for the most part to have been conventionally hostile to young men. Except for the Sausage-Seller in *Knights*, all Aristophanic heroes are older men; rejuvenation is a popular theme; and sexual success is the almost exclusive prerogative of older men.[14]

But, as Finley notes, there were myriad attitudes toward the elderly in the surviving literature of ancient Athens, and Aristophanes is not as admiring of the old as he might appear:

> If one searches through the surviving poetry, drama, histories, political and forensic speeches, philosophical treatises and essays, one will find, not at all surprisingly, passages running the gamut of possible attitudes and conceptions of the elderly. Quotations are available to support almost any judgment. At one extreme there is the wise old voice of experience . . . At the other extreme are the jokes about the aged that fill comedy and satire; the *Wasps* of Aristophanes alone contains a sufficient quarry to keep a music-hall comedian in material for a season. The jokes become especially brutal when they touch on the sexual desires of older women, as in the two last surviving plays of Aristophanes.[15]

In line with Finley, and contra Henderson and Cartledge, I argue the representation is more clearly a negative one throughout *Knights*. Old age—in the figure of Demos—is repeatedly associated here with senility, not wisdom. Moreover, the rejuvenation of Demos at the end of the play should give us pause before we approach Aristophanes as sympathetic to old men—their reward is not wisdom, but a return of their youth. Salvation from Paphlagon comes not from the advantages of age, but from a younger man (the Sausage Seller) who boils down the old man Demos into a reinvigorated incarnation of his earlier self (and representing an earlier Athens). The old man is the central protagonist, but he's also been an unwitting dupe. Aristophanes' critique of Athenian democratic politics relies on this. He is clearly ridiculing a *demos* that thinks it controls the demagogues, even as those politicians swindle and corrupt them. If the old man is an admirable hero, a repository of wisdom, the comedic edge fizzles.

Moreover, the discussion of old age in the parabasis amplifies the negative portrayal. Aristophanes' playfulness with the multiple meanings of old age here also serves the critical purpose of distinguishing him from other would-be flatterers or *parrhesiastes*; not only does he profess to be on their side (although not out of love, but because of a common enemy), but he *is indeed* like the city itself—aging, anxious about it, and eager to maintain his powers. Aristophanes has the chorus explain why he waited so long to produce his own play (*Knights* was his first self-produced play, but his fourth performed play). Part of the problem is, as is mentioned time and again throughout Aristophanes' corpus (and as noted by Cleon in the Mytilenean Debate), the fickleness of *demos*. The chorus notes, "he was long aware that your tastes change every year, and that you abandoned his predecessors as they grew older" (518). The *demos* tosses aside the old poets because they—the *demos*—are *epeteioi* (changing, like the seasons) *and* because those poets have lost their comedic edge, becoming washed-up has-beens.[16] Here we see Aristophanes imitating at least the second half of that critique back at the *demos* twofold, showing how Paphlagon treats Demos as decrepit and Aristophanes casting the *demos* as decrepit as well. The multiple layers here, moving between literal and figurative levels, engage the audience's intellect, pushing them to consider their own role in the sort of problems they see on stage, while also engaged them affectively, getting them laughing at Demos, and perhaps at themselves.[17]

Still, the point is not primarily that the audience is fickle or even that Aristophanes treated the audience in the same way that they treated the old poets, but that individuals—including those in the audience and Aristophanes himself—have well-founded anxieties about old age:

> He knew what happened to Magnes as soon as the grey hairs appeared . . . in his old age, though never in his prime, he ended up getting booed off the stage, veteran that he was, because his powers of mockery had deserted him. Then he recalled Cratinus . . . you see him driveling around town, his frets falling out, his tuning gone and his shapeliness all disjointed, but you feel no pity; no, he's just an old man doddering about, like Conn-ass wearing a withered crown and perishing of thirst.
>
> (518–34)

Unlike other plays, in which he explicitly mocks his rivals for their lack of originality (see, for example, the first parabasis in *Clouds*), in *Knights*, he ironically pities the other comedians for their agedness. Even as this false pity is meant to draw attention to those comedians' more general failings in the theater, the choice of old age as the cause of their poor showings remains significant here, as it invokes particular understandings. More than the attitudes of fickleness or legitimate mockery of the unworthy, the choice of elderly status here allows Aristophanes to connect with the audience, as he links the loss of intellectual power with aging—a process which all humans must confront, including Aristophanes, thus making "himself part of the broader community and . . . his social criticism more palatable."[18] The effect is to make the presentation of Demos's tolerance for the buffoonery of Paphlagon—and therefore the presentation of *demos*'s tolerance for dangerous demagogues like Cleon—less threatening to the audience he hopes will digest his larger critique. We will all age—even the playwright is anxious about it. He knows what may happen to his own intellectual powers and reviews the dangers in careful detail for the audience who would prefer to ignore their own literal and figurative weaknesses. This is Aristophanes' way of both connecting with the audience by revealing himself as vulnerable to these same dynamics and at the same time throwing that condition in their faces so that they may not ignore it. We can each recognize this in ourselves and in Demos. Yet that doesn't make the decline any less serious. Like the poets—and like the individual audience members in the future—Demos's powers have faded over time. Meanwhile, the Athenian *demos* has figuratively gone through a similar process. A persistent nostalgia for the past is present in *Knights* as well: "we want to praise our forebears for being gentlemen worthy of this land and the Robe" (565). But the critique here depends on more than nostalgia for the past or a generational conflict—for here we also have "litigious old fogeys" (978) and Aristophanes is clearly trying to avoid the loss of intellect that he claims has befallen his aged predecessors. Being old is not only difficult because the young are so troublesome or unworthy compared to their forebears, but because being old is just so difficult (in this particular view). It is a time of loss and corruption, rather than ascendance and power. The *right* way to be is full of youthful energy—capable, independent, able to reign in shameless flatterers, and take control of one's own household (or polis).

Keep in mind that democratic Athens was elsewhere known for its restlessness and vigor—and for an arrogant faith in its own powers. During the Corinthian Speech at Sparta in Thucydides' history, Athens is described as:

> [g]iven to innovation and quick to form plans and to put their decisions into execution . . . bold beyond their strength, venturesome beyond their better judgment, and sanguine in the face of dangers . . . they use their bodies in the service of their country as though they were the bodies of quite other men, but their minds as though they were wholly their own, so as to accomplish anything on her behalf . . . they were born neither to have peace themselves nor to let other men have it.
>
> (I.70)

This portrait calls to mind an Athens of youthful energy. This may of course be the same energy that gives rise to the sophistic revolution and the *pleonexia* that leads to the spectacular defeats of the Peloponnesian War, but their intellectual strength and vigor is also a source of great pride for the Athenians. Yet they have succumbed to flatterers like Cleon.

This critique is not just metaphorical. It works because it solicits anxieties that audience members could have about their own prospects as they age. Whether it is salient for us or not, we all know we will age (or at least we all hope to be around long enough to age). Unlike other conditions or events often considered to be shared human experiences—birth, childhood, family, love, sex—aging and the prospect of death can carry their dark edges right up front. Simone De Beauvoir argues:

> Old age is not a mere statistical fact; it is the prolongation and last stage of a certain process. What does this process consist of? In other words, what does growing old mean? The notion is bound up with that of change. Yet the life of the foetus, of the new-born baby and of the child is one of continuous change. Must we therefore say, as some have said, that our life is a gradual death? Certainly not. A paradox of this kind disregards the basic truth of life—life is an unstable system in which balance is continually lost and continually recovered: it is inertia that is synonymous with death. Change is the law of life. And it is a particular kind of change that distinguishes ageing—an irreversible, unfavourable change; a decline.[19]

In this view—and this is not the only possible view of aging, to be sure—once past young adulthood, biological change becomes a much more onerous process, as individuals face the possibility of both physical and mental decline, instead of the sense of possibility and improvement that often marks childhood and adolescence. Of course, childhood and adolescence can also be times of great anxiety and unwelcome change, especially for girls in a patriarchal society. But the dominant cultural narrative generally follows De Beauvoir's lines. As we age, bodies are less resilient and intellects may not be as sharp. Moreover, as people age, they often find themselves dependent on others—similar to children, but having already enjoyed a sense of autonomy and freedom that children do not yet know. And unlike children, adults know the general contours of what awaits them as they age: eventual physical and mental decline. Yes, there are advantages to age—wisdom and authority, most obviously—and there is no way to ultimately prevent the decline, even if good self-care may delay it or mitigate some of the most difficult aspects. One simply must deal with it in some way.

In the end, the way to fix the city in this particular play is not to find a better leader, but to abandon its corrupt, passive politics.[20] "The *Knights* enacts a cure of Demos, a cure that includes a rejection of his role as spectator in a theater of politics . . . the Athenians must learn to see through the costumes, props, and role-playing of those who claim to love the city." Meanwhile, would-be leaders like

Cleon must move from roles as performers to mere spectators.[21] Yet Aristophanes seems to go even further, as Demos is counseled to leave the city altogether. Demos must return to his country ways: "if Demos ever returns to his peaceful life on the farm . . . he'll realize the many benefits you beat him out of with your state pay" (805–7). The Sausage Seller advises the rejuvenated Demos to "keep your language pure, everyone; close your mouths, call no more witnesses, shut up the lawcourts that this city's so fond of, and on the occasion of our revolutionary good luck, let the audience sing a paeon!" (1316–19). To restore Demos, we get the boiling down and transformation of Demos from ugly (*aischron*) to beautiful (*kalon*) (1321). Demos emerges refreshed; he now "lives in the violet-crowned Athens of old . . . when his messmates were Aristides and Miltiades" (1322–5). He wears a golden cricket—the symbol of Athenian autochthony, enjoying peace rather than days spent at the Assembly. This is not a reformation of politics so much as an abandonment of it.[22] Instead of regaining control over the demagogues, the citizens will avoid them. Likewise, Demos does not learn to deal with the difficulties of his elderly state, but is fantastically transformed into a rejuvenated version of his younger self—the self with the physical and mental prowess to take control of his own affairs. In many ways, this is not so different from Demos's earlier reliance on the panderers who claim to serve Demos, allowing him an escape from complex and exhausting processes of democratic freedom by outsourcing the work to others. Either way, Demos thinks he is getting what he really wants, that he is really the one in control. This is much like Anker's characterization of post-9/11 US politics, in which citizens' fantasies of sovereign freedom ironically led to a willingness to give the state wide latitude in restricting freedom. In both cases, the desire for a *sovereign* sort of freedom leads to citizens willing to turn the hard and messy practice of judgment over to others, just as long as those in charge stoke the public's beliefs in its own power.

Either way, the fantasy of escape from age is tied here to a desire to avoid the challenges of democratic citizenship that has caused so much strife for Demos. Although such escapism offers little opportunity for political solutions to problems of democratic freedom or rhetoric, it does highlight the difficulty of such problems and perhaps highlights the limits of comedy as an antidote. At the same time, we also see that a particular understanding of old age emerges over the course of the play—one that relies on an idea of youthful adulthood as the time of real power and true freedom. And once this vision is put into an intergenerational context, the elderly status becomes especially troublesome.

★★★

In *Knights*, Aristophanes portrays the apparent difficulties of growing old; in this account, the Athenian *demos*, like the elderly Demos, is too decrepit to deal with the likes of Cleon. Yet Aristophanes uses the old man figure throughout his work, not just in this one play. Is there something about growing and being old that is especially resonant in a democratic polity? True, we may lose—or fear we will lose—some of our mental and physical powers and that is frustrating in and of itself. Even more than such individual anxieties, however, old age calls to mind our intersubjective vulnerability. This is a condition faced by all members of a democratic community, who find themselves reliant upon others for recognition, participation, and meaningful action. Yet this reality is especially frustrating in a democracy when freedom is conceived of as an ability to control events around us—as we see in *Clouds*.

As Sheldon Wolin argues, "democracy began as a demand for a 'share' of power in the institutions for making and interpreting the laws and deciding questions of diplomacy and warfare."[23] But democracy, as Wolin goes on to discuss, it not a matter of sharing in the bureaucratic state. It has an "eruptive character" and is marked by a striking level of freedom: "democracy permits all manner of dress, behavior, belief: it is *informal*, indifferent for *form*alities. Democracy is as careless about obeying the law as it is about respecting distinctions of age or social status."[24] Democracy is momentary, impossible to institutionalize; it is a demand to take back power from the state apparatus. Democracy promises freedom to citizens, an ability to shape the as-yet-undetermined future.

Such a refusal of limits, however, can bleed into tyranny—as Plato long ago noted (*Republic*, 562–4; in fact, Plato uses intergenerational chaos to illustrate that point!). This is not the tyranny of evil autocrats, but an understandable desire to live without limits and to create the world anew. Arlene Saxonhouse explains:

> The word *tyranny* . . . deriving from the ancient Greek *tyrannos*, is far richer than the popular image of an individual who abuses power might suggest. Indeed, it uncovers for us the meaning of rule without limits, whether moral, physical, or historical. The *tyrannos* is the new ruler, the one who has come to power in the city by means other than birth or established precedent. Therewith his illegitimacy—but also his freedom. The ruler as tyrant becomes the paradigm of the free individual, the one self-perceived as unrestrained, able to carry forth thought into deed. Among the ancient Greeks, tyranny incorporated a freedom to break away from what was old and limiting. Released from traditions, the tyrant could transform the world in which people lived. The tyrannical impulse was not necessarily evil but could indicate a creativity and a freedom to transcend the limits inherited from the past.[25]

Whereas tyranny takes freedom to the extreme, that fantasy of sovereignty—of living without the externally imposed limits of others and masterfully controlling one's circumstances—also makes democracy deeply appealing for many. Still, the tyrannical impulse makes democratic life impossible, given that plurality is also a condition of our lives. In Oedipus' case (which inspires Saxonhouse's essay), he finds that he is not the sole author of his own life and that despite his cunning, history refuses to relinquish its hold on him. In the end, his entire family—save Ismene and Creon—die violently because of his arrogant faith in himself. Of course, freedom does not inevitably lead to tragedy. On a positive note, Wolin offers examples of "democratic moments," born of our freedom: "individuals who concert their powers for low-income housing, worker ownership of factories, better schools."[26] These are not tyrannical episodes, but moments of communal action. Freedom, for Wolin, involves the collaborative use of power; it is not simply an individualistic, sovereigntist view of freedom. Yet those moments must be fleeting to remain democratic; democracy is the "taking back of one's powers" and is not suited to organizing all aspects of modern life.[27] One's powers may be joined with others, but it is a tenuous connection, one that can always be severed when routine and order block the energetic freedom and spontaneity of true democracy (which is why Wolin argues it is not helpful to think of democracy as a complete political system in the modern era). Freedom—the ability to determine our own actions—is key to the democratic ethos, yet its full expression is limited by the fact that we must interact with others to "constitute a collaborative world."[28]

But it is in this most familiar idea of the able-bodied, powerful individual where frustration and anxiety enter so easily. As we can accomplish very little on our own (although the fantasy that we did it ourselves may persist), and since we cannot control others, the simultaneous promises of freedom and power that animate democracy can contrast sharply with the need to live among similarly free people and to use power collaboratively. This is the difficult circumstance of democratic life. Add now to this the fact that these frustrations are amplified by living in an intergenerational context. We are born into a particular historical environment that shapes the very terms of our political action. Thus, our freedom is not only limited by the fact that we must live with others, but by the fact that the conditions of our lives have been fashioned by people who came before us and whom we cannot call to account. We do not get to begin with a clean slate, but must deal with a set of choices that we had no part in creating. Yet the intergenerational frustration is even deeper if we take the older person as our embodiment of the democratic subject. The frustration is born of our *finitude*, which has two aspects. The first refers to the fact that when we make choices, we close off others.[29] We are finite beings, in that not everything is infinitely possible. Thus, as time passes, we find our freedom limited by the choices we have made before. As more choices are made, more possibilities are closed off. Although new circumstances then result, opening new possibilities as well, our potential becomes history as we age. At this point in my life, I'm fairly certain that I will never become a medical doctor or Bruce Springsteen's manager. When I was 20 years old, these were possibilities (even if unlikely). Although this closure might provide a sense of relief and security, there is also a loss and potential frustration here—I must continue on the choose-your-own-adventure path laid out for me by previous exercises of my freedom. If those choices did not turn out how I might have hoped, they can feel especially constraining. As we age, this sense of finitude can build, which may be perceived as deeply undesirable if we do not develop means to cope with that reality.

In this way, I myself am a sort of *assemblage*, a collection of fitted together decisions, moods, experiences, which may or may not conflict with one another. Shelley Park describes an assemblage as "a collection of multiplicities including both organic and nonorganic forces that can be neither divided (broken) nor unified (blended), but only transformed."[30] Thinking in terms of assemblages, rather than individual unified wholes, highlights qualities like temporality, heterogeneity, and fluidity. Internally, the assemblage is marked by difference and irreducibility. Externally, the assemblage must be seen over time in order to be understood—no single snapshot would prove sufficient. Action here is *emergent*, arising from the interactions between members, rather than being a sum of individual actions. Because the theory of assemblages also directs our attention to nonorganic forces, the *assembled self* (rather than the *sovereign self*) would also leave more room to account for the material, ideological, and discursive social constructions that shape individual desire and set the terms for the self to make choices and act in the world.[31] The *assembled self* would then be the collection of the self at different moments in time—like a 4-D version of the 3-D self that exists at any single moment. Who one is in the present is the emergent assemblage of previous selves, of decisions and identities shaped by both internal and external forces. These are not unrelated, random bits, but neither must they spring from some stable (indeed, sovereign) core that dictates a relatively coherent set of decisions.[32] This assemblage view of the self can also lead to frustrations and regrets, especially if one sees one's former self as particularly unwise and foolish. But as Joan Didion writes:

> I think we are well advised to keep on nodding terms with the people we used to be, whether we find them attractive company or not. Otherwise they turn up unannounced and surprise us, come hammering on the mind's door at 4 a.m. of a bad night and demand to know who deserted them, who betrayed them, who is going to make amends.[33]

The present self as a sovereign, self-determining agent with a stable core cannot really handle the knock of the former—and perhaps unlikeable—selves. Taken at a single point in time, an individual may appear to act with sovereign authority (at least over herself), but that becomes even more untenable if we put time back into motion. This notion of the assembled self has important implications for agency—that is, our ability to have an impact on the world. Instead of a single agentic moment, agency here is *distributed* over time. It also accounts for the *out-of-jointness* of time, the ways in which the past comes hammering on the door of the present. One's ability to act depends on many previous decisions (made by the self and by others). That is, no action exists in a neutral, single moment that was fully created and controlled by the person acting. Instead, our agency is distributed over time (it is also distributed over members of larger assemblages, as I will discuss in Chapter 4).

The second, and potentially more disruptive, element of our finitude is related to the very fact of aging—our mortality. Because we have a finite amount of time in life, we all must face the prospect of handing over the world to others. Moreover, because of the decline in our abilities before we die, we must often become accustomed to a mental and physical loss of power while we are still around to be frustrated by the loss. The elderly have had their shot at freedom, have created something anew, and now must relinquish control. The promise of freedom and the possibilities of action have been realized—however imperfectly and however nostalgically glorified—and now that generation must give up their projects to the succeeding generation, who may in fact ruin it all. Anything they did manage to accomplish will now be out of their hands. Finitude always provides a hard limit to even the most powerful individual—not only because we are enfeebled by age or limited by choices we ourselves made, but also because the next generation is there, ready to use their own freedom. Transgenerational projects, contra Jefferson, are the norm. But, just as an individual cannot actually and assuredly control events (even when commanding them), neither can a generational cohort fully own a project. Even a single moment—say, the flooding of New Orleans after Hurricane Katrina—will live on in time, shaped and reshaped by those who follow. And this lack of control amidst democratic aspirations to *archê* as sovereign power—is revealed in Aristophanes' work to produce destructive anxieties. I do not mean that Aristophanes knew this or was himself commenting on a dangerous conflation of freedom with control. Instead, his work shows the absurd violence resulting when individual control is demanded yet not afforded (and in my reading, this occurs as demands for control are inevitably thwarted because action is a social and temporal phenomenon).

We see these frustrations quite clearly in Aristophanes' *Clouds*. Whereas the elderly Demos struggles with politicians in *Knights*, we see an explicitly intergenerational battle in *Clouds*. This struggle is not simply the result of diminished intellectual powers or decrepit cynicism, but springs from the protagonist's inability to direct events once he puts them into motion. Faced with his own mortality, the protagonist must rely on his son and finds that events slip out of his control. In fact, he unwittingly creates the conditions for his own overthrow. This play is most well-known for its critique of Socrates and philosophy, but the intergenerational tension is what propels our protagonist, Strepsiades, to the Thinkery in the first place, and Strepsiades' frustration with his son's education (which he ordered his son to undertake) ultimately leads to the arson that destroys Socrates' school.

In *Clouds*, the audience meets the old Strepsiades, an Athenian shouldering great debts because of his wife's and son's profligate ways—another old man unable to control his household. He decides that the way out of his predicament is to send his son to Socrates' Thinkery to learn how to argue his way out of the family debts. His son, Phidippides, refuses: "Yuk! That scum. I know them: you mean the charlatans" (*Clouds*, 102). Although Phidippides had earlier promised to obey his father, he rejects his father's authority, confident that "My uncle Megacles won't stand by and see me go horseless" (124–5). Strepsiades decides to enter the school himself, although he is an old man, "forgetful and dense" (129). Throughout the text, Strepsiades' age gets noted—he is an "oldster born long ago" (358). Although he is old, the Clouds encourage Socrates to try to teach him. After several attempts with the "inept, brainless, and forgetful" Strepsiades (627), Socrates gives up on the "old coot" (790). His age leads not to mental acuity or wisdom, but, as we saw in *Knights*, to dim-wittedness. The Clouds advise the old man to send his son to the school instead, questioning Strepsiades' willingness to give in to Phidippides' refusals. The father manages to coax his son into joining the Thinkery, although Phidippides remains insulting for a good while. Finally, Strepsiades is getting what he wants—a younger, more capable mind to represent him to his creditors, a son who will do his bidding as his own powers wane. But, as the Chorus of Clouds notes: "this sort of business has a way of taking unexpected turns" (811–12). The desire to recreate the world on terms more favorable to his own sense of sovereign freedom is thwarted by the intersubjective vulnerability he faces as he must rely on his son—who has his own ideas— to actually carry through his plans.

Aristophanes reiterates the intergenerational tensions in the battle scene between the Better and Worse Arguments about halfway through the play. The Better Argument calls the Worse "a parricide" (912) who "defiles . . . [the] younger generation" (927–8). The Chorus invites the Better Argument to demonstrate its superiority, noting how it "crowned the older generation with many good traits of character" (960). The Better Argument focuses on how the old education followed custom and tradition, maintaining respect for elders and modesty; this education led to the Marathon generation, a far better group than the shameless, elder-disrespecting generation that inhabits the agora and bathhouses today (961–99). The glories of the bygone era of Cronus get mentioned as well (1029). The argument appears to be that if Athenians could just maintain the course charted for the city by their predecessors, things would end well.[34] But, just as Cronus is overthrown, it's all for naught—the Worse Argument wins with an argument about being "wide-arsed," leaving the Worse Argument to educate Phidippides in oratory. Again, the Chorus warns Strepsiades: "As for you, I think you'll come to regret this" (114). The father has hatched a plan, but he is unable to carry it out because of his advanced age; Strepsiades will instead deal with finitude by demanding that his son take over his ignoble attempt to thwart convention by arguing his way out of his debts. There is a desire to both command and control those actions, a desire that *must* be frustrated because it refuses to acknowledge the actual conditions of human life. Strepsiades wants to control what he begins—an understandable desire for a democratic citizen, yet one that remains forever out of our reach.

Here is where connecting sovereignty with its analogue *archê* is especially fruitful. The Greek *archê*, usually translated as "rule" (as in *archon*) actually has another meaning of "beginning"—as in origin or foundation. Markell, working from Arendt, describes the loss entailed by the eventual dominance of the former over the latter meaning:

> [t]he dominance of "rule" in this sense [as power of command over others], Arendt claims, actually represents the loss of a vital ambiguity in the Greek words *archê* and *archein*, the terms that now conventionally translated into English as the noun "rule" and the verb "to rule". . . . These Greek words, Arendt observes, originally had to do with "beginning," with setting something into motion, as well as with leading.[35]

And from Arendt: "To act, in the most general sense, means to take an initiative, to begin (as the Greek word *archein*, 'to begin,' 'to lead,' and eventually 'to rule' indicates), to set something into motion."[36] As political actors, we set things into motion; as Markell points out, that means taking the world as it is and then *beginning* from there (10). Both Arendt and Markell want to salvage the sense of beginning from the term and to disentangle it from rule and sovereign power. For Arendt, the Platonic tradition leaves us with the idea that one could substitute "making for acting in order to bestow upon the realm of human affairs the solidity inherent in work and fabrication." It is the equivocal nature of the original Greek that allows Plato to focus on rulership, which eventually overwhelms the meaning of *archê* as beginning.[37] According to Arendt:

> Escape from the frailty of human affairs into the solidity of quiet and order has in fact so much to recommend it that the greater part of political philosophy since Plato could easily be interpreted as various attempts to find theoretical foundations and practical ways for an escape from politics altogether . . . The problem, as Plato saw it, was to make sure the beginner would remain the complete master of what he had begun, not needing the help of others to carry it through.[38]

This does not mean Plato was the first to use *archê* to indicate rule over others; that usage has deep roots and appears in Aristophanes as well (see *Knights*, 797). Regardless, in such cases as these, the urge is to insulate a subject from uncertainty, ambiguity, and vulnerability; with *beginning* as *command*, there is an expectation of final authority over action. We have been told and retell a particular story about what it means to be the origin of something in the world. We can now tell a different story, as Arendt and Markell do. One person is not the sole author of the meaning of their actions, neither can we know where things one sets into motion through action may end. Consider anti-abortion activists' use of the Dred Scott case, or invocations of the battle for black civil rights as a model for gay civil rights.

Archê, Finitude, and Community in Aristophanes 81

The original actors do not determine the whole scope of those events—although they obviously have a hand in them. They have begun something, but those meanings expand beyond them, get taken up and reworked, transformed beyond their original intents, perhaps unrecognizable to the original actors. Markell's work explores this, thinking of events as beginnings in that they provoke response, rather than own their meanings.

Still, for many in our particular historical and ideological landscape, to be the origin implies authorship and authorship implies control—even if this desire for sovereign rule is born out of a confusion of the *fabrication* of our working life with the *action* proper to political life. Although Plato's formulation is antipolitical, it also highlights a critical irony: because action is a beginning, action—using our freedom—then leads to a loss of control—a sense that our freedom is not really so free. When we found something or create a point of departure, others begin to respond to it. We lose control over it, as it slips from our hands to the hands of others. Things may go badly, in fact. Seen from this perspective, we can better understand why Wolin sees democracy as a fleeting moment; it occurs in those rare moments when our own sense of freedom and our collaboration with others aligns—a rare and momentary occurrence. Thus, there is a frustration that arises out of the realization that Arendt is right. In the best cases, individuals come to understand that retaining control over what they have begun would effectively be the end of freedom. And then we can work to deploy and enliven other notions of freedom.[39]

This dynamic is also coupled with the fact of generations. Not only must citizens deal with the fact of plurality, but as they age, they must share the political stage with newcomers, people with whom they may not yet share a history and who they may feel owe them a certain amount of deference. This new generation arrives (partially and intermittently) with different experiences, languages, and touchstones—and their own desire for authorship. Even as we still participate in politics, these newcomers take the results of our actions and reshape them before us. Although this is always a possibility in a plural world, it is amplified in the multigenerational polity over time. Natality animates us *and* it gives rise to others, who are also animated with their own wills. As Aristophanes reminds us, this happens as we find our own capacities waning over time, our physical and intellectual powers weakening relative to those to whom we gave birth. Cronus is overthrown by Zeus, and Polemarchus inherits Cephalus' argument. We cannot remain politically active forever and we must inevitably lose even the possibility of control over the products of our freedom. Our lives have limits, but the generations keep proceeding. The loss and frustration—the affective forces—stemming from this physical and mental experience can be destructive, as my reading of the ending of *Clouds* shows.

Meanwhile, Arendt's vision of freedom for a plural generation of newcomers in the world—her story of *archê*, as well as Markell's use and expansion of it—offers a different way of thinking about political life, one that gets at the intersubjective vulnerability faced by every person and one that acknowledges our place in a temporal continuum. Just as people often experience with their own offspring (especially in more authoritarian parenting styles), some citizens find themselves trying to retain control over uncontrollable forces. One may feel a sense of ownership and want to keep what they have made within their control. This desire for control may happen in any number of situations across time and space; it is not a *natural* or *necessary* feature of human personality. But couple that possibility—a contingent, sometimes occurring urge—with the Western emphasis on freedom as an individual quality with sovereignty as its ideal—and now *archê* as a moment of beginning comes to have a too-frequent expectation of control. Aristophanes' comedies, however, reveal the dangers that arise when citizens cannot let go.

Once Phidippides is educated by the Worse Argument, he returns to his father, but is little help with the creditors, instead arguing with his father about the turning of the month (1170–200). When the creditors arrive, it is Strepsiades who argues with them until they leave. Soon, however, Strepsiades finds himself being beaten by his own son. This action begins offstage, apparently because the son refused to sing for his father, claiming that Simonides and Aeschylus were bad poets and quoting from the younger Euripides instead (1361–76). Phidippides proudly explains why beating one's father is proper. Strepsiades reminds his son how he cared for him in his infancy (1380–90) and of the respect due a father. Yet Strepsiades is impressed with his son's argumentative skills, and concedes the point (1436–8). His son goes further then, arguing that it would also be just to beat his mother. At this point, Strepsiades sees that his son has gone too far; he asks the Chorus of Clouds why they allowed him to go down such a path. They reply that Strepsiades set himself down this path with his quest to weasel out of his debts (1454–5) and that he needed to relearn respect for the gods himself (1458–61).

Strepsiades gets the message and regrets his attempts at deception. Yet the anger continues. He first asks Phidippides to help him destroy Socrates and Chaerephon, but the son ironically refuses because "I couldn't do my teachers any harm!" (1467). Further enraged, Strepsiades decides he must burn down the Thinkery. The final scene in the play consists of Strepsiades attacking the school with a torch and hatchet. It is not a silly, happy ending where Strepsiades finds himself renewed or his problems solved by retiring to the country to live the simple and good life. Instead, Strepsiades is chasing after the Thinkery's inhabitants, yelling about their impiety as the Chorus abruptly pronounces: "Lead the dancers on their way: we've done enough performing for today" (1510–11). Meanwhile, his son exited the stage without any remorse for his ways, having rebuffed his father's pleas to help him destroy the school. The play ends in a fit of violence, leading Peter Euben to call it a "hybrid"—both tragedy and comedy.[40] In the end, no one wins at all. Strepsiades craved control, but never got it; his reaction is to destroy the perceived cause of his troubles. At the same time, the audience should be aware that it's not simply the Thinkery that is to blame for

Strepsiades' bad state—he began the play complaining about his difficulties and hatched the plan to outsmart his creditors himself. The old man is no hero, but instead an aged buffoon, taken in by the false promises of fancy rhetoric and ultimately vulnerable to his son's greater skills. Strepsiades has been slapped in the face with his attempt to triumph over his own finitude. The alternative is not just a matter of affirming a different story of the self, but of helping people deal with an existential frustration—life ends. At times and for some people, this will be enormously frustrating, regardless of the dominant story. Interpreting narratives about that frustration and offering citizens opportunities for affective and intellectual engagement is key to working toward a new social ethos adequate to the challenge of intergenerational justice.

★★★

My reading of Aristophanes highlights the importance of thinking through freedom from multiple perspectives—or, rather, multiple embodiments. Once we do, the tensions and difficulties of intergenerational justice and the dangers posed by the allure of sovereign freedom come into clearer focus. We must be conscious of the very serious frustrations posed by finitude and living in a multigenerational polity that aspires to democratic freedom. Appreciation of this can also help us better understand the general difficulties of trying to balance those impulses within an intersubjective, transgenerational context. While the dynamics are more pronounced for the still-existing previous generations, the limits on democratic freedom are something we all face at moments in our lives. With our aspiration to freedom and the particular meaning freedom has taken on in the Western political tradition, efforts to attend to intergenerational justice must take into account what a monumental shift this would be.

Aristophanes also reminds us of one way of cultivating an awareness of these dynamics and frustrations: the theater. Whereas theater played a prominent role in ancient Athens that we cannot recapture, it does point us to the possibility of communal efforts at memorializing, discussing, and parodying our political life in other ways. This may be critical to the health of our democracy. As Allen asks: "Is it possible that democratic citizens have a special need for symbols and the world of fantasy precisely because their real political world does not and cannot give them the autonomy, freedom, and sovereignty it promises?"[41] This is precisely what we see in Aristophanes. The plays not only offer a critique of various problems in Athenian democracy, but they draw out other anxieties, exorcising the tensions that may otherwise lead to violence. The laughter generated by his work is both straight comedy and consequential—Aristophanes is funny *and* politically engaged, often targeting specific practices and individuals for parody or condemnation. We thus see a "perpetual tension between the spirit of celebratory, playful release and the force of derisive antagonism."[42] Both plays discussed here ridicule their central character—old men with serious flaws and weaknesses who, like the audience members, are lured in by the fantasy of freedom and control. Through the laughter, the play builds a democratic community through self-scrutiny, exploring the difficulties that mark the political community and offering laughter as a way of processing those tensions. As we see here, comedy can help readers and audiences see the tensions between freedom, power, and the passage of time and recognize this as a central problem of democratic life. Yet Aristophanes seems to counsel the impossible: removing ourselves from the problems of community, moving to an idealized pastoral life and leaving it all behind (or else burning it all down). This is a fantasy, but perhaps it is the only option because we cannot yet give up on the idea of insulating ourselves from vulnerability. The ends of the plays then might be more fruitfully read as another warning against the sovereigntist urge. Thus, we need to come to a new relationship with our democratic identity. We are not starting completely fresh though, as our actual experience—read for what it is, not for the aspiration to sovereignty we are told we deserve—tells us that we are not in *control*. We do in fact rely on others in order to make our mark on the world and, indeed, to develop our own sense of our selves that appears to drive that mark-making. As this chapter shows, we can look to our own finitude within a single life to see that the "I" is actually a collection of selves over time, an assemblage of one. It also means we cannot possibly control events in the far future, even events that spring out of our most ambitious and capable plans. Recognizing our own agency as already distributed is a promising possibility for creating further cracks in the fiction of the sovereign self so enthralling to us now—and so dangerous for them, in the future.

Notes

1 Portions of this chapter appeared in "As If We Were Codgers: Flattery, *Parrhesia*, and Old Man Demos in Aristophanes' *Knights*," POLIS 29, no. 1 (2012): 108–29.
2 See John Zumbrunnen, *Aristophanic Comedy and the Challenge of Democratic Citizenship*.
3 Andrew Scholtz, "Friends, Lovers, Flatterers: Demophilic Courtship in Aristophanes' *Knights*," *Transactions of the American Philological Association* 134 (2004): 275.
4 Rosanna Lauriola, "Aristophanes' Criticism: Some Lexical Considerations," *AION* 32 (2010): 42–3.
5 Rosanna Lauriola, "Athena and the Paphlagonian in Aristophanes' 'Knights': Reconsidering 'Equites' 1090–5," *Mnemosyne* 59, no. 1 (2006): 75–94, 84.
6 For further discussion, especially on politician-as-*erastes* in *Knights*, see Scholtz, "Friends, Lovers, Flatterers."
7 See Lowell Edmunds, "The Aristophanic Cleon's 'Disturbance' of Athens," *The American Journal of Philology* 108, no. 2 (Summer 1987): 233–63.
8 For a similar line of argument, see Slater, *Spectator Politics*, 82–3.
9 For more on the dangers of flattery, see Yuval Eylon and David Heyd, "Flattery," *Philosophy and Phenomenological Research* 77, no. 3 (November 2008): 685–704; Richard Stengel, *You're Too Kind: A Brief History of Flattery* (New York: Touchstone Books, 2000).
10 Jeffrey Henderson, "The *Demos* and Comic Competition" in *Nothing to Do with Dionysos? Athenian Drama in Its Social Context*, eds. John J. Winkler and Froma I. Zeitlin, 308–9.

11 Thomas K. Hubbard, *The Mask of Comedy: Aristophanes and the Intertextual Parabasis* (Ithaca, NY: Cornell University Press, 1991), 14.
12 Paul Cartledge, *Aristophanes and His Theatre of the Absurd* (London: Duckworth, 1995), 47.
13 Jeffrey Henderson, "Older Women in Attic Old Comedy," *Transactions of the American Philological Association* 117 (1987): 108.
14 Ibid., 109.
15 M. I. Finley, "The Elderly in Classical Antiquity," *Greece & Rome* 28, no. 2 (October 1981): 164.
16 For Cratinus' response to Aristophanes' critique, see Slater, *Spectator Politics*, 77.
17 For more on the parabasis as a bond between the poet and audience, see Hubbard, *The Mask of Comedy*.
18 Ibid., 14–15.
19 Simone de Beauvoir, *The Coming of Age*, trans. Patrick O'Brian (New York: W.W. Norton, 1996), 10.
20 Zumbrunnen (*Aristophanic Comedy and the Challenge of Democratic Citizenship*) argues in reference to *Acharnians* and *Knights* "that the wry, ironic vision that cleverness yields . . . is not by itself a sufficient response to the challenge of democratic citizenship" (98). To offer a further account, he turns to fantasy (in *Assemblywomen* and *Wealth*) to develop a theory of "comic recognition."
21 Slater, *Spectator Politics*, 84, 77.
22 For further discussion and an argument for a dual solution to the problem, see R.W. Brock, "The Double Plot in Aristophanes' *Knights*," *Greek, Roman, and Byzantine Studies* 27 (1986): 15–27. At the same time, the particular action in *Knights* offers citizen-spectators a meditation on some of the problems confronting democracy, while the interplay of flattery and truth-telling within the play itself may help to cultivate the ability of citizens to better discern trustworthy speakers and see through the rhetorical trickery of demagogues like Cleon (for more on this, see Lauriola, "Aristophanes' Criticisms," 53–5 or Zumbrunnen, *Aristophanic Comedy and the Challenge of Democratic Citizenship*).
23 Sheldon S. Wolin, "Norm and Form," 36.
24 Ibid., 50.
25 Arlene Saxonhouse. "The Tyranny of Reason in the World of the Polis," *American Political Science Review* 82, no. 4 (December 1988): 1261.
26 Wolin, "Norm and Form," 58.
27 Ibid., 57.
28 Wolin, *The Presence of the Past*, 154.
29 This first sense comes from Jean Paul Sartre, *Being and Nothingness*, while the second sense of finitude seems to be the more common usage, coming out of Heidegger; the two senses are clearly related.
30 Shelley M. Park, *Mothering Queerly, Queering Motherhood: Resisting Monomaternalism in Adoptive, Lesbian, Blended, and Polygamous Families* (Albany, NY: SUNY Press, 2013), 163.
31 See Nancy Hirschmann, *The Subject of Liberty* and Markovits and Bickford, "Constructing Freedom."
32 For more on this debate, see Krause, *Freedom beyond Sovereignty*.
33 Joan Didion, *Slouching towards Bethlehem* (New York: Farrar, Straus and Giroux, 2008), 139.
34 I agree with Peter Euben, who argues that it's not at all clear that Aristophanes is offering a conservative critique of New Education or Athenian democracy. The Old Education might not be all it's cracked up to be, especially given Strepsiades' own failings, the inability of the Better Argument to fully defend the achievements of the Old Education, and the "tragic" ending of the play. See Euben, *Corrupting the Youth*, Chapter 5. For more on *Clouds* as tragedy, see M. S. Silk, *Aristotle and the Definition of Comedy* (New York: Oxford University Press, 2000).

35 Markell, "The Rule of the People," 4. To be fair, Markell here is trying to draw our attention away from the seeming paradox between democracy and rule that he sees throughout political theory; to do so, he draws on Arendt's conception of *archê*, which he argues can reorient debates in political theory by directing our attention to action as a moment for responsiveness (rather than the tension between rule and freedom). Meanwhile, I want to dwell on the ambiguity because it helps us to better understand intergenerational tensions (even if we ultimately should move beyond it).
36 Arendt, *The Human Condition*, 177.
37 Ibid., 225.
38 Ibid., 222.
39 Think here of Joan Cocks's ideas about "natural freedom": "This is the freedom to enjoy bodily life as one element of a non-dystopian universe, in which all species can exist at the level of, not bare life, but flourishing life. For our species, this means, quite banally, the freedom to breathe clean air, drink unpolluted water, and be outdoors without fear of catastrophic changes in the weather. But it also means the freedom to indulge in sensory delights to be had in the physical world around us, including the delights of meeting natural life forms that are entrancing because they are neither like us nor for us" (*On Sovereignty and other Political Delusions*, 138).
40 Euben, *Corrupting Youth*, 137. Again, see also Silk, *Aristotle and the Definition of Comedy*.
41 Allen, *Talking to Strangers*, 22.
42 Halliwell, "The Uses of Laughter in Greek Culture," 292.

4
MOTHERS, POWERLESSNESS, AND INTERGENERATIONAL AGENCY IN EURIPIDES

> Unless carefree, mother love was a killer.
> –Toni Morrison, *Beloved*

> The mother's battle for her child—with sickness, with poverty, with war, with all the forces of exploitation and callousness that cheapen human life—needs to become a common human battle, waged in love and in the passion for survival. But for this to happen, the institution of motherhood must be destroyed.
> –Adrienne Rich, *Of Women Born*

What does it mean to have the "powerless responsibility for human lives," as Adrienne Rich describes aspects of motherhood?[1] Exploring the peculiar position of mothers, this chapter argues that they are figures who usefully complicate the notion of discrete individuals set into generations apart from others. Because of this, this particular embodiment of humanity clarifies the role of distributed agency in intergenerational justice. Not only is the present individual an assemblage of all her previous selves, but she is also part of a much larger assemblage, spread across an extended temporal landscape. After some contextualizing discussion, I first focus on Euripides' *Trojan Women*—a play in which mothers suffer incredibly as they confront apparent powerlessness in the face of the erasure of both their past and future. I then move on to Euripides' *Medea*—a play in which a mother causes incredible suffering as she chooses to attend to the future by destroying it. The first part of the chapter focuses on ways in which women were removed from the political life of the city. The second half highlights how women also transgress that construction, doing so in ways that also violate their ascribed responsibility within the familial assemblage, pushing readers to reconsider the bounds of identity, as well as the power of one generation over another. This works because we already see women (embodied as mothers here) as members of assemblages, contributing to distributed agency, yet retaining responsibility. That is, mothers are not seen as autonomous, individual actors—their agency is never entirely their own. This has long been problematic and a root cause of women's oppression in a tradition that prizes sovereign individualism. But I also want to claim it here strategically and selectively to argue that if we can focus on the parent as this sort of liminal figure between generations, we might be able to think about ways of eroding the aspiration to sovereign individualism that pits generation against generation.

In contrast to that powerless responsibility of mothers, my earlier examination of Aristophanes' *Knights* and *Clouds* revealed two elderly men (Demos and Strepsiades) who felt entitled to power but who generally denied responsibility for their part in actions that exceeded their will. It's not surprising that their refusal is tied to their elderly status—having moved from an idealized masculine position of autonomy and strength, they now find themselves more and more vulnerable as their physical and mental powers decline. Thus, we saw the frustrations borne from their inevitable realization that they are not free to control events around them, able to impose their will across generations. The fact of finitude—often ignored but nevertheless there—means that the aspiration to sovereign control will always be thwarted. The frustration arising from this unfulfilled expectation can have disastrous, even if comical, effects. People often cannot deal with the upsetting reality that their own decisions were shaped by the choices of previous generations, as well as their own previous choices, which may now seem strange or inexplicable. Similarly, there is often frustration that one's agency is deeply dependent on context and the future responsiveness of others. Instead, like Strepsiades, some would rather burn it all down and retreat to the country (or a gated community or into a denial of climate science).

What is another way forward? How might we close the gap between successive generations, recognizing the future as having a right to as wide a field for making political decisions as possible, but also recognizing how temporality fixes the field in some ways? Here is where the figure of the mother enters. The mother is a liminal figure, occupying a space between generations, often seen as operating in more relational and less individualistic terms. Of course, fathers can occupy this space as well, but given mothers' traditional—both in Athens and in contemporary life—role in caring for children, mothers are more obviously connected to the future generation. As more co-parenting arrangements spread, thanks in part to structural changes in family policies, this should change. Still, motherhood is often constructed as alert responsiveness to others' needs, rooted in the material practices of motherhood, which then shape a particular consciousness. These material practices of carework—feeding, clothing, caressing—link individuals into a networked assemblage. Acknowledging this reality, over and against the aspirational ideal of the sovereign self, reveals how a parentally inspired notion of distributed agency offers a pathway to the cultivation of intergenerational justice.

★★★

How exactly is the mother tied to the future? Occupying a place between generations, women do a disproportionate amount of dependency work on behalf of children and elders. Care ethicists have long argued that the relations of care springing from this encourage mothers, in particular, to be closely attuned to the needs of others. Especially early on in a child's life, the caregiver must be aware of subtle cues and daily patterns to know when the child is hungry, tired, unclean, etc. (or else risk constant unhappiness and crying—and a child who becomes accustomed to being ignored and unattached to other humans). Being attuned to the needs of others ideally involves an understanding of one's inability to control events and the choices of others. The toddler cannot legitimately be forced to consume a particular food; the teenager cannot be forced to respect or love another person. Unlike the ideal liberal (male) individual, with his freedom to act in the world, this work has shaped a widespread view of mothers as creatures of necessity, bound to the needs of others and, in turn, dependent themselves upon the recognition and uptake provided by their associated and publicly acting males.

Various theorists have taken up this line of thought over the years. Simone De Beauvoir offered a crushing critique of how this situation affects women, offering a vision of mothers as smothering, resentful, distorted humans.[2] In this case, motherhood is a deficiency and constraint—and hopefully a temporary interruption in one's *real* life. Attaching an intensely needy dependent to the individual trying to make her mark upon the world can indeed seem akin to tossing a heavy anchor behind a moving boat. Later theorists redeemed motherhood as a life project, viewing it as providing an alternative ethical model, focused on interdependency among people and the welcome need to provide care for those who need it (rather than contractual relations among atomistic individuals).[3] For example, according to Sara Ruddick, the day-to-day material experience of mothering (which she decouples from gender; "mothers are not identified by fixed biological or legal relationships to children but by the work they set out to do"[4]) shapes a particular consciousness on the part of the caregiver, leading to a specifically "maternal thinking," rooted in the mother's responsiveness to three core needs of the child: preservation, growth, and social acceptability.[5] Because the demands of the dependent run all over the place in unpredictable ways, the maternal thinker must also be flexible and deeply sensitive to the child. (Contrast this with Strepsiades' attempt to use his son as a tool, controlling him, and never recognizing the legitimacy of his son's distinctiveness.) This is not a romanticized, universal, or conflict-free view of maternal work; Ruddick is attempting to explain one way of being in the world that takes the raising of children as its primary focus (which does not mean that mothers engage in maternal thinking *all* the time either). Operating within this mode, it is more likely that one would be less wedded to the idea of action as authoritative and sovereign. Instead, action is directed at and, in a sense, *by* another (dependent) person and requires their uptake for its meaning. At its best, it is not action that is dominated by another (as in slavery). There is little pretense of a lone will creating something in the world over which she is the final authority.

A critical part of this work is figuring out where the lines between selves fall—that is, *recognition* of one another as distinct yet deeply interconnected entities. Too often, the mother is *misrecognized*—seen as subsumed completely in parenting, a means-to-the-end of the child. After all, if her *telos* is children, it becomes hard to see her as an individual in her own right. Jessica Benjamin's work, *The Bonds of Love*, describes the difficulties as the self emerges from interactions between mother and child.[6] Given the historical landscape and social structure in which we live:

> No psychological theory has adequately articulated the mother's independent existence. Thus even the accounts of the mother-infant relationship which do consider parental responsiveness always revert to a view of the mother as the baby's vehicle for growth, an object of the baby's needs. The mother is the baby's first object of attachment, and later, the object of desire. She is provider, interlocutor, caregiver, contingent reinforcer, significant other, empathic understander, mirror. She is also a secure presence to walk away from, a setter of limits, an optimal frustrator, a shockingly real outside otherness. She is external reality—but she is rarely regarded as another subject with a purpose apart from her existence for her child.[7]

Feminist theory and activism have done tremendous work in breaking down that erasure, but the tenacity of that ideology, as well as material demands of caring for young children, conspire to keep at least significant elements in place.[8] Nevertheless, in Benjamin's view, the healthy process of recognizing another requires a "paradoxical mixture of otherness and togetherness: You belong to me, yet you are not (any longer) part of me. The joy I take in your existence must include *both* my connection to you *and* your independent existence."[9] Whereas the early days of parenting often involve total control over the child, who must be fed, clothed, changed, etc. and cannot do any of those things on its own, the later practices of parenting move from directing action ("drink this milk") to setting the terms of action and arranging options to be chosen ("there is milk in the refrigerator"). That is, the child does not have free reign—it must live with an adult, who provides an array of options and choices, but who ultimately cannot (legitimately) force the child to eat this or that or choose this or that life path. One key to facilitating this relationship is reciprocal attunement—"a dance of interaction in which the partners are so attuned that they move together in unison."[10] In these interactions between parent and child, parent and child are neither opposed (the child is no anchor behind a moving boat) nor a singular unit (with either mother or child subsumed in the other). Instead, they are responsive to one another and relishing in the sense of affirmative recognition emerging from that attunement.

At the same time, concerns about essentialism and fears that dependent relationships and motherhood are over-romanticized are entirely warranted. I do not want to structure an argument around the idea that "women" have some essential access to a privileged form of subjectivity and that they should cultivate a family-based life, forsaking other interests or aspirations, in order to magically save the future from the destructive forces of liberal individualism. Not at all. First, that's a caricature of the arguments. The point is that this perspective shows, at the very least, how closely tied the practices of motherhood are with the general idea of the future. This attention to the future generation is not rooted in some feminine essence, but in the material practices of parenting (which could be done by any person caring for another—although, as Catherine MacKinnon notes, given our current gender relations, women are valued for the care they give others—and so these ideas are generally associated with female parents).[11] Since women—mothers or not—are often expected to care for others, including older relatives, siblings, community members, these dynamics are also relatively easy to extrapolate beyond motherhood. Finally, I should note that these are also idealized versions of those practices; when parenting is done well, it is attuned to the other, who is not perceived as cleanly outside the self, but deeply intertwined with it. It also does not mean that the parent is a martyr, sacrificing herself completely to the needs of the child, as motherhood has too often been idealized. That false construction depends again on the self–other dynamic against which I want to push. All this adds up to the idea that perhaps we can think through specific maternal practices—and, in tragedy, explorations of the meaning of those practices—in order to develop a self-conscious and constructed idea of how to tear down the boundaries between generations.

Nevertheless, society's relationship with women as primary parents remains an ambivalent one, perhaps in part because of this tremendous responsibility yet its traditionally gendered and marginalized status. Ideologically, mainstream culture pushes women to consider their primary responsibility to be to their families.[12] These constructions help shape women's very desires and understanding of themselves—as well as those of employers, family, friends, educators.[13] At the same time, there is also tremendous anxiety about the association of mothers with the development of future generations, especially regarding the mothering activities of women of color and working class women.[14] Being a "good" mother is conditioned by racial and class constructions, yet we tend to see it in terms of an individual's moral worth as a caregiver. If children are left alone in a single-family home for hours so the white, well-to-do mother can go to lunch alone, no one is likely to even notice. If children are left at a table in a shopping mall food court while the African-American working-class mother goes to a job interview 30 feet away, she is arrested.[15] Being able to provide enough resources, education, and time for one's children is first and foremost a question of social structure. Yet it's much more often understood in terms of the mother's individual psychological fitness for motherhood and ability to sacrifice all for her children. Thus, we live with an ambivalent vision of motherhood in which she is both saint and sinner, the backbone of society and a threat to civilization.

The Athenian myth of autochthony reveals a similar ambivalence about mothers and their (powerless) responsibility for future generations.[16] For the Athenians, women produced children and were charged with maintaining the *oikos*, ensuring the work of the household and the provision of new Athenian citizens. As Nicole Loraux notes, "A woman can accomplish her *telos* (her goal) only in giving birth, and although there is no female citizenship, motherhood nonetheless counts as a civic activity."[17] Women's worth was contained in their role as producers of future citizens; their tie to the contemporaneous world was dependent on their *kurios*, their adult male guardians. Meanwhile, men focused on politics and "in ancient Greece, the public world could only be defined in terms of war. Political leaders were military leaders. Political life entailed the preservation of the city through war."[18] In contrast to her male counterpart who found fulfillment in the world of the polis, the woman's life took place entirely inside the family—a family she created through her own power to give birth. I do not mean to draw too strict a boundary between the two spheres—both males and females maintained an interest in each realm, and the private and public life depended upon one another in interesting, complex ways, as Helene Foley has shown.[19] Yet an unmistakable separation and, for women, confinement, existed:

> Unlike the ambiguity of other divisions . . . there was no ambiguity about the difference between male and female, between those who fought the city's battles, debated the city's policies, and voted in its assemblies and those who bore the child, wove the cloth, and stayed within.[20]

Given the ideology of male supremacy in Athens, the biological fact of maternity and the social fact of female child-rearing is hard to reckon with. How could an inferior (female) version of an Athenian produce and nurture the superior (male) version? "Every formal inquiry into origins necessarily confronts males (and masculine society) with what they know but would often like to circumvent or even deny—namely, that man is from women born."[21] In Athens, this effort to deny maternity is revealed in the myth of autochthony. Although the term initially referred to the idea that the Athenian citizens were native to Attica—that is, not settlers, colonizers, or invaders—over time it developed into a complex story of earth-born men with multiple narrative branches and interpretations. Thus, autochthony could refer to a story in which all Athenian men were born from the earth or a version in which the first Athenian, Erichthonios, was born from the earth (Ge) after Athena wiped the pursuing Hephaistos' sperm from her leg. In this latter version, the earth-born founder of the Athenian bloodline named the city after his protector and foster-parent, Athena, forever linking the city to the goddess—herself an ambiguously gendered, virgin figure born from the head of her father Zeus—and further shoring up the exclusion of women from this civic imaginary. Meanwhile, woman "embodies not her native land but that of her husband"—a field to be ploughed by an earthborn son of the city, in order to produce more earthborn sons for the city.[22]

This exclusion also enabled the polis to link its citizens to one another through shared parentage and an erasure of generational division. Kasimis notes that "the ideology of autochthony emboldened a citizenship politics concerned with ancestry through a discourse that transcended generational time so that each citizen could appear to be the unmediated offspring of the land."[23] In this story, there is one timeless family of blood-tied, motherless, male citizens; individual families (which nonetheless continued to play a part in the life of the city, to be sure) were erased, freeing up the field of loyalties for the polis to take center stage. There was no role for human mothers within that imaginary—and the whole problem of women could be sidestepped. Perversely, denying biology also meant instantiating its value—for the Athenians limited citizenship based on bloodlines (in the autochthonic version, blood ties to the land). This also ended up highlighting the division between one generation of citizens and the next, as Athenian fathers were the key requirement (although the Periclean citizenship law later enhanced the status of mothers, requiring both an Athenian father and mother).

The city also attempted to limit the power of mothers in other ways, ways that required acknowledging the power of the bond between mother and child. Bonnie Honig demonstrates how the mourning practices of democratic Athens pushed away from the (Homeric) emphasis on the unique irreplaceability of an individual and instead privileged the dead's contribution to the city—clearly evident in Pericles' Funeral Oration, among other places.[24] The person to whom that irreplaceability is most deeply felt is, unsurprisingly, the mother—the person who gestated that body, who nursed him in infancy, and who nurtured his growth into manhood. Likewise, Loraux chronicles the city's regulation of mourning practices and its attempts to position the polis as true mother of the citizens. As a rival claimant to the citizen's body, mothers and their "feminine excess" posed a particular threat to the polis. Thus, laws designating who could mourn for the dead, and how, evolved in Athens, beginning with Solon. Mourning and lamentation were "ideally . . . hermetically sealed inside the house" and women's role in public funerals was to be unnoticed.[25] As Loraux also notes, mothers are notably absent from Pericles' Funeral Oration (the word "parent" is used when Pericles encourages those of childbearing age to just have more children). Mothers may mourn, but only in ways that do not disrupt the polis and its activities; they are just another member of a group of mourners, if they are recognized at all. The suppression of mothers' lamentation for their dead children allows the city to control any claim of mothers over their children's lives and to regulate the intimate "body-memory of mothers."[26] Of course, the city will not survive without actual mothers since no new soldiers would be born and men would be unable to continue their family lines. Thus, the erasure is never complete and these remainders—these mothers, with their disruptive grief—must find some sort of voice in order to avoid more violent ruptures. Tragedy becomes the space in which the threat of a woman's claim to her children can be explored and contained.

According to Honig:

> This institution of exception was also a regulated, disciplined domain within which some subversion was tolerated. Permitted, approved, if still also transgressive tragedy was a relatively safe venue that allowed and even occasioned emotions like, but not the same as, the emotions once solicited by female mourners, some of whom were "professionals" not unlike the actors who performed in the dramas. In tragic theater, emotions once exercised in now forbidden mourning rites are transformed into something else and exercised in moderation in a polis-centered and policed form.[27]

And so we arrive at tragedy, the one place within Athens where a mother's bond with her child could be publicly acknowledged, critiqued, and celebrated (admittedly, by men, rather than the women themselves).

★★★

Of the three major tragedians from Athens, Euripides may be the most difficult to make determinative claims about. Scholars differ as to whether he was an innovator or traditionalist, sophist or not, misogynist or not.[28] Without resolving where Euripides stood in these debates, we know his work reflects the intellectual currents of late 5th-century Athens. Euripides critiques *and* praises the Olympian gods, the new philosophical currents, women's aspirations to autonomy, and so on. As Donald Mastronarde explains:

> In sum, Euripidean tragedy, probably to a greater degree than other Greek tragedy, imposes on its viewer and interpreter a significant burden of *aporia* and compels a thoughtful recipient to acknowledge difficulty and uncertainty, to perceive the fragility of cherished structures and values, and to accept the insufficiency of man, whether in isolation or in a social and political group.[29]

In this spirit, I want to note that for each play, I am offering *a* reading—not the only one or even the most prominent or likely one. My interest is in whether mothers might help us theorize new ways to take up the cause of future generations, tempering the frustrations brought on by hopes for generational sovereignty and ending the misrecognition that results in the absence of intergenerational concerns from mainstream democratic theory and politics. Regardless, a few generalizations can be made. Euripides' gods, more so than in other tragedians' work, do seem more human—as in, more awful and bound by petty desires and grievances. For example, at the start of *Trojan Women*, Poseidon announces his departure from Troy—"when cruel desolation comes over a city, worship suffers, and the gods no longer receive their honors" (26–7)—as if the destroyed city is failing to keep up a bargain he had made with it. No sacrifices? I'm out of here. Meanwhile, Athena arrives to bargain with her former rival, intent on causing the Greek fleet misery for Ajax's rape of Cassandra in her temple. Instead of sources of wisdom (through the suffering they inflict) or otherworldly beings, Euripidean gods are retributive, inconstant, and often fractious, helping to amplify the sense of human powerlessness that marks so much of his work. "They serve him as dramatic incarnations of the capricious, irrational forces which his tragic vision saw as the determinants of the fate of mankind."[30] And as humanity seems more helpless in Euripides' work, more buffeted by chance and bad luck, we also get deep psychological exploration, with a focus on the interior motivations and struggles of individuals.[31]

Even more relevant to my argument, women occupy a central place in Euripides' plays. In many of the plays, women are the primary locus of action and, even when they are not, their portrayals are often the most moving within a play (so even as the *Bacchae* focuses on Dionysus and Pentheus, it is Agave's plight that most moves us). Although our record is partial, his portrayals appear to me much more sympathetic than the traditional Aristophanic criticism. Case in point: for a child-murdering mother, Medea is remarkably compelling—and remains unpunished in the end, heading off to Athens with the bodies of her dead boys. Over and over again, we hear of the burdens born by women—childbirth, child-rearing, bad marriages, the need to manage reputation carefully, the powerlessness—and women's attempts to push back against or to just negotiate those limits. Often the results are horrifying, but one does not get the sense that these women are *simply* terrible. It is not so much women who are singularly indicted for the tragedies that befall or are committed by them. Instead, Euripides' work brings the tensions and oversimplified binaries of Athenian gender roles to the surface, presenting viewers with a world turned upside down, in which mothers murder their children for revenge, women bargain for power, glorious battles are shown to be unsparing disasters, and familiar heroes are indecisive and unable to impose their will on the world. Through narratives that invite "exploration of routine assumptions and recognition of complexity and indeterminacy," the plays here detail the inescapable connections between generations that are rooted in the everyday practices of mothers.[32] And within these narratives, there is unparalleled suffering, vividly and concretely described.

★★★

Trojan Women (also known as *Troades*) was performed in 415 BCE, winning second prize. This dating puts it after the Melian massacre and as Athens prepared for the disastrous Sicilian Expedition. Thus, many have read the play for its anti-imperialist, anti-war messages.[33] However, the play also contains praise for Athens, the "sacred country of Theseus" (219), and the captive Trojan wives pray to go anywhere but Sparta (also the home of Helen), revealing Athenian chauvinism amidst possible critique (210–11). The action of the play concerns the immediate aftermath of the Trojan War. The city has fallen and only the women remain, about to be divvyed up among the conquering Greeks. The play focuses on Hecuba—the queen, Priam's widow, mother of Paris, Hector, Cassandra (and others). Throughout, Hecuba laments what has become of Troy, the losses incurred by her family, and her dire future—assigned as a slave to Odysseus. She has endured the abuse of Hector's corpse by Achilles, watched as Priam was killed at their household altar (481–4) by Neoptolemus, son of Achilles (and the new husband to Andromache, Hector's widow), and now must resign herself to the final destruction of her family line and erasure of Troy. The play opens with Poseidon's recounting of the horrors of the war and proceeds to focus on "poor Hecuba... weeping many tears for many reasons" (36–44).

Given all she has suffered, it is no surprise that the play is basically an extended lament (*threnos*). A practice so tightly regulated in the city itself, here it is unleashed in front of the audience, with little else going on in the play to absorb the viewer's attention. Francis Dunn notes the atypical structure of the play; for example, Euripides' other plays have a set pattern of elements in the epilogue, but those elements—*deus ex machina*, prophecy, etc.—occur here in the prologue instead.[34] This leads Dunn to argue "the finality of the prologue, which suggests that the plot is finished rather than about to begin, focuses attention in the following scenes upon the human agents, and upon how they cope with their dead-end situation."[35] There are, however, a few moments of action and movement in the play—the murder of Astyanax and the "trial" of Helen. Nevertheless, it is true that the play is markedly stationary and doesn't have the reversals and dramatic downfalls (they are already fallen) typical of tragedy. Readers must instead concentrate on the pain endured by Hecuba, Cassandra, and Andromache as they face a series of revelations and commands in which there can be very little freedom to act.

Instead of plot and heroic action, we get "from both the minute technical, and overall structural, point of view, a lament."[36] The play actually consists of a series of laments, with one complete lament (1287–on, for the city of Troy) and five reduced laments (one for Troy; one for Hector; three for Astyanax).[37] But it's not just that the play contains laments—it is itself, in fact, an extended lament. Ann Suter goes on to argue that every scene of the play, not just the formal laments, recalls lamentation for lost loved ones in its themes. Moreover, the movement between individual speaker (often Hecuba) and the chorus—solo and group—echoes the antiphony of formal laments. Finally, the focus on the impending sea voyage (in which the Trojan women will finally die, although they do not yet know it) and "remarriage" of the Trojan wives (as concubines and slaves) evoke the traditional associations of death as a voyage or marriage.[38]

Given the regulations on lament and its relegation to privatized space in the democratic polis, the presentation of an extended series of laments as part of the Great Dionysia is notable. Suter argues that this shows that lament was not as repressed as others argue, but that is not logically necessary. This could be a spot where Euripidean theater offers an opportunity for exception, a forum in which the repressed seeped back out, releasing tensions generated by the original repression (and, perhaps, reminding some why that repression was ordained in the first place and reminding others of why the repression was so problematic).[39] Tragedy here expresses what would be forbidden outside the theater and, in the midst of the Peloponnesian War, the audience would be well-versed in the officially sanctioned and anti-individualistic public funeral rites. Just as Cassandra is granted a reprieve for her harsh words against the Greeks (on account of her madness, 408–23), the *Trojan Women* can offer a reprieve from the state-restrictions on mothers' mourning.

Nevertheless, why write a play in which almost nothing happens? I want to suggest it is because lament—the mobilization of affect—is what is left when one is in a position with so little power (and then Athens attempts to take even lament away from women). The women are enslaved, their kin slaughtered, and their familial homes destroyed. There is never any clear reason for their suffering, no higher purpose or wisdom to be gleaned, no options for heroic action (in contrast with Medea). The only thing to do is somehow endure or to kill one's self (a worry Talthybius expresses at 299–302). As the characters repeatedly remind viewers, men have the potential for greatness in war, dying honorable deaths in defense of their city—and the women are left to accept whatever happens. This vulnerability and inability to confront it in an efficacious way mirrors the predicament of anyone living within a context of extreme inequality. Nussbaum argues that "through the not uncommon social reality of a woman's life . . . we come to see a possibility for all human life."[40] And although I think this is true, especially in contrast to the sovereign-power sought by Aristophanic old men, I do not want to lose sight of the unique position of the mothers here.

For women, this powerlessness was coupled with responsibility for producing the next generation. In the Greek world, a women's life's work was to prepare for marriage, to produce children, and then to raise them to be citizens/soldiers and their wives. In these tasks, Hecuba excelled:

> No woman, Greek nor yet barbarian, could boast that she gave birth to their like. These sons I beheld slain by the Greek spear . . . the virgin daughters I raised to be deemed worthy of husbands of great station I raised for others' benefit, and they have been taken from me.
>
> (477–86)

Her identity, her self, is never separate from the family she has formed with her children. Each individual's existence is constructed by the others' existence. The affective power of Hecuba's suffering lies in the completeness of her loss even as she must carry on existing. With no other family members left, it is unclear that there is anything left worth living for. This is not just the misery of an individual forced by the structures of patriarchy into her role as mother; this is the misery of a person constituted by her membership in an assemblage.

Thus, the family, extending from dependent/caregiver relationships, can be more usefully thought of as an *assemblage*, just as the individual self over time can be. The family is not an indivisible, organic whole, of which each part is an inextricable member and without which the family ceases to be a family. Instead, families take shape, form, emerge, crumble, re-emerge, disappear. It is a configuration of assembled parts, each of which fundamentally shapes—but does not determine—the overall assemblage, but without which the assemblage may continue—although differently than it would with that particular part. As Jane Bennett writes: "Each member and proto-member of the assemblage has a certain vital force, but there is also an effectivity proper to the grouping as such: the agency of the assemblage."[41] To understand the family as assemblage, we cannot see the parent as acting one way and then add the child to the scene. Instead, we see the parents' intentions and actions as shaped by the very presence of the child and vice versa. Moreover, an assemblage also includes non-organic elements—here, social structures, broader ideologies, language, personal histories, housing—which also shape desire and agency. As Nancy Hirschmann has argued in her feminist theory of freedom:

> Because "women's 'experience' is thoroughly constructed, historically and culturally varied, and interpreted without end," the self is not merely *embedded* in social relations but *constituted* by them. The self is only made possible by its social relations. It could not exist—logically, materially, discursively—outside of them.[42]

Her theory aligns nicely with a view of the family as an assemblage—multiple individuals, as well as other material and discursive elements, lead to the emergence of particular desires, actions, and outcomes, none of which would be the same without the interactions between elements. Shelley Park's analysis of queer families as assemblage also expands such a view. She argues "as an indivisible multiplicity that undergoes transformation, its form is rhizomatic, it relies on connectivity rather than reproduction, and it is a site of territorialization, deterritorialization, and reterritorialization."[43] In terms of assemblage theory, these emergent but relatively stable configurations are marked by what Manuel DeLanda terms *relations of exteriority*:

> [t]he reason why the properties of a whole cannot be reduced to those of its parts is that they are the result not of an aggregation of the components'

own properties but of the actual exercise of their capacities. These capacities do depend on a component's properties but cannot be reduced to them since they involve reference to the properties of other interacting entities. Relations of exteriority guarantee that assemblages may be taken apart while at the same time allowing that the interactions between parts may result in a true synthesis.[44]

At the same time, this fluidity should not be overstated. This is not the simple substitution, division, or addition of, say, playing with building blocks. The dismantling of an assemblage can have catastrophic effects, as we see in Euripides' work. The critical point here is that the capacity for agency does not reside in a single, autonomous individual. When we move to thinking in terms of assemblages, we see agency as *distributed*, rather than sovereign. "The relationship between tendencies and outcomes or between trajectories and effects is imagined as more porous, tenuous, and thus indirect."[45] Thus, motivation for action can come from a number of sources—corporeal, mental, and non-human (even as humans retain a particular responsibility for action springing from their capacity for self-reflection).[46]

Thus, a family may in fact be composed of individual units, who are able to enter and exit the assemblage, and lack a fundamental stability and fixed position. But *Trojan Women* shows us the friction involved in this fluidity—it is incredibly painful and changes the agentic properties of the assemblage. True, detached from the whole (widowed, childless), these women live on. That is, the organism—the family—did not exhaust their meaning or require their obliteration upon its destruction. In fact, the tragedy is driven by the persistence of the mother outside of her familial assemblage. Although children are their necessary function, and the men their voice in the larger world, the women find that, in fact, their family is only *contingently obligatory*, to draw on DeLanda's language. And without that larger assemblage, Hecuba's success as a queen seems meaningless now. Her family has been destroyed by the actions of the men around her, including her son, Paris. With her first-born, the great warrior Hector, gone, she has no one to come to her aid. The mother's relationship to men is a complex one—as wife and mother to men, she provides critical maternal care and the only possibility for continuing the family line. At the same time, she is dependent on their protection and deeply vulnerable when they cannot or will not provide it. As the Trojan War progresses, the boundaries between warfare and *oikos* that protected the assemblage of which she was part are erased, destroying her life's work, and leaving the individual mother exposed to the enemy.

Moreover, this is not simply the loss of any regular life's project or collection of assembled parts. As Andromache laments her seemingly pointless mothering work after receiving the news that the Greeks intend to throw Astyanax from the city walls, ensuring no Trojan heir to refound the city, she makes clear the deep physical connection between mother and child:

> O child that my arms have held when young, so dear to your mother, O sweet fragrance of your flesh! It was for nothing, it seems, that this breast of mine suckled you when you were in swaddling clothes, and all in vain was my labor and the pain of my toil! Now, and never again, kiss your mother, fall into my embrace, put your arms around me and press your lips against mine.
>
> (757–63)

These children were not only the culmination of a woman's life work or fellow members of an assemblage. The physical connection between them actually blurs the lines between autonomous individuals. Andromache laments not only her labor and nursing efforts that are about to be rendered pointless, but also the impending loss of this piece of herself and the bond of love it had generated.

The resignation with which they must face this destruction drives the tragic *pathos* of the work. After a series of antiphonic exchanges between Hecuba and Andromache, Hecuba cries "terrible is the force of necessity" (616). There seems to be no choice here, no possibility for choosing another way forward (aside from suicide). Moreover, this lack of freedom is compounded by the pain of knowing that earlier decisions—points at which a woman could choose to be one way or another, albeit within a narrow framework—have only worsened the current situation. Andromache speaks jealously of Polyxena's death because her sister-in-law knows "nothing of her own misfortune" (641–on). Instead, Andromache is all too aware that her position in the familial assemblage is what now brings her pain:

> But I, though I aimed at a good name and hit that mark well, failed to hit good fortune. Everything that women have discovered of modest behavior I practiced diligently in the house of Hector. First, whether or not there is anything blameworthy in a woman's conduct, the very fact that she goes out of the house draws criticism. I let go all longing for this and stayed in the house. I did not admit within my walls women with their clever talk but was content to have within myself a good teacher, my own mind. I kept my tongue quiet and my gaze tranquil before my husband. I knew where I ought to be the winner over my husband and where I should yield the victory to him. When the report of this reached the Greek army, it was my undoing.
>
> (643–58)

Her seamless interweaving of self and family led to her exemplary reputation and now causes Achilles' son, Neoptolemus, to claim her as his. And so she must make a new home in the "house of people who have killed my own kin" (660–1). It also seems clear from this passage that this role of the modest, cloistered wife is not entirely natural, but an arduous practice, cultivated successfully by Andromache. She chose to do this thing that not every woman can achieve just by virtue of being female, but then pays for it. And now the choices involve only negatives—betray Hector's memory or suffer her new husband's wrath (661–8). She is in an impossible situation, unable to fulfill her role as wife, and her role as a mother is coming to a painful, brutal end. Andromache was charged with birthing and raising the future king of Troy, yet is unable to protect this piece of herself—a powerless responsibility indeed.

One of the most painful moments of the play occurs as Hecuba prepares Astyanax's body for burial, as multiple temporal positions—pasts, futures—collide into the present. Andromache has been forced to leave Troy too quickly with her new husband and has asked Hecuba to complete the task of burying her young son. Placing the boy into Hector's shield, Hecuba delivers one of the longest speeches of the play, in which she curses the Greek fear of the child and mourns her dead grandson. The pain of his death is fueled by the end of the potential it indicates: "if you have attained manhood and marriage and godlike kingship and been killed defending the city, you would have been blessed, if blessedness lies in any of these things" (1168–70). As she dresses the body, she lists the now impossible futures for him—"victory in horsemanship or bowcraft . . . your marriage" (1209–10, 1218).

> Her lament over Astyanax is like the lament over a fallen warrior, which this child will never grow up to be. The shield is a monument of a sort to Hector, but its presence is a reminder of Hector's defeat and the failure of his efforts and sufferings, *ponoi*, to which the shield physically attests.[47]

Hecuba's familial line ends with Astyanax's death, mirroring the end of the city of Troy. "The land's name shall be wiped out! In one place one thing, in another another vanishes away, and poor Troy is no more!" (1322–4). As a mother (of the future king, Hector) and grandmother (of his son, Astyanax), Hecuba was uniquely connected to the future of her city. She crossed three generations of power (and physically built the great warrior Hector within and then with her own body). And so it is Hecuba who is best suited to bear final witness to the (attempted) erasure of her city. Given the rigid association of women with home and childrearing, the matriarch is the one who most painfully bears this total loss of the future, both metaphorically and literally represented by children. In this way, her laments push back against "the destruction of the creative energies and powers of parents—especially female parents—and the loss of attention to specific individuals."[48] Yet Hecuba's liminal status between the powerful adult generation (of male warriors, including ones she bore) and the powerless (children, as well as the other women) provides her with little power to influence the course of action, even as it ensures her deep sense of loss. Yet her inescapable responsibility for the future continues to shape her response to the world—a response that can only be rendered as lament, given her powerlessness. Of all figures, the idealized Greek mother is most attuned to the loss of future possibilities because her identity is bound up in helping the future generation come into its own power—her familial assemblage had a particular *telos*, which has been now rendered pointless. Yet, as a woman, she is least able to prevent the destruction of Troy. Is this perhaps part of the "psychological wage" enjoyed by those *with* power—charge another marginalized group with responsibility for the material practices (rather than lofty proclamations or even legal authority) that bring the future generation into existence, but be sure the mothers' perspective will cause no alteration to the decisions made by those with power? Leaving those most marginalized figures with primary responsibility for the future ensures that the future does not impose a burden on those with power, allowing the larger political assemblage to disregard the intersubjective vulnerability that challenges its aspirations to sovereign power, continuing the fantasy that has too long animated democratic political life. Like Cassandra, the mother can really see what's going on and the costs incurred, but just like Hecuba's daughter, there is no uptake.

Lament appears to be the most agentic act available to the women of Troy. Talthybius, the Greek messenger, counsels Andromache to "nobly bear the pain of your misfortune"—just as he delivers the news that her son will be killed.

> Since you are weak, do not suppose that you have power. You have no one anywhere to defend you. Consider: your city and your husband are gone, and you are in the power of others, and we are strong enough to fight against a single woman.
>
> (729–32)

Yet there are still some decisions to be made—for if she chooses to fight or insult the Greeks, they may still take away her opportunity to provide a burial for her son. Her choices are extremely limited—so much so that to speak of freedom would be nonsensical. Yet Andromache has some agency. As Krause argues:

> [h]owever disabling social inequality may be as a general matter, the alchemy of agency makes individual instances of agency unpredictable—sometimes unpredictably forceful. Moreover, agency is never an all-or-nothing affair; we should think of it as existing on a continuum.[49]

She is *involved*, but not *in control*. Andromache's behavior is hardly transgressive or surprising though; she relents to the Greek demands, and provides instructions to Hecuba for the burial of her son. What would the transgressive act here be, in any case? How could a woman raised to identify as the mother of her children act transgressively, given this set of options (this situation reminds me of Sethe in *Beloved* and Morrison's insistent question from the Foreword: "what 'free' could possibly mean to women"[50]). She makes a choice to refrain from insulting the Greeks or trying to physically rebel, but that's hardly a *choice* in this case, given Andromache's continued obligation to Astyanax and his decent burial. Acting in

Mothers, Powerlessness, Agency in Euripides 103

a transgressive way might make her a heroic individual (akin to Antigone), but it would violate her sense of self as a mother, even as it might salvage her sense of self as a Trojan or a Hector's wife.

Hecuba likens their situation to that of a ship in a storm:

> When sailors encounter a storm that is not too violent to bear, they show an eagerness to win their way out of their troubles to safety . . . but if a heavy and agitated sea overwhelms them, they surrender to luck and yield themselves to the running of the waves. So too I, suffering so many misfortunes, am mute, letting my troubles go and holding my tongue. For the wave of misery sent by the gods overwhelms me.
>
> (688–96)

There is nothing to do but resign oneself to one's lot. Curiously, however, Hecuba is not silent, as she claims here. She laments—indeed, as more misfortune arises (she is about to hear of Astayanax's death sentence), Hecuba continues her public mourning. This—the lament—*is* the transgressive option amid systematic social inequality. Here we have the Trojan queen freely lamenting the loss borne by women as a result of men's excesses during wartime (engaging in a practice banned in the city of Athens itself). She is not acting as a free individual, but as a constituent (and unequal) member of a series of much larger assemblages (family, royal household, Troy, Greek slaves, and so on).

When Adrienne Rich writes about the "powerless responsibility" of mothers, she taps into this dynamic. Rich refers to the kind of women's powerlessness she notes in the epigraph to this chapter—the lack of access to resources, the glass ceilings, the outright discrimination and violence, the legal obstacles to real equality with men, etc. The *Trojan Woman* shows us an even more brutal version of those structural injustices. But there is a second, deeper, and more positive notion of powerlessness here. In another essay, Rich writes:

> [t]o hold power over others means that the powerful is permitted a kind of short-cut through the complexity of human personality. He does not have to enter intuitively into the souls of the powerless, or to hear what they are saying in their many languages, including the language of silence.[51]

Along such lines, power is power-over-others—the attempt to reduce another individual to a particular characterization in order to shore up one's own sense of sovereignty (connecting here with Markell's understanding of "misrecognition"). In this sense, parenting at its best means refusing power over the child and instead grappling with the messiness of a developing human personality, staying attuned to the unpredictable other in order to fulfill one's responsibility, despite our inability to determine what will happen (or, as we see in *Trojan Women* or with climate change, to change what has already happened). The mother is powerless in this very particular sense; she cannot *control* the child, she must instead see the child and its personality and learn to work within those limits to bring about the desired ends (preserving life, fostering growth, socialization). The mothers' agency here is not sovereign, and instead reveals that power is located within the larger assemblage, across longer temporal frames, and dependent upon one's willingness to shoulder the burden of responsibility.

With this move to a non-sovereign view of agency, the power of agency-as-involvement, rather than agency-as-control, emerges. Thus, each member of the family is involved in an assemblage that shapes the context in which she finds herself, which shapes the very terms of her action in the world. She is not sole author, neither is she able to act with sovereign authority. This does not absolve one of responsibility, of course:

> To define agency as the affirmation of one's subjective existence through concrete action in the world is therefore to locate the experience of agency in a self that is reflexive, potent, and individuated but not sovereign. If the experience of human agency is located in the individual, however, the sources of agency are more widely distributed, as the material dimensions of agency reveal.[52]

Only if we require a sovereign self to take action do we require complete control in order to bear responsibility. This is the familiar critique of responsibility-as-liability, as opposed to Young's vision of a "social connection model of responsibility" in which injustices are social and structural, often invisible, often springing from everyday actions. The burden of responsibility is both extended and deepened by the acknowledgment that the *assembled self* and the *self-as-member-of-assemblage* do not fully control the outcomes but may only contribute to it. Thus, the experience of caring for a younger person and being cared for in this way seems to have a unique potential for making a connection across generations, provided we understand agency as shaped by membership in an assemblage.

It is not that the mother must abnegate her own self to fulfill her responsibility. In this ideal view, she is also not set into competition with these dependents. Instead, they mutually construct one another. For example, in the very first weeks after I had my first child, I was deeply struck by the sense of necessity involved, as if this child's needs were an obstacle to fulfilling my own. If I wanted a sandwich or medicine from the shop down the street, I couldn't just walk out the door. If I wanted a shower, I had to be sure he was safe and asleep or with someone else before I could go ahead and do that. Since I was feeding my child with my body (which was now also suddenly unfamiliar to me), my own physical being—and not just my will to do this or that—was tied to this child and would cause me physical pain if separated from him for more than a few hours. A few days before, I had freedom of movement and, suddenly, it was gone. This sort of constraint was unlike anything I had experienced before in my life.[53] At first, it felt like that anchor I mentioned earlier—tossed behind me as I was speeding along through my life. Over time, though, this need to be deeply sensitive and responsive to my children became part of who I was—but without the feeling of constant sacrifice and near erasure I felt during those first days. When I have a decision to make, their needs are just part of it. It's not that our needs never differ—they do—but it doesn't always feel like it's me vs. them. Our shared assemblage roots my own sense of self, like another deep interest or desire or constraint—akin to my own need to eat—except that it concerns other persons, ones who now form a central part of my own identity.

This does not mean there is never conflict because we are still in fact separate minds *at the same time*. This emotional intertwining is similar to how Young describes pregnancy, an experience that begins parenthood for many caregivers: it "challenges the integration of my body experience by rendering fluid the boundary between what is within, myself, and what is outside, separate. I experience my insides as the space of another, yet my own body."[54] The atomistic view of distinct individuals gives way to something that much better acknowledges the inescapability of connection and responsibility we have to one another. The physical boundaries between individuals become more fluid. Moreover, given that my children's lives should outlast mine and given that they have needs beyond my own, I have also extended my time frame for thinking about decisions. Travel to this conference or put the money into the college account? Given increasing inequality, should I also be thinking about saving a 'nest egg' beyond a college fund for them? If we want to move to Florida, will the school system be adequate for their long-term needs? Will the state address the rising possibility of significant impacts from climate change during their lifetimes or does it make more sense to settle in a place with longer-term potential?

★★★

There are two other moments of potential power in the play—Cassandra's curses on the Greeks and Hecuba's "prosecution" of Helen. Early in the play, Cassandra emerges carrying a torch (suggesting both marriage and the Erinyes, or Furies), singing of her impending "marriage" and calling on her mother to "dance . . . joining with me in the joyful step!" (332–4). After she is interrupted and the chorus and Hecuba make clear that she is in the throes of madness, Cassandra continues on to prophesy great tragedy for the Greeks and to recount the glory of Troy. She also dwells on the Greek losses in the war, during which their men died in an unfamiliar land, far from the relatives who would honor them, while Greek women were left widowed and childless. In contrast to other Trojan women, Cassandra's words are powerful and active, and indicate a refusal to bow down to the Greek victors. (They also provide much of the anti-war sentiment in the play—for if even the victors lose so much, what could the point of such "glorious" wars be?) At the same time, because of their divine inspiration, her comments are quickly disregarded by Talthybius: "If Apollo had not struck your wits awry, you would pay dearly for sending my generals from the land with such words" (408–10). The audience knows Cassandra's prophecies will indeed come to pass, but since there is no uptake by those around her, they do nothing to change the scene in front of us—no one acts any differently because of her words. She is not recognized. This is not the action of someone using their freedom in the world or trying to affect others; instead, Cassandra's power lies in her role as a mouthpiece for preordained fates.

One other scene bears examination as well. At line 860, Menelaus arrives on the scene, looking to take Helen back to Greece in order to be killed there. Helen pleads for permission to argue against her death sentence; Menelaus is not inclined to grant it until Hecuba intercedes, also requesting that she (Hecuba) be able to speak in favor of Helen's execution. Menelaus allows it and Helen defends herself, arguing that Paris—son of Hecuba—was to blame, as were the goddesses that staged the contest in which Helen was the prize. Helen argues that she also tried to flee Troy after Paris' death but was unable to do so. After her speech ends, the Chorus Leader implores Hecuba to "come to the rescue of your children and country by destroying the persuasive force of her words" (966–8). Hecuba here is positioned as the last savior of the future of Troy (at least its future as a memory)—an actor, able to affect the outcome of a particular situation. In a long speech (969–1032), Hecuba defends the goddesses and argues that instead of trying to flee Troy at every chance, Helen instead kept her eyes focused on who was winning and changed her loyalties to suit. Hecuba also notes that Helen never tried to kill herself, "actions which a noble woman would do if she longed for her former husband." Instead, Helen enjoyed her elevated status among the barbarian women—an arrogance she continues through to the current scene by appearing in fine clothing. Menelaus agrees with Hecuba's assessment and promises death to Helen. In the final moments, Helen pleads for forgiveness, as Hecuba warns Menelaus to ignore his wife. These last words from Hecuba receive an icy response from the king: "Old woman, cease! I pay her no heed" (1046). We are quickly reminded that Hecuba's ability to intercede is limited; she is not able to speak freely, but only granted a turn to speak by the victor, who will not listen unless he wants to do so. After he abruptly admonishes Hecuba, however, Menelaus actually listens to her, heeding her warning to not travel with Helen, as his love for her might undermine his plans (and thus undermine the possibility that her "wretched death . . . will cause all women to be chaste" (1055–7)). Nevertheless, we see the limits of Hecuba's persuasive power—always dependent on the uptake of Menelaus, who has absolutely no obligation to—and little patience for—Hecuba and the women of Troy. She has power only when those with actual power decide she may have a bit. Moreover, this is not an openness to Hecuba's pleas to spare her grandchild or to keep one part of Troy on the face of the earth. It is only a willingness to allow the most aggrieved woman in Troy to lend legitimacy to a death sentence for her former daughter-in-law, whom Menelaus must know Hecuba hates. Although Hecuba plays a role and uses speech to persuade, it is much more like Cassandra's speech or Andromache's choice (to not rebel)—it does not fundamentally change our expectations or transgress norms. There may be some element of freedom and choice, but there is no imaginative unpredictability and no improvement in the prospects for future generations.

In *Trojan Women*, we see a landscape marked by necessity, one in which the only way to exercise freedom is to lament. The individuals who inhabit that space in between generations, charged with responsibility for future individuals—parts of a larger assemblage that both outruns and yet depends on their individual agency—no longer have any power to shape future conditions (if they ever had much at all). As the Greek and Trojan generals exercise their own freedom, the end point is the complete annihilation of the Trojan future (ensured by the murder of Astyanax). The women of Troy can only lament their losses. Instead of railing against their inability to impose their will on the world, the women, with no expectation of sovereign freedom, move to commemoration and grief. The lamentations here rebuke the future-destroying wars of the men, if only as a reminder of the future that is now lost—and the depth of the pain engendered by that loss. Given the transgressive status of women's unbridled lamentation in democratic Athens, the effort to memorialize both the past and the impossible imagined future reveals a possibility of women's agency despite powerlessness. Through lamentation, we have "the affirmation of one's subjective existence . . . through concrete action in the world."[55] This agency is not sovereign power and would be almost unrecognizable to anyone expecting the power to influence the present—the lamentations do not change the situation for the women or for Troy. However, lamentation here provides future generations with an opportunity to remember the city (although it will not be Trojans doing the remembering but Athenian theater-goers). Those who cared for the interests of the future generations were unable to ensure that a future would come to pass, especially given that those in power had a narrow focus on the immediate, bound to "[destroy] what he loved best for the sake of what he hated most, surrendering to his brother his own pleasure in his children for a woman's sake" (370–4). That's the tragedy of the play and the affective push to engage more deeply with questions of intergenerational justice. Yet, even as action will not recuperate the future Hecuba had envisioned, there is a way to accept and honor the responsibility to that future. Thus, the women are left to use their limited agency to lament. In this effort, they begin a process of memorializing an impossible future. This is the agency of grief, of marking and condemning the disaster that has already come to pass.[56] In this way, the Trojan mothers *are* engaged in the process of collective world-making and thereby exercising agency. Throughout the succeeding generations, we continue to recognize their grief and their lost visions of the future, and to reflect on the tragedy that befell the mothers of Troy. And those Athenian citizens gathered at the Great Dionysia were also called upon to consider the restrictions on those charged with the work of producing a future polis, as well as the fact of their own vulnerability—and, perhaps, find ways to manage the frustrations and anxieties generated by it.

★★★

But what happens when women are the ones who destroy the future generation, lobbing off critical parts of the assemblage in order to achieve the sovereign control that the royal women of Troy so clearly lacked? Performed in 431, Euripides' *Medea* has long fascinated and revolted audiences. Likely an innovation on the original story (in which she only accidentally kills the children or in which the Corinthians do so as revenge for the murder of Creon and the princess), Euripides' version calls on the audience to confront the "heroic" struggles of a woman who takes revenge on her unfaithful husband by murdering the products of their union, their two young male children (in addition to her husband's new wife and father-in-law). What is the point of the murders? To shock us? Is it a "therapeutic exploration of violence?"[57] Is it to show how close to a savage beast a woman, especially a foreign one, really is?

The play could include those readings. But the one I want to offer focuses on the ways in which this play further reveals the intertwining of selves and the family as an assemblage (versus the family as an organism with the father as head). The family—and Medea's decisions on behalf of it—is not just a collection of individuals, but a new entity. From this perspective, we see the ways in which Medea's sense of self is bound up in her own identity as Jason's partner (not just dependent wife; that is, she sees herself as one who is worthy of reciprocity) *and* her own identity as mother to these children, *and* her own identity as a spirited (*thumotic*) individual.[58] Yet her political reality is the life of a relatively powerless dependent on a selfish male. In contrast, Jason acts as if his actions are his alone; even when he makes arguments that he has indeed considered Medea and their sons' position, most readers—and certainly Medea—find him self-serving and arrogant. Euripides never presents us with a Jason who struggles with his commitment to others, trying to find a path balancing his own desires and his responsibility for Medea and the children. Unlike Jason, Medea is very aware of the interdependent relationships between the central characters here, and how she does not fully exist apart from them (or, later, their memory). In this way, it is more useful to see action in the context of the larger familial assemblage and in terms of distributed agency: both of these individuals—Jason and Medea—contribute to the children's deaths. Medea is the final locus, of course, and retains legal responsibility for their murders (which also means her own suffering, as she and the children can never be entirely separate). But to deny Jason's role in the events is to ignore the structural injustices faced by a woman in Medea's position—without rights, unprotected, unrepresented—and to excuse those who contribute to the perpetuation of such structural injustices, even if only through everyday, "normal" actions. Jason has made choices, taking advantage of Medea's apparent powerlessness, and setting up a configuration in which Medea must either acquiesce, losing all sense of individual self and drifting into a future akin to that of Hecuba and the other Trojan women, or else take horrifying action, destroying the assemblage that also gives her life meaning. We see Medea struggle with the physical presence of her children—the affective pull of their soft skin and their kisses. We see how the very materiality of her children (and not just their unique personas) shape that moment of choice. Despite her own will's intention to take revenge by murdering her children, her action is forcibly slowed by the affective connection she has with the physical presence of her children.

This is not to exculpate Medea; she remains a child-murderer, after all. As she well knows ("how wretched my self-will has made me!" (1029)), her own personality means that vulnerability is unacceptable to her and she is willing to go to any length to salvage her honor—even murdering her own children. Since she has no armor or battlefield, her children become the weapon. To use them in this way means she must conquer her own attachment to them and proceed despite her status as their mother. Her needs as a spirited, sovereignty-seeking individual and her needs as a member of this assemblage are the core conflict in the story—not her conflict with Jason. This is why the play remains both a gripping and painful account, instead of just frivolous violence. It is the story of an individual following one line of the logic of her self (her spirited individuality), but with full awareness of the cost to the rest of herself (her involvement in an assemblage). Jason is clueless, pitiable, forgettable. Medea is quite aware of her self, her status, and her family ties. The result of Medea's spirited individuality dominating her affective connection to assemblage is both grotesque and unforgettable. The tragedy is that she must act like the male—dominate and destroy others—in order to be seen as a person. There is no space to *not* kill the children in this logic of sovereign control, even as her own lived experiences tell her doing so will cause her tremendous suffering. But what if she acted—if she had been able to act—as part of the assemblage that she, at other times, clearly recognizes as part of her core identity?

Thus, the play can't help but lead many to question traditional masculine values—honor, bravery, justice (as helping friends, harming enemies (809–10))—which Medea has appropriated. It is tempting to then see the possibility of motherhood—but motherhood done *right*—as an alternative. But that's not quite the point either. Euripides makes much of the connection between mother and child—but also notes the general precariousness of parenthood and how it outruns the parent's best intentions:

> I say that those mortals who are utterly without experience of children and have never borne them have the advantage in good fortune over those who have . . . But those who have in their house the sweet gift of children, them I see worn down their whole life with care: first, how they shall raise their

children well and how they may leave them some livelihood. And after that it is unclear whether all their toil is expended on worthless or worthy objects. But the last of all misfortunes for all mortals I shall mention. Suppose they have found a sufficient livelihood, suppose the children have arrived at young manhood and their character is good: yet if their destiny so chances, off goes death carrying the children's bodies to Hades.

(1090–111)

To be a parent means that one is bound to the unpredictability of the future in a specific and intense way—through the lives of others with wills and fortunes of their own. Just because mothers are seen to be *more* closely linked to this, in part because of their "body-memory" and also through their material practices, does not mean this is *not* a more generalizable condition—or that mothers prove immune to the yearning for sovereign control, as we see in Medea. The choosing of one response to the world or another—our character—is within our power. And the forces outside of us always lead us back to a non-sovereign understanding of freedom—if we can only really see them as they are. According to the Chorus here, parents experience that inability to control the products of their labor most acutely. And when they either ignore that condition (Jason) or refuse its constraint on their individuality (Medea), the results are terrible and self-destructive. Medea can only control the meaning of the lives of her children (for herself and for Jason) through the ending of those lives—no more unpredictability. Moreover, that the play is not so much about women's capacity for violence or even their relative powerlessness vis-à-vis men is supported by the closing lines of the play: "What men look for is not brought to pass, but a god finds a way to achieve the unexpected. Such is the outcome of this story" (1417–19).

This is not to argue that gender is not a central theme of the play. Medea tacks back and forth between a conventional understanding of femininity and motherhood (interdependence and distributed agency) and a more transgressive appropriation of male virtues (individuality and sovereign power). We see Medea as a powerless female *and* as a strong (masculine), even heroic, actor. We see the hero Jason, leader of the Argonauts, free to do what he wants *and* utterly broken and powerless. Medea consistently draws gendered distinctions and recounts stereotypes. She then uses those naturalized ascriptions *and* rejects them. Early in the play, she recounts the challenges facing women:

> Of all the creatures that have breath and sensation we women are the most unfortunate. First at an exorbitant price we must buy a husband and take a master for our bodies . . . the outcome of our life's striving hangs on this, whether we take a bad or a good husband . . . When a woman comes into the new customs and practices of her husband's house, she must somehow divine, since she has not learned it at home, how she shall best deal with her husband. If after we have spent great efforts on these tasks our

husbands live with us without resenting the marriage yoke, our life is enviable. Otherwise, death is preferable. A man, whenever he is annoyed with the company of those in the house, goes elsewhere and thus rids his soul of its boredom. But we must fix our gaze on one person only. Men say that we live a life free from danger at home while they fight with the spear. How wrong they are! I would rather stand three times with a shield in battle than give birth once!

(230–51)

Here, Medea famously challenges the traditional justification for male supremacy over females. Women must endure myriad challenges with little preparation and very little assurance of success. Everything hinges on a single individual—her husband, who has near complete control over her life. And, as Medea now knows, a poor choice can leave a woman—especially one who murdered her brother and betrayed her father for that husband—completely exposed. Moreover, Medea rejects the idea that women have it easy by foregoing war in order to give birth to children. Medea would prefer the male role three times over, in fact. The physical difficulty of giving birth is clear, but Medea's reference here is broader, given the challenge she will face in overcoming her love for her children in order to take her revenge. Having children is not only physically dangerous, but the emotional connection to them leaves her forever vulnerable to their pull, unable to act with the freedom that would make her plans easier to execute (of course, without children, she would not have this plan).

At the start of the play, the Nurse fears for the children—Medea is inconsolably depressed, but she also has a fierce, unpredictable temper and the nurse believes that she now loathes her children by Jason (36). Throughout the first half of the play, we hear little from Medea regarding her family, aside from her regret for betraying her family of origin and her hatred for Jason. But as the time approaches for her to fulfill her plan, her love for her children is made clear. In a long speech beginning at 1019, she laments her children, in ways reminiscent of the laments in *Trojan Women*. She bemoans the fact that she will never see them married and cries, "It was all in vain, I see, that I brought you up, all in vain that I labored and was racked with toils, enduring harsh pains in childbirth." She recounts all that she will lose—their company in old age, "the bright faces of the children," and "hands and lips so dear to me." Her resolve wavers at 1040–8: "Why should I wound their father with their pain and win for myself pain twice as great?" Her membership in this assemblage shapes her own agency, and seems to overcome her desire to be seen as a sovereign individual. Her fear of mockery and letting her enemies win out steels her once again, but she still longs to kiss the children and "wish you happiness—but in that other place." She is "overwhelmed with pain" to end her children's lives—but insists she must do so because Jason has left her no option. In her final monologue urging herself into the house to complete the murders, she must goad herself on (1236–50).

At this point, the messenger has recounted the gruesome deaths of Creon and his daughter, so Medea admonishes herself: "I must not, by lingering, deliver my children for murder to a less kindly hand. They must die at all events, and since they must, I who gave them birth shall kill them" (1238–41). But it is a task she knows will bring her unfathomable pain:

> Come, luckless hand, take the sword, take it and go to your life's miserable goal! Do not weaken, do not remember that you love the children, that you gave them life. Instead, for this brief day forget them—and mourn hereafter: for even if you kill them, they were dear to you. Oh, what an unhappy woman I am!
>
> (1244–50)

If the *telos* of women is motherhood, then what to make of a woman who destroys her children? The sight of her son's corpse should be "*pathos* in the highest degree," as Loraux describes such scenes elsewhere in tragedy.[59] With the death of her children, the Athenian woman has no meaning left, no purpose. The assemblage is assumed to give her entire life meaning; a self outside the family simply does not compute. But Medea is a more complex figure, of course, and helps us appreciate that even when ideology conceives of the self in particular ways, human action outruns those prescriptions. Medea's love for the children is real—and so her murder of them demonstrates how seriously Jason has harmed her, as well as her perversely heroic strength. She's not simply a deviant, horrifying mother. Instead, we can also view her as a heroic individual, able to overcome all pain to re-establish her honor.[60] And she must kill her own children to do this; it is not enough to kill Jason or his new bride. Instead, the pain of childlessness will be worse than death for Jason, especially as he enters old age (1396). Loraux notes how figures like Medea:

> [k]ill their own children better to destroy their husbands. But then they always kill sons, hence depriving their spouse of the arrogant tranquility of a father whose sons will perpetuate his name and lineage. It is not that these heartbroken mothers kill the children to whom they gave birth, but because the father annexed them to his own power, they thereby destroy the father in the husband.[61]

By destroying his future, she is better able to destroy Jason in the present. Once again, different temporal frames collide. To do this, she must become master of herself, the sovereign authority over her assemblage (and thus no longer felt as an assemblage, but the children treated—at least in this moment—as mere appendages to be used as means to an end).

Medea openly laments her children *before* the murders, and there are moments where it seems that her grief will win out. But Medea's "virtue" is that she is able to harness her grief and move ahead with her plan. Like the heroic solder in battle, Medea becomes a sovereign actor, able to impose her will on the world, despite constraints. She is well aware that these murders will cause great harm to herself (1029–30)—and not because she will be punished, because she has already secured a promise of refuge from Aegeus. Medea still sees the intertwining of selves here, but is committed to victory. Like some Achillean figure, she is willing to suffer terribly in order to achieve greatness. She recalls the soft skin of her children (Loraux's body-memory of mothers), their sweet breath, and their bright eyes, and she thinks of their lost future. But she masters all those feelings and is able to proceed with her plans to defeat her enemies.

Medea masters her words as well—demonstrating both verbal autonomy and verbal self-restraint, in ways reminiscent of the Greek male ideal in battle.[62] Brad Levett discusses how Medea is able to use language as both the stereotypical deceitful female (as Medea herself notes), but also as an active male. She self-consciously draws on stereotypes of women to convince Creon and Jason when it's necessary to do so, but she also remains tight-lipped and immune to persuasion—even her own—when need be.[63] On multiple levels, we see her self-sufficiency and masterful control. Moreover, Medea is much more masculine than feminine in the way she moves in the world—she comes outside the house, converses openly with males.[64] In these ways, Medea appears heroic—a figure more masculine than maternal. Up until she kills her children, Euripides is developing her response in a way that reminds us of Achilles' wrath.[65] Of course, the play ends much differently than Priam and Achilles in Homer, as Medea refuses to allow Jason to even touch the bodies of his dead sons.[66] And because she is now a child-murderer, no one can celebrate her the way in which one would celebrate Achilles.

Part of the perversity of her response stems from the disjuncture between the particular position Medea is in and the particular position she *thought* she was in. Throughout the play, Medea often positions herself *not* as a powerless female, but as an individual who is exchanging favors with other equals (with Jason, with Aegeus; only with Creon do we see her play the part of powerless female). Medea imagined her marriage as a reciprocal friendship between Jason and herself.[67] She helped him in his earlier quest, violating her own obligations to her family, and expected that he would honor his oaths to her, given the obligations incurred by her earlier assistance, which he now belittles (522–44). With his new marriage, that partnership is destroyed. One member of the familial assemblage has left, creating a void. Given that this particular member is also the public representation of the familial assemblage, this loss is especially debilitating. Jason has left her particularly powerless—in a strange place, suspect to everyone, and now without a *kurios*. Euripides' characterization of Jason makes this clear—we are sympathetic to her plight and to the losses she has incurred in order to help Jason, who now thoughtlessly abandons her when something better comes along. In some ways, what transpires is not just because Medea has this deeply *thumotic* character that requires revenge (although that is also true), but because she really has no choice. That is, it's not simply her own psychological failing or perversity, but also the structural conditions of her life that lead to the murders. Earlier in the story, she betrayed her male relatives—those who would otherwise come to her aid in such a situation—to aid Jason. She now lacks male representation because Jason has proven to be a faithless man—but she is unwilling to abide by that powerlessness, given her character.

Does powerlessness of this sort—overwhelmed by circumstance because of marginalizable status, even as Medea tried to do the "right" thing and make sacrifices for her husband—lead to her horrifying response? When one fears that one is nothing but someone else's means to an end, when one feels disposable, is that when a person does the most horrible things just to prove her efficaciousness? In many ways, she's like Hecuba: powerless. Her life's project—the familial assemblage she has created with Jason, embodied by the sons that will carry on after they are dead—is slipping away and there is nothing she can reasonably do about it. Unlike the situation in *Trojan Women*, though, there is a single, obvious enemy—Jason—who is also the person to whom she's dedicated her life's work, destroying her own family of origin (a different assemblage) in the process. And Medea is no Hecuba—Medea is vengeful, driven by her spiritedness, and willing to take on risks normally the province of men. But what Medea reveals in her quest for sovereign authority akin to the men around her is the perversity of the ideal, as well as the structural inequalities that leave her without other recourse. She must repress her love for her sons in order to achieve her goals and we recognize the false win it is. "For Medea understands that her decision to abide by her decision to kill the children entails detriment to herself [e.g. 1029–30]. Thus, Medea's 'victory' of self-control comes only at the price of viewing herself as an enemy to be resisted."[68] By claiming sovereign agency and denying power's distributed origins (here, her sons' own desire to live), her story becomes tragedy.

We also see the problematic nature of this quest for sovereign freedom in Euripides' portrayal of Jason. Jason tries to control his situation and plan for the future. Tellingly, his desire for autonomy even extends to reproduction (as it did for Athenians): "Mortals ought to beget children from some other source, and there should be no female sex. Then mankind would have no trouble" (573–5). If only he could wipe women from the earth, he could live as he really wants! He makes efforts to persuade others of the wisdom of his plan (which ring hollow), aiming to proceed with his new marriage without encumbrance. But, in the end, the gender reversal is clear, as an impotent Jason becomes the lamenter, left brideless, positionless, and childless. Ultimately, his failure springs from his own misrecognition of the fundamental unpredictability of others. Jason thinks he can act as if she really is how he wants to see her: a weak female, in the same position as the women in Troy. But Medea is driven by her honor and she has given up a great deal for him and so will not easily submit—although she will exploit his stereotypical assumptions to her advantage. And, although he cannot see it, she *does* have some power over him, given his love for his children (or at least his family line). Thus, Jason lacks the sovereign freedom that Greek men would expect to have.[69] In fact, not only does he lack that power, but his assumption that he does in fact possess it enables Medea to so fully destroy him and his plans.

The murder of children for the parents' sins or needs is a near constant theme throughout Greek tragedy (and even in Medea's story—for she continues on to Athens, marries Aegeus, whose involvement in the death of King Minos' son will require the sacrifice of 14 Athenian youth to the minotaur every 9 years). When it's a "sacrifice," it is an individual, often heroic, man murdering a child, often a daughter. Medea shocks us because here we have a mother, whose children are nominally safe and who is not commanded by any divinity to undertake the murders. Instead, Medea chooses to kill the children she loves because she sees no other way to reclaim her individual honor from the person she hates so deeply. Here, a member of one generation uses what little power she has to determine future (im)possibilities, using those younger persons as a means to an end. She does this as all other efforts to attend to the future fail. She can get no uptake from Jason—he has left her and her position leaves her powerless to do anything else. Given that her (masculine *thumotic*) identity is so deeply bound up in her honor and her need to win out over her enemies, the murder of the children, which requires her to overcome her very real bond with them, her existence in that assemblage—is the only option available to her.

It is not entirely accurate to say that Medea uses her children as a means to an end, however. She does not see them as distinctly separate beings from their father or from herself. To hurt them is to hurt him—even as she herself is hurt by her actions. There is no tidy way to exit a familial assemblage, just as no generation can truly refrain from affecting another. In Medea's case, her own self remains bound up in the children—not because of some magical maternal essence, but because of the social relations and material practices linking her to them. The children's survival and the *thumotic* aspects of her identity are irreconcilable because the children *are* her (only) power. Of course, the children are more often understood as the property of their father—and here are just reappropriated by Medea, who even absconds with their bodies in the end. But she is the one whose daily life is connected to the children, while Jason has begun over again with his new wife, claiming (unbelievably) that the children's position will be improved by his new marriage.

Given the disconcerting triumphalism at the end of the play, one of the most interesting questions is whether Medea actually self-destructs, as many commentators imply. We know the larger assemblage (of her and her children) is part of her core identity, as her laments make clear. We see Medea tame her connection to her future (her children), as she struggles to push them from her mind in order to get the power to exert her will upon the world and punish her former husband. To do this, she must draw lines between individuals—lines which we cannot actually accept and whose erasure drives the drama. Medea rejects her liminal position between Jason and the children, the past and the future.

The Trojan mothers' agency of grief will not suffice for Medea. She refuses her responsibility to the future in order to achieve sovereign power, but the horror of the play shows the falsity of this achievement. She may get the power for which she longs. Her refusal of her *powerless* responsibility is in fact a form of agency—but it comes at too high a cost. It is the only thing Medea can do—sacrifice the future, her own assemblage. This particular reading of Euripides' play also contains a cruel Platonic irony.[70] We pity and condemn Medea, losing sight of how not-so-very-different we are and how often we ourselves draw such lines, separating our futures from those of others, sacrificing those less powerful in the present (the future generations) because we also feel like it's the only thing we can do. Our attempts to exert our own power (even as, much like Jason, we convince ourselves that this will be a benefit for them as well) can too often destroy opportunities for any sort of freedom in the future.

In order to broaden the self beyond a quest for sovereign power, we can look instead to those denied even the possibility of such a quest—the mothers required by context to form an identity rooted in interdependence and a larger assemblage over which they are charged with primary responsibility. Yet *Trojan Women* and *Medea* also move us with a portrayal of the misery of this formation, as it is coupled with powerlessness and a reliance on proxy representatives who can too easily sacrifice them. Instead, we need a vision of transgenerational connection—one coupled with political power.

Notes

1 Adrienne Rich, *Of Woman Born: Motherhood as Experience and Institution* (New York: W.W. Norton, 1995), 277.
2 Simone de Beauvoir, *The Second Sex* (New York: Vintage, 1949/2011).
3 Virginia Held, *Feminist Morality: Transforming Culture, Society, and Politics* (Chicago, IL: University of Chicago Press, 1993); Eva Feder Kittay, *Love's Labor: Essays on Women, Equality, and Dependency* (New York: Routledge, 1999); Sara Ruddick, *Maternal Thinking: Toward a Politics of Peace* (New York: Ballantine Books, 1989); Joan Tronto, *Moral Boundaries: A Political Argument for an Ethic of Care* (New York: Routledge, 1994) and *Caring Democracy: Markets, Equality, and Justice* (New York: NYU Press, 2013).
4 Ruddick, *Maternal Thinking*, xi.
5 Ibid., 17.
6 Jessica Benjamin, *The Bonds of Love: Psychoanalysis, Feminism, and the Problem of Domination* (New York: Pantheon Books, 1988).
7 Ibid., 22–3.
8 For a powerful fictional take on this, see Elisa Albert, *After Birth* (New York: Mariner Books, 2016).
9 Benjamin, *The Bonds of Love*, 15.
10 Ibid., 27.
11 Catherine MacKinnon, *Feminism Unmodified: Discourses on Life and Law* (Cambridge, MA: Harvard University Press, 1987), 39.
12 Susan Moller Okin, *Justice, Gender, and the Family* (New York: Basic Books, 1989); Pew Research Center, "Modern Parenthood: Roles of Moms and Dads Converge as They Balance Work and Family" (2013): www.pewsocialtrends.org/2013/03/14/modern-parenthood-roles-of-moms-and-dadsconverge-as-they-balance-work-and-family/.

13 Markovits and Bickford, "Constructing Freedom."
14 Ange-Marie Hancock, *The Politics of Disgust: The Public Identity of the Welfare Queen* (New York: NYU Press, 2004); Patricia Hill Collins, *Black Feminist Thought* (New York: Routledge, 2000); Markovits and Bickford, "Constructing Freedom"; Dorothy Roberts, *Killing the Black Body: Race, Reproduction and the Meaning of Liberty* (New York: Vintage, 1998) and *Shattered Bonds: The Color of Child Welfare* (New York: Basic Civitas Books, 2003); Joe Soss, Richard C. Fording, and Sanford F. Schram, *Persistent Power of Race* (Chicago, IL: University of Chicago Press, 2011).
15 www.khou.com/story/news/local/2015/07/17/houston-mom-charged-with-abandoning-children-during-job-interview/30307379/.
16 I do not mean to erase the dramatic differences between ancient Athens and the contemporary US. But with regard to women and their role in society, the relevant social relations make the leap less irresponsible than might seem. Bernard Williams is helpful here: compared to attitudes about slavery, "modern prejudice [about women] is to a much vaster extent the same as ancient. Quite apart from the fact that prejudice based on traditional religious conceptions flourishes in the contemporary world, the idea that gender roles are imposed by nature is alive in "modern," scientistic forms. In particular, the more crassly unreflective contributions of sociobiology to this subject represent little more than continuations of Aristotelian anthropology by other means" (*Shame and Necessity*, Berkeley, CA: University of California Press, 1993, 125).
17 Nicole Loraux, *Mothers in Mourning* (Ithaca, NY: Cornell University Press, 1998), 12.
18 Arlene Saxonhouse, "Men, Women, War, and Politics: Family and Polis in Aristophanes and Euripides," *Political Theory* 8, no. 1 (1980): 66.
19 Helene Foley, "The Conceptions of Women in Athenian Drama," in *Reflections of Women in Antiquity*, ed. Helene P. Foley (New York: Gordon and Breach, 1981), 127–68.
20 Arlene Saxonhouse, *Fear of Diversity: The Birth of Political Science in Ancient Greek Thought* (Chicago, IL: University of Chicago Press, 1992), 8.
21 Froma Zeitlin, "Foreword," in Nicole Loraux, *The Children of Athena: Athenian Ideas about Citizenship and the Division Between the Sexes* (Princeton, NJ: Princeton University Press, 1993), xii.
22 Jean-Pierre Vernant, *Myth and Thought among the Greeks* (New York: Zone Books, 2006), 172.
23 Kasimis, "The Tragedy of Blood-Based Membership," 234.
24 Bonnie Honig, "Antigone's Laments, Creon's Grief: Mourning, Membership, and the Politics of Exception," *Political Theory* 37, no. 1 (February 2009): 5–43; *Antigone Interrupted* (New York: Cambridge University Press, 2013).
25 Loraux, *Mothers in Mourning*, 25.
26 Ibid., 37.
27 Honig, "Antigone's Laments, Creon's Grief," 13.
28 R. P. Winnington-Ingram, John Gould, P. E. Easterling, and B. M. W. Knox, "Tragedy" in *The Cambridge History of Classical Literature*, eds. P. E. Easterling and Bernard M. W. Knox (New York: Cambridge University Press, 1985), 258–345; Ann Michelini, "Euripides: Conformist, Deviant, Neo-Conservative?" *Arion: A Journal of Humanities and the Classics* 4, no. 3 (Winter 1997): 208–22.
29 Donald J. Mastronarde, *The Art of Euripides: Dramatic Technique and Social Context* (New York: Cambridge University Press, 2010), 311.
30 Winnington-Ingram *et al.* "Tragedy," 325.
31 Ibid., 327.
32 Mastronarde, *The Art of Euripides*, 246.
33 Suzanne Said, "Tragedy and Politics," *Democracy, Empire, and the Arts in Fifth-Century Athens*, eds. Debora Boedeker and Kurt Raaflaub (Cambridge, MA: Harvard University Press, 1998), 284.
34 Francis M. Dunn, "Beginning at the End in Euripides' *Trojan Women*," *Rheinishes Museum für Philologie*. Neue Folge 136. Bd. H. 1 (1993): 22–35.

35 Ibid., 32.
36 Ann Suter, "Lament in Euripides' *Trojan Women*," *Mnemosyne* 56, no. 1 (2003): 1.
37 Ibid., 5. Suter lists the elements of a formal lament: expression of grief and loss, contrast between past and present, praise for the dead, anger at the dead for abandoning the living, anger and desire for vengeance against those responsible, desire of mourner to die, description of mourning and funeral rites offered (3). A "reduced" lament has some, but not all, these elements; full or reduced does not refer to length, but rather to these elements.
38 Ibid., 13.
39 See also, Charles Segal, *Euripides and the Poetics of Sorrow: Art, Gender, and Commemoration in* Alcestis, Hippolytus, *and* Hecuba (Durham, NC: Duke University Press, 1993).
40 Martha Nussbaum, *The Fragility of Goodness: Luck and Ethics in Greek Tragedy and Philosophy* (Cambridge, UK: Cambridge University Press, 1986), 413.
41 Jane Bennett, *Vibrant Matter: A Political Ecology of Things* (Durham, NC: Duke University Press, 2010), 24.
42 Hirschmann, *The Subject of Liberty*, 203–4.
43 Park, *Mothering Queerly, Queering Motherhood*, 163.
44 Manuel DeLanda, *A New Philosophy of Society: Assemblage Theory and Social Complexity* (London: Continuum: 2006), 11.
45 Bennett, *Vibrant Matter*, 36.
46 This is where I part ways with many new or vital materialists (like Bennett). I would not ascribe agency to electrons or an electrical grid. Instead, I agree with Sharon Krause that humans (and very likely other animals) have a particular capacity for self-reflexive action and an outsized responsibility for the things we do in the world. Thus, "we need to recognize the ways that individual agency is corporeal and distributed but also to make room for responsibility and normativity . . . rather than being located exclusively within the individual, or construed simply as an internal capacity, agency is better understood as a product of the bodily encounters, self-understandings, and social interpretations through which one's identity finds affirmations in one's deeds." Sharon Krause, "Bodies in Action: Corporeal Agency and Democratic Politics," *Political Theory* 39, no. 3 (2011), 300, 308.
47 Segal, *Euripides and the Poetics of Sorrow*, 29.
48 Arlene Saxonhouse. "Aeschylus' *Oresteia*: Misogyny, Filogyny and Justice," *Women and Politics* 4 (1984): 13.
49 Krause, *Freedom beyond Sovereignty*, 17.
50 Toni Morrison, *Beloved* (New York: Vintage, 2004), xvi.
51 Rich, *Of Woman Born*, 65.
52 Krause, "Bodies in Action," 304.
53 See the description here of the relationship between the choice to *not* have a second child and "to continuous and intense nature of childrearing": www.washingtonpost.com/news/to-your-health/wp/2015/08/11/the-most-depressing-statistic-imaginable-about-being-a-new-parent/?tid=sm_fb.
54 Iris Marion Young, *On Female Body Experience: "Throwing Like a Girl" and Other Essays* (New York: Oxford University Press, 2005), 49.
55 Krause, *Freedom beyond Sovereignty*, 4.
56 For much more on the democratic potentials of mourning, see David McIvor, *Mourning in America*.
57 Pietro Pucci, *The Violence of Pity in Euripides' Medea* (Ithaca, NY: Cornell University Press, 1980).
58 Aristide Tessitore, "Euripides' *Medea* and the Problem of Spiritedness," *The Review of Politics* 53, no. 4 (1991): 587–601.
59 Loraux, *Mothers in Mourning*, 37.

60 Marianne Hopman, "Revenge and Mythopoiesis in Euripides' *Medea*," *Transactions of the American Philological Association* 138, no. 1 (Spring 2008): 155–83; Brad Levett, "Verbal Autonomy and Verbal Self-Restraint in Euripides' *Medea*," *Classical Philology* 105, no. 1 (January 2010): 54–68.
61 Loraux, *Mothers in Mourning*, 51.
62 Levett, "Verbal Autonomy and Verbal Self-Restraint in Euripides' *Medea*," 54–5.
63 Ibid., 62. See also Mastronarde, *The Art of Euripides*, 272.
64 Mastronarde, *The Art of Euripides*, 252.
65 Hopman, "Revenge and Mythopoiesis in Euripides' *Medea*."
66 Ibid., 171.
67 Ibid., 158.
68 Levett, "Verbal Autonomy and Verbal Self-Restraint in Euripides' *Medea*," 64.
69 See Mastronarde, *The Art of Euripides*, chapter 8.
70 "The *Euthyphro* makes it easy for us to take Socrates' side and to feel a contempt for Euthyphro that, in reality, we should also feel for ourselves. In each case, Plato provides a different reason for the incomprehension with which Socrates' interlocutors react to him. One of these reasons is bound to become our own excuse ... In fact, our situation is in some ways worse than Euthyphro's. For Plato puts us in the position of believing that we know what is better and of doing what is worse: we tell ourselves and our students that Socrates is right and Euthyphro wrong, and yet we refuse the kind of life our agreement with Socrates demands. But as Plato has Socrates argue throughout his early dialogues, there is not such as knowing the better and doing the worse: there is only ignorance of the better." Alexander Nehamas, *The Art of Living: Socratic Reflections from Plato to Foucault* (Berkeley, CA: University of California Press, 1998), 43.

5

FREEDOM, RESPONSIBILITY, AND TRANSGENERATIONAL ORIENTATION IN AESCHYLUS[1]

> Every generation, by virtue of being born into a historical continuum, is burdened by the sins of the fathers as it is blessed with the deeds of the ancestors.
> —Hannah Arendt, *Eichmann in Jerusalem*

> Thus in all these ways we will transmit this City, not only not less, but greater and more beautiful than it was transmitted to us.
> —*Ephebic Oath of Ancient Athens*

What would it look like to have responsibility for the future, without expectation of control but with some power to shape the political landscape? The old men of *Knights* and *Clouds* demand control, only to be thwarted by the reality of human plurality and interdependence, as well as their own finitude. The comedies mock our quest for freedom as sovereignty, and remind us that the ideal of generational sovereignty posited by Jefferson and others remains a democratically inspired yet anti-democratic fantasy—a source of cruel optimism, to use Lauren Berlant's language.[2] Meanwhile, Euripides' work moves us from recognition and mockery to consider the tragedy of the willingness to accept responsibility for the future when that willingness is met with complete powerlessness. Democratic action requires a broader view of the entire assemblage of which the individual is part— and this broader view is one in which a commitment to intergenerational justice might take root. At the same time, women's "powerless responsibility" reveals the critical need to preserve a space for meaningful agency on an individual level, even as it is embedded in the networks formed by care relations. In this chapter, then, I want to ask how institutions might help balance the tension between a desire for freedom and the limits on that power presented by the fact of transgenerational democratic life marked by assemblages and distributed agency.

An examination of Aeschylus' *Oresteia* directs our attention to these questions, while making clear the central place intergenerational concerns played in ancient understandings of democracy and suggesting ways in which democratic institutions might begin to address these difficulties. Reading the trilogy as I do here once again highlights the importance of political aesthetics and of paying attention to a citizenry's "particular style of imagining peoplehood."[3] Over the course of the three plays that compose the *Oresteia*, audience members and readers are invited to consider the need for and difficulties of intergenerational responsibility as the central characters deal with the tension between freedom and claims of necessity, set amidst the backdrop of the development of their own familiar Athenian legal institutions. Given that the trilogy was performed before a recently democratized polis, the tragedy exemplifies democratic efforts at political judgment in difficult circumstances marked by conflicting imperatives. Because these particular plays so clearly link intergenerational responsibility with Athenian democratic ideology, they helped to promote a transgenerational *orientation* suitable for negotiating intergenerational tensions (by orientation, I refer to what Benjamin McKean has described as "how we get our bearings in our social world by identifying those features we habitually regard as the most salient features of the landscape"[4]). That is, citizens might develop an understanding of political life in which a temporally expansive perspective figures prominently, in which the transgenerational assemblage is seen as a central actor in democratic political life. The significance of the trilogy is not simply that legal institutions come to replace blood feuds or that the polis is founded via these legal institutions and dependent on the exclusion of women—two important readings well established in the literature.[5] Alongside those readings, it is also worthwhile to attend to the ways the trilogy focuses audience attention on problems of intergenerational justice within a specifically democratic polis, encouraging the development of this particular democratic orientation among citizens. The audience sees a single individual—Orestes—let go of claims to sovereign control over his life and instead acknowledge the assemblages within which he acts (his family-across-generations, as well as Athenian democratic institutions), working within the bounds of their emergent possibilities. Orestes does not willingly acquiesce his control—the sovereign model—but instead should be seen as recognizing the actual reality of distributed agency in which he exists. He is part of a much larger, complex system, full of diverse, sometimes conflicting elements, which shape the array of possibilities before him—and which will be shaped in turn by his contributions. By looking at these political actors across time (and referencing an even longer story of parent–child conflict), the plays immediately set up each actor as a member of a larger assemblage, whose actions are not the product of sovereign mastery, but rather take place amid an already existing and constraining background that urgently calls for attention, allowing no retreat to Aristophanes' fantasy of country life without politics. The actors who try to control events on their own—Agamemnon, Clytemnestra—only continue the brutal legacy of the house. Those who move away from the sovereigntist approach—relying on mechanisms of accountability while acknowledging their expansive temporal intersubjective vulnerability—achieve democratic freedom. And in watching this democratic spectacle, citizens see an image of non-sovereign freedom that admits to their own finitude and temporality. Focusing on the plays once again shows us the utility of seeing intergenerational justice not as a technical problem of distribution but one of affective motivation, imagination, and institutional engagement.

I begin by introducing the plays and the attendant intergenerational themes. After outlining a theory of democratic responsibility, I examine the ways that Aeschylus' trilogy addresses intergenerational justice through a consideration of the ways successive characters deal with the past and either refuse or affirm responsibility for their actions in light of it. Engaging with the *Oresteia* does not provide prescriptions or analytical categories that can make our path clearer, but it does clarify the stakes of these questions, indicating the democratic orientation necessary to deal with them, and providing affective materials for reshaping our understanding of democratic embodiment in a way that does not valorize the sovereign individualism that fuels today's cruel optimism. Instead, this reading sees the characters as embedded in larger assemblages of which their individual agency is only part of a larger distribution of power that helps to mobilize a transgenerational orientation attuned to the challenges of future-oriented justice.

★★★

In 458 BCE, Aeschylus presented the *Oresteia* as a trilogy (comprised of *Agamemnon*, *Libation Bearers*, and *Eumenides*) at the Great Dionysia, winning first prize.[6] It presents the story of the House of Atreus in Argos and dramatizes Athens' move from a traditional system of reciprocal violence—personified by the Erinyes (The Furies)—to the judicial processes of the polis.[7] Some commentators also argue that the *Oresteia* reflects Aeschylus' perspective on the important political issues of the day (namely, Ephialtes' reforms of the Areopagus or the Argive alliance); others maintain that the play cannot be reduced to a particular message in such a way.[8] Of particular interest to theorists has been the play's exploration of gender conflict and its legitimation of women's exclusion from the polis.[9] These themes are undoubtedly key to understanding the plays' political significance. Moreover, the intergenerational and gender conflicts are closely connected. The trilogy tempers the intergenerational conflict in the end only by denying the role of the mother in producing future generations. At the same time, the trilogy's intergenerational dimensions and their relation to a *democratic* polis remain largely unexplored.[10] By linking this particular story with the establishment of citizen-directed judicial processes and presenting it to a democratic audience, Aeschylus ties democracy—and not just the polis more generally—to the promise of intergenerational justice. Yet it is not simply that the existence of such institutions as the lawcourt can absolve the present of responsibility for past injustice. Rather, the trilogy shows us that dealing with these questions requires a democratic sense of intergenerational responsibility that depends on acknowledgment of intersubjective vulnerability and distributed agency. These elements can inform a specifically democratic orientation in the face of threats of violence and injustice that span across generations.

We can better appreciate the critical place of intergenerational themes in the plays by reviewing the mythological backstory of the plays. The family history of the House of Atreus extended much further than the action of this particular tragedy and is replete with stories of children suffering as a result of their parents' folly. According to Greek mythology, it began with Tantalos, a son of Zeus, who was invited to dine with the gods on Olympus. In a display of arrogance, he serves his own son, Pelops, disguised as dinner, to the gods. The gods bring Pelops back to life and he becomes king of Mycenae, going on to have two sons, Atreus and Thyestes. After a battle over which son has rightful claim to the throne, Atreus finds out that his wife, Aerope, and Thyestes were lovers. In revenge, Atreus kills Thyestes' sons and serves them to him—another terrible feast. Thyestes' has one more son, Aegisthus, who, according to some accounts, kills Atreus and exiles his sons, Agamemnon and Menelaus, to Sparta. Agamemon later returns, overthrowing Thyestes and Aegisthus (in the play here, however, Aegisthus is exiled while still a baby and only returns when Agamemnon is away at Troy; *Ag.* 1605), and ruling Mycenae until he leaves for the Trojan War with his brother, husband of Helen, who was sister to Agamemnon's wife, Clytemnestra. The fleet gathers at Aulis, waiting to depart for Troy under the brothers' command. However, the winds stall as a result of Artemis' anger after she sees a pregnant hare devoured by two eagles. The expedition's seer reveals that to appease Artemis, Agamemnon has to sacrifice his daughter Iphigenia. Agamemnon is put in the position of either giving up the expedition (in front of his allies and against Zeus' command) or killing his daughter. He at first struggles with the decision, but ultimately chooses to sacrifice Iphigenia: "How can I become a deserter of the fleet, losing my alliance? That they should long with intense passion for a sacrifice to end the winds and for the blood of a maiden is quite natural" (*Ag.* 212–16). The winds pick up after the murder and Agamemnon's fleet is able to sail to Troy; while he is away, Aegisthus plots with Clytemnestra to usurp Agamemnon. The action of the trilogy begins when Clytemnestra learns of Agamemnon's imminent return.

Although we do have instances of violence between siblings and spouses, and although the gods and fate play a defining role, the plays' motivating tragic elements focus on intergenerational violence. This backstory, which would be known to the Athenian audience, is invoked right from the start of *Agamemnon*: the watchman's opening speech is marked by fear and silence—"About other matters I say nothing; a great ox has stepped upon my tongue" (*Ag.* 35–7). The choral ode that immediately follows consists of the aged of Argos, lamenting both the war and their inability to have taken part in it—the power of their generation has waned. They liken their situation to that of children, reminding us of the impotence of both groups: "But we, who because of our ancient flesh could not then contribute to the force in support, and were left behind, remain here, guiding our childlike strength upon staffs" (*Ag.* 72–5). The chorus then delves into the story of the events leading up to the war and the scene of the two eagles, stand-ins for Agamemnon and Menelaus, eating the pregnant hare, bringing to mind the family's tragic history; the chorus goes on to tell the story of Agamemnon's sacrifice of Iphigenia. Like the Athenian audience, the chorus knows the family's history and watches as the new rounds of violence unfold.

The action of the trilogy also explicitly calls to mind the intergenerational tensions of the characters' present. It includes two important child-as-avenger images—a lion cub in *Agamemnon* (716–26) and a suckling snake in *Libation Bearers* (527–50). *Libation Bearers* is replete with references to salvation through the children, as the elders (chorus) wait for Orestes to avenge Agamemnon's murder: "Children, saviours of your father's hearth" (264–5); "these hateful sufferings are a reproach to the father and even more so to the children" (379). The tensions between the generations are evident in the refusal to acknowledge the role of the mother in the birth and upbringing of the child: Apollo's story of gestation in *Eumenides*, Elektra's refusal of her mother at the start of *Libation Bearers*, and the role of Orestes' nurse in place of his biological mother. The resolution of these tensions leads to the institutionalized exclusion of the female from the public realm. (I will also draw attention to the relations of care that surround Orestes, even as the biological mother herself refuses that connection.) Moreover, not only is Orestes a true child—that is, politically irrelevant—when the plays begin, he becomes a potentially accountable adult by the trilogy's end, highlighting the changing position of offspring. The intergenerational conflict also extends beyond the human world. *Eumenides* repeatedly notes the relationship between the bearers of the old laws (the Erinyes) and the younger generation of the Olympian gods and their usurpation of the former's powers: "Ió, you younger gods, you have ridden roughshod over the ancient laws and taken them out of my hands into your own!" (*E.* 778–9 and 808–9). Aeschylus presents for the audience exaggerated intergenerational tensions that characterize human life, setting up the drama and resolution in terms of the conflicts between those who have held power in the past and those who have arrived to demand their share of it.

Because the story is so fully framed by problems of intergenerational justice and culminates in the founding of civic institutions in Athens, the *Oresteia* invites us to think about two components of a democratic approach to the problem. These components often seem to lie in tension with one another, but living with that tension can help temper the longing for generational sovereignty. First, intergenerational justice requires an acceptance of responsibility across generational time. Each generation must take responsibility not only for the conditions it creates, but also for the conditions in which it finds itself, even as those conditions are unchosen.[11] This responsibility contrasts with the Jeffersonian urge to generational sovereignty and instead sees each generation as embedded in a temporally larger system of actions and response; that is, it helps to cultivate a transgenerational orientation.

Weighing on the other side of the equation is freedom. Intergenerational justice involves not only accepting things as they are and owning one's actions, but also acknowledging the promise of freedom in democracy (even if that promise was left unfulfilled in one's own experience). In a democratic context, this means not simply refraining from harming future generations, but also from severely circumscribing their potential range of actions. Freedom here is conceived of not as sovereign control, but in Krause's plural formulation.[12] That is, freedom comes in a number of forms—non-interference, non-domination, non-oppression, and collective world-making—which collectively help support the idea of agency as having a recognizable impact on the world. Thus, freedom for future generations means leaving them as much range as possible to bring about their own impact on the world. Whereas it may seem contradictory to argue that we must take responsibility for our actions—including small roles we play in larger structures—instead of attributing them to necessity or to others, and then that we must not bind the generations that follow to similar expectations, this argument is meant to highlight the odd burden placed on each generation. As one comes into full political citizenship, one inherits both a demand to own the past and intersubjective present—accepting the constraint on one's own freedom that responsibility poses—and an obligation to keep open the potentials for democratic deliberation among future generations.[13] This is not to say that we must *represent* future interests as in the generational representation approach. Instead, this is a matter of preserving the capacity of future generations to participate as widely as possible in setting the terms of their own actions.

Confronting this tension is the hallmark of political adulthood in Aeschylus' trilogy. The action culminates in the development of a transgenerational conception of responsibility capable of negotiating the conflicting imperatives that arise in an intergenerational, assembled context, although the plays stop far short of a seamless resolution. Aeschylus' work legitimates problematic exclusions in the polity and highlights the ways in which democratic procedures fall short of their often idealized status. However, the playwright nonetheless memorializes that mythical founding moment in which the bargain is struck between freedom and responsibility, highlighting finitude, plurality, and interdependence, and encouraging the audience to bring the democratic ethos engendered by that moment to their institutional life. The plays craft an image of democratic citizenship rooted in a transgenerational orientation and move the audience to take it up as their own project by placing it at the very establishment of Athenian democratic institutions.

Of course, questions of responsibility are even more difficult in a world marked by gods who take an active role in human affairs. Did Aeschylus' characters make choices, or simply act according to divinely ordained necessity? There are actually two questions here: first, what was the ancient idea of choice?

Second, what role does Greek religion play in those choices? Clearly, the characters are not autonomous choosers of the modern, liberal sort. Yet neither are they passive actors, listlessly encountering a god-determined future. Instead, we should view the actions on which responsibility rests as the result of decisions emanating from an individual's character, drawing on Aristotle's idea of *prohairesis* (usually translated as either decision or choice). In his view, a decision comes about after deliberation; *prohairesis* thus refers not simply to voluntarily action, but to thoughtful voluntary action.[14] After this process of thoughtfulness, we then come to desire to do certain things, which motivates us to act. These actions in turn shape our character, which reflexively shapes the choices we make in the future.[15] Moreover, our character and actions are shaped by the environment in which we are raised and live—and, in turn, our decisions and character then help shape that context. Because of this, we can be said to be responsible for both our characters and actions—and bear at least some responsibility for the community in which we live. What we choose is what we are responsible for, even if that choice emanates from deep within our character, as Aristotle would have it, and therefore is not truly "free" in our modern—that is, sovereign—sense of the word. Instead, we might think of our character along the lines of the assembled self of Chapter 3, or the larger familial assemblage of Chapter 4.

Hirschmann's turn to feminist theory to rethink contemporary liberal notions of freedom and liberty echo Aristotle's claims here. According to Hirschmann, the dichotomy between inner and external motivation is a false and artificial binary. Instead, understanding choices requires attention to both individual desires that seem to emanate from within the individual, as well as the external forces that not only constrain or enable the expression of those desires, but also have a hand in shaping them in the first place:

> If . . . freedom consists in the power of the self to make choices and act on them, but the self that makes these choices, including her desires and self-understanding, is socially constructed, then to analyze freedom theorists must examine specific concrete situations in which that construction takes place. Viewing freedom as a *political* question requires applying general theoretical conceptions not just to specific events—a sexual assault, losing a job to a less qualified male, being forbidden by religious edict to leave the house, blocked entry to an abortion clinic, coerced sex with your boss—but to the broader contexts that construct both the events and the individuals who participate in them.[16]

To argue that social constructions shape our character is not to deny our responsibility for our choices but only to acknowledge the reality of human freedom. Moreover, each of our choices then loops back into contributing both to the character we have formed (and which remains ever evolving through our lives—the assemblage of selves) and to the social constructions which will continue to shape our character (and that of others). So not only do other people shape our field of action—as we saw in Chapters 3 and 4—but we also contribute in this more subtle (but no less powerful) way to the very desires we and others have. Again, our agency is part of a much broader network of forces and desires.

But even this understanding of choice does not answer the question of whether Aeschylus' characters are in fact choosing to act. Do these actions emanate from the individual's character or are they fated? And in fact, Aeschylus is writing at precisely the moment at which the Athenians are beginning to work this out—do human actions originate from within or without the self?[17] Was Agamemnon compelled by divine forces or did he choose—in the Aristotelian sense—to act as he did? Was he deaf to his daughters' cries because he had a blameworthy character or because this was the only way to complete the deed, which had to be done, as Bernard Williams argues?[18] Yet it may be that both necessity and choice are at work, much as they are still now. According to Jean-Pierre Vernant and Pierre Vidal-Naquet:

> Since the origin of action lies both in man himself and outside him, the same character appears now as an agent, the cause and source of his actions, and now as acted upon, engulfed in a force that is beyond him and sweeps him away . . . it is not that these are two mutually exclusive categories and that, depending on the degree of initiative on the part of the subject, his actions may fall into either the one or the other; rather, depending on the point of view, these same actions present two contrary yet indissociable aspects.[19]

This reading is supported by the fact that the sacrifice occurs in a particular way that seems to be in keeping with Agamemnon's character and lust for war—he first weighs the conflicting imperatives, then moves forward: "his mental wind veering in a direction that was impious, impure, unholy, from that point he turned to a mindset that would stop at nothing" (*Ag.* 219–21). Although the demand for the sacrifice comes from Artemis, the way in which it occurs is the result of decisions made by Agamemnon. Together—and alongside the war and the longer history of the cursed House of Atreus, as well as Iphigenia—they form an assemblage. Yet we would never hold Agamemnon blameless for the murder, neither would we blame Iphigenia for it (one can imagine that her sweet excitement, coming to the encampment expecting to become betrothed to Achilles, was so heartbreaking to her father that he had to steel himself in this way, given who he was). The relevant question for this project is how the characters themselves confront this relationship between their actions and the necessity placed upon them by forces which remain outside, yet closely linked, to them. Do they acknowledge their (albeit constrained) decision to act in the particular way they did and their role in a larger assemblage? Or do they refuse responsibility for their role in events? Even in conditions not of our own making and where necessity seems to be bearing down on us, each moment provides opportunities for the character to make some choices. This is why responsibility can still exist within a framework of assemblages and distributed agency. It is precisely the acceptance of this constraint as a condition of our action that drives this analysis. As Williams notes:

> Living in a world in which such forces or necessities operate does not, then, mean that you cannot do anything, or that you think that you cannot do anything. You can act; you can deliberate; and so you can think about what different things would have happened if you had acted differently.[20]

And, as Williams goes on to point out, living in such a condition may not be as foreign to contemporary experience as we might think, gods and oracles notwithstanding.[21]

★★★

So what exactly is this bargain between non-sovereign freedom and intergenerational responsibility in a democracy? It occurs at the moment in which one acknowledges the fact of interdependency and distributed agency, and thereby commits oneself to collective judgment, considered in light of both history and future commitments. We see it when a citizen—or generation—takes responsibility for her actions by recognizing that her freedom is constrained by collective decision-making institutions *and* when that decision-making assemblage includes efforts to balance responsibilities generated by the past with attention to freedom of action for the future. This requires being open to the possibility that submitting to that decision may entail sacrifice on the citizen's (or generation's) part or that he will have to work to ameliorate the pain that the decision causes others. As Allen discusses, sacrifices must be just ones:

> [s]acrifice is a special sort of problem in a democracy. Democracies are supposed to rest on consent and open access to happiness for their citizens. In the dreamscape of democracy, for instance á la Rousseau, every citizen consents to every policy with glad enthusiasm. No one ever leaves the public arena at odds with the communal choice; no one must accept political loss or suffer the imposition of laws to which she has not consented. But that is a dream. An honest account of collective democratic action must begin by acknowledging that communal decisions inevitably benefit some citizens at the expense of others, even when the whole community generally benefits.[22]

According to Allen, sacrifices must be voluntary. But because she is not focused on intergenerational issues, the real difficulty of sacrifice is not quite apparent. That is, no sacrifice on the part of future generations can be voluntarily made, simply because of non-existence at the point in time in which the decision is made. Allen also argues that the sacrifice must be acknowledged as such, honored, and not consistently taken by one party. Even without the actual presence of future individuals, these other criteria provide some guidance and constraint when thinking about the future. Moreover, present and future generations might very well find themselves forced to make sacrifices because of the decisions of past generations. Attention to honoring and memorializing these sacrifices would be key. Yet we must first recognize the intergenerational entanglements. As Hannah Arendt argues with characteristic matter-of-factness:

> When Napoleon, seizing power in France after the Revolution, said: I shall assume the responsibility for everything France ever did from Saint Louis to the Committee of Public Safety, he was only stating somewhat emphatically one of the basic facts of all political life. It means hardly more, generally speaking, than that every generation, by virtue of being born into a historical continuum, is burdened by the sins of the fathers as it is blessed with the deeds of the ancestors.[23]

According to Arendt, even if particular individuals are not personally responsible for past events, those individuals remain politically responsible by virtue of their (involuntary) membership in the polity.[24] This is not guilt: "there is such a thing as responsibility for [those acts]. But there is no such thing as being or feeling guilty for things that happened without oneself actively participating in them."[25] This view of justice and injustice is mirrored in Young's arguments about structural injustice (versus responsibility as liability; see Chapter 2). To reiterate, Young argues that structural injustice occurs as people participate in widely accepted and everyday actions that end up leading to harm—like buying cheap clothing produced in a sweat shop far out of sight or procuring a mortgage from financial institutions with a history of redlining African-American applicants. They are part of an unjust network or assemblage. In the case of Arendtian responsibility, though, it's not *just* that there is no single agent who committed a specific harm against an individual victim. The temporal component is also key. Participation in structures—specifically here, communities *in time*—is the key link between harm and responsibility. One may be part of a much larger assemblage—a generation—and agency may in fact be quite distributed. But individual moral and political responsibility remains, provided we move to a non-sovereign view of agency. As Krause argues:

> Furthermore, while the assemblage approach undercuts strict responsibility, there is another sense in which it is likely to make more people responsible for more things, or to broaden the scope of properly attributed responsibility. The close connection between agency and (reflexive, norm-sensitive but non-sovereign) subjectivity allows us to call people to account for a wider range of outcomes than is possible on a view that narrowly equates

agency with conscious intention and control. In this sense, the distributed, material approach to agency poses no threat to the concept of responsibility but rather enhances it.[26]

Even if the terms of the inheritance are patently unjust and the scope of action incredibly circumscribed, the politically responsible adult does what she believes must be done without excusing it as a necessary result of decisions made long before her arrival or simply because it was not her—and her alone—intention. Thus, one of the first components of a democratic conception of intergenerational responsibility must be an acceptance of conditions as they are and an acknowledgment of one's place in a historical continuum, which may require great sacrifice. This relation to others may be deeply unwanted and resented, but as Butler argues (in reference to Levinas and persecution, but I think the sense of givenness is useful here):

> *We do not take responsibility for the Other's acts as if we authored those acts.* On the contrary, we affirm the unfreedom at the heart of our relations. I cannot disavow my relation to the Other, regardless of what the Other does, regardless of what I might will. Indeed, responsibility is not a matter of cultivating a will, but of making use of an unwilled susceptibility as a resource for becoming responsive to the Other.[27]

That is, responsibility is an acknowledgment of the conditions of our lives, conditions often created by others over whom we have no control or influence. It is not a matter of creating something from nothing, but of taking what is there and responding to it. The imagined figure of the sovereign individual is godlike, able to create the conditions under which he acts, self-sufficiently. He is able to *overcome* whatever conditions are initially present and re-create the world according to his will. In this view, responsibility is warranted, but *only* for those actions clearly undertaken by the sovereign figure. But if we imagine a figure born into a larger assemblage, a network of histories, power relations, material elements, and other acting, unpredictable figures, then two choices remain: no responsibility (so all belongs to the assemblage and none to the individual—a false choice) or distributed responsibility, in which actors acknowledge that the individual did not control the extant conditions but must begin with them and take them up to act.

Political life is about those moments when we choose to act, within these networks of conditions. Democratic politics at its best is *action* (in Arendt's terms), which includes both speech and what we more commonly think of as action; it reveals our "unique distinctness."[28] Action is different from the other forms of activity (labor and work) because it is marked by uncertainty and the attempt to create something new (the overlooked meaning of *archein* discussed earlier). The interesting thing is that attempts to create something new—action—become more limited the greater the acceptance of responsibility as a result of someone else's past actions becomes. The entire field of imaginative and desired actions is no longer open. For example, perhaps college admissions should be based solely on "meritocratic" test scores; but if you accept that elementary and secondary schools in the US bear the marks of multigenerational institutionalized racism and class segregation, then that option is off the board. So creating a fair system of college admissions is limited by an acceptance of a responsibility to the past, which limits what might be created in the future. In this regard, one sense of our natality (the fact that we are born into a particular historical and political environment) is closely related to and sometimes in tension with another sense of our natality (our ability to give birth to new things). A democratic conception of intergenerational responsibility not only involves an acceptance of things as they are, but also a commitment to preserving future potentials, using one's own freedom to ensure the possibility of future politics for those who come after. So begins again the cycle of accepting things as they truly are (rather than as we had hoped they would be) and then acting to open future possibilities.

Moreover, one cannot accept necessity and take responsibility, which depends on choice, *without* freedom. These two concepts are not so much opposed as intertwined, enabling aspects of politics. The conditions may very well not be of one's own making, but what one does with those conditions reflects a particular choice for which one can be assigned responsibility. Also, one may deny choice, but that does not mean it did not exist. We see this repeatedly in the *Oresteia* (and in contemporary politics)—an actor had no choice, gods (or the situation) dictated it. Yet even when freedom is most severely constrained, there are choices to be made (for example, in how one should approach deliberation or how one should handle the aftermath of the decision). In fact, as Markell notes, the relevant distinction is not so much about alternating between constraint and freedom; instead it is about the character of one's response to events in the world:

> There is no way to undo what has been done, no way *not* to suffer it—but you can do more than merely suffer it: you can take it as your point of departure. You can, in short, begin . . . whether your activity is a beginning is not wholly under your control: it is, instead, a matter of the character of the responses and reactions it provokes (or fails to provoke) in you and others.[29]

It is our ability to experience events and to respond to them in unique ways that characterizes democratic political life. It is not our ability to *control* events. Thus, by taking responsibility for the conditions in which we find ourselves by responding to them, we exercise our freedom.

What we take responsibility for rests on the choices we make and, as noted earlier, this involves deliberation (in the broader, Aristotelian sense of considering different sides of a question with uncertain answers, rather than a more specific or rule-bound sense used by some deliberative democrats). One must weigh various options, since choices are there to be made and actions will have some effect on the situation. Now one can do this more or less fully and more or less well, but deliberation must still occur—even if attempts are made to minimize the importance of deliberation later or even if the situation feels compelling in one way or another. Thus we can, at least in part, judge the extent and quality of responsibility by the quality of deliberation. Finally, because it is a *democratic* conception, it must involve recognition of others as worthy of moral respect and political power—that is, as equals—and a willingness to engage in the practices of accountability that flow from this recognition. One must acknowledge the equality of others, offer justification for decisions, and accept the collective judgments of the democratic groups. Thus, a democratic conception of intergenerational responsibility involves an acceptance of the conditions of one's actions (even though one did not make them) and a commitment to maintaining the opportunities for future generations (considered equally worthy of freedom to act) to engage in democratic politics themselves. It also requires a willingness to deliberate about the proper course of action, explain one's own position, and submit oneself to the collective judgment of equals, despite continued conflict and irreconcilability.

★★★

The tension between claims of necessity and responsibility run throughout the *Oresteia*, alongside the development of a democratic ethos of intergenerational responsibility. It begins with the story of Agamemnon's murder of Iphigenia. Did Agamemnon act here because of necessity (*anangke*)? Was Agamemnon just a pawn in the longer line of familial tragedy? Agamemnon's murder of Iphigenia and excesses in Troy are, in this view, simply the unavoidable result of fate, all put into motion by the terrible feasts served up by his forefathers. As Daniel Tompkins argues, however, the term *anangke* was highly ambiguous—it is a starting point for discussing agency, rather than an alternative explanation for action.[30] Agamemnon makes a decision to act as he did. At first, he wrestles with the god's command:

> It is a grievous doom not to comply, and a grievous one if I am to slay my child, the delight of my house, polluting a father's hands with streams of a slaughtered maiden's blood close by the altar. Which of these options is free from evil?
>
> (*Ag.* 206–11)

He felt compelled, but that does not mean he did not come to desire it himself:

> And when he put on the yokestrap of necessity . . . from that point he turned to a mindset that would stop at nothing . . . he brought himself to become the sacrificer of his daughter, to further a war of revenge over a woman and as a preliminary rite to the fleet's departure.
>
> (*Ag.* 218–27)

It is an unjust sacrifice, desired by Agamemnon and left unhonored. We do not see a Medea-like suffering grief here, only a commitment to his own actions.

Not only does he see himself as a lone actor, able to sacrifice others to achieve his own end, Agamemnon then refuses the responsibility laid upon him by this murder-sacrifice. As Nussbaum argues, "he adopted an inappropriate attitude towards his conflict, killing a human child with no more agony, no more revulsion of feeling, than if she had indeed been an animal of a different species."[31] Like the generations before him that seem to confuse human and animal, Agamemnon sees his own child as an instrument in service to other ends and refuses the responsibilities generated by this act. Rather than seeing her as another human being with desires of her own or even simply as part of his own familial assemblage (and thus part of his own self-understanding), Iphigenia becomes a disposable means to the parent's end. Attention to Iphigenia's cries would distract him from what he feels must be done. Although Agamemnon acts under more complicated motives than hubris or revenge (unlike his forefathers), the sacrifice of his daughter is not attended by the necessary conflict that it should have engendered. "He becomes a changed man, unable to recognize that part of himself and the world he had cherished just a moment before. Now blinded, he becomes one-sided, partial, unjust."[32] Once he makes his decision to proceed in the way he does, he can only see and desire that option; no others are acknowledged. He later returns to Argos with no mention of his dead daughter; meanwhile, the chorus anxiously awaited Agamemnon, warning of the "black furies" that may yet await the king for the excesses at Troy (*Ag.* 461–8). We see that Agamemnon denies his connection with others, and thereby his responsibility for his actions; he quickly moves on as if his deeds were decisive closings, rather than new occasions for response.

This problem repeats itself with Clytemnestra. Does she act on her own or is she just part of the long-standing tragedy that follows the House of Atreus? Clytemnestra often invokes Agamemnon's actions as the true cause of her own: "Why, the offspring that I conceived by him, the much-bewailed Iphigenia, was sacrificed by her father. He is suffering his deserts for an action that deserved them" (*Ag.* 1525–7). Here we have a vision distributed agency at its most worrisome. In her view, she is not responsible because she did not set up these events. Of course, she is right, just as Medea is right that the death of her children is not entirely and only the result of her action. Both situations were set into motion long before. The chorus highlights the sense of unavoidability, as well as the anxieties generated by the logic of inherited guilt and retribution:

> But now, if he pays for the blood shed by his forefathers and by dying causes the dead to exact further deaths as a penalty, what mortal, hearing this, can boast that he was born to a destiny free from harm?
>
> (*Ag.* 1338–42)

In the context of kin-led reciprocal violence that marked murder-justice prior to the establishment of courts, Clytemnestra's actions might make sense to the

Athenians, were it not for their transgression of traditional gender roles, which the chorus repeatedly points out after its initial period of confusion (*Ag.* 1346–71). A more typical woman would likely have acted differently. Like Medea, Clytemnestra's actions are strange and reveal her to be more male than female. This deviation also indicates Clytemnestra's actions are *motivated*, not simply automated; the standard feminine response would have been deference to her husband, but Clytemnestra breaks out of this model, indicating choice in the matter. Moreover, the immediacy of a god's command and a stalled fleet do not play the same prominent role here as earlier. The audience understands that these actions are rooted in the family's tragic legacy, but they are nonetheless the result of Clytemnestra's particular character.

Clytemnestra's response to the action improves on Agamemnon's, but she never takes real responsibility for the results of her decisions. She does not deny her part in the murders of Agamemnon and Cassandra neither does she seek to erase the past as Agamemnon did:

> Then I struck him twice, and on the spot, in the space of two cries, his limbs gave way; and when he had fallen I added a third stroke, in thanksgiving to the Zeus of the underworld, the saviour of the dead, for the fulfillment of my prayers.
>
> (*Ag.* 1384–7)

She relishes the act: "I rejoiced no less than the growing corn rejoices in the liquid blessing granted by Zeus when the sheathed ears swell to birth . . . I glory in it!" (*Ag.* 1391–2, 1394). She confidently and repeatedly asserts her justification for the deeds—Agamemnon's murder of Iphigenia and his forefather's similar slaughter of his own children. The king had "sacrificed his own child," (*Ag.* 1417) and her act meted out the "Justice that was due for my child" (*Ag.* 1432), as "the ancient, bitter avenging spirit of Atreus, the furnisher of the cruel banquet, has taken the likeness of this corpse's wife and paid him out, adding a full-grown sacrificial victim to the young ones" (*Ag.* 1500–4). Clytemnestra also believes that her murder of Agamemnon has stopped the cycle of bloodshed that marks this family, a cycle that was certainly devastating to the women who bore these children and were charged with maintaining the familial assemblage:

> I am willing to make a sworn agreement with the spirit of the Pleisthenids [an alternative family name for the Atreids] that I will be content with what has happened, hard though it is to endure; but that for the future it should leave this house and vex some other family with internecine killings. Even if I am left with only a small part of our possessions anything is enough for me if I can remove the madness of mutual slaughter from our house.
>
> (*Ag.* 1568–76)

Again, action is described as a decisive and necessary closure to unjust conditions (caused by others), rather than a chosen response that calls for further responses. Nonetheless, she acknowledges her actions and offers justifications, believing she can end the claims of necessity and the violence, freeing future generations from the familial legacy.

However, Aeschylus' characterization of Clytemnestra ensures little audience sympathy for her approach. She relishes the deed *too much*, secure in her hatred of Agamemnon and referring to his sexual infidelities abroad. "Here lies this abuser of his wife, the charmer of Chryseis and the rest at Troy, and with him this captive . . . this cheap whore of the ship's benches" (*Ag.* 1437–43); she then goes on to discuss her extra pleasure for the murder of Cassandra, "a choice side-dish to the pleasure in which I luxuriate" (*Ag.* 1446–7). There is little conflict but much certainty in her righteous claims of justification for Agamemnon's murder at the end of the first play. At other times, she refuses to take full responsibility: "Destiny, my child, shares the responsibility for these events" (*LB.* 910). We also see her rejection of her living children. By the second play, she is a mother trying to control her family to the point of lobbing off parts of that assemblage. She basically turns Elektra into a household slave and sends Orestes away, denying him his patrimony (*LB.* 135–6). Clytemnestra thus also refuses to acknowledge the enduring difficulties of her decision to act. Elektra speaks ruefully of being "dishonoured, treated as worthless; shut up in the bowels of the house, like a dangerous dog" (*LB.* 445–7) and laments "the pains we have suffered, and from a parent too" (*LB.* 418–19). The only reason Clytemnestra releases Elektra to pour libations is because of a dream she has about a suckling serpent. After her claims of acting on behalf of her murdered child, Clytemnestra has rejected her living children. Real responsibility for her actions would surely not involve punishing her children like this in an effort to protect her position in the household, trying to foreclose their opportunities to respond to events. It would instead require acknowledging the new dynamics, incorporating the members of the family in a way that does not require their erasure. Although she provides justification for her actions, she fails on the other counts of democratic, intergenerational responsibility: she refuses to acknowledge her children and their shared formation, the sacrifices entailed by her choices, and the unintended results of her actions.

With Orestes, the plays show another attempt to move out of these failures to balance freedom and responsibility, although it remains incomplete. It is significant that we see this as Orestes grows into manhood over this period, becoming a politically important actor for the first time. To accomplish this, he first pretends to be dead—representing a symbolic rebirth into adulthood. We see this transition in a narrative format, which—unlike other forms—is able to reveal the ways in which Orestes exists over time, inhabiting a particular world and struggling to make sense of it *as* he moves through it. By the end of this struggle, Orestes comes to represent a new way of being in the world, contrasted with his parents who continue the cycle of violence because of their refusals of responsibility for their actions. Of course, his range of action remains narrowed by what has come before. As N. G. L. Hammond writes:

> Heredity is a part of anyone's *moira* or apportionment. In some cases heredity may restrict the choice open to an individual, because he inherits a particular dilemma. Orestes is in such a position. He is drawn onwards by a variety of powers: the fortune of his father . . . the dead man's desire for revenge, the demands of justice, daughter of Zeus, who speaks through the oracular response of Apollo.[33]

Given the context of the plays as part of civic education in Athens, as well as the political import of monarchical struggles, this is not an issue solely of personal responsibility. Instead, Orestes faces a political problem, trying to create stability and justice in Argos in the wake of his family's crimes against one another. Whether he truly desires to or not (that is, he may simply be motivated by terror), Orestes takes on responsibility for the larger assemblage, not just his own self. As the time unfolds across the three plays, this process of creating a new beginning from an inherited legacy is intimately connected to the founding of legal procedures in Athens. With the help of Athena, Orestes becomes a model of transgenerational democratic orientation, accountable and responsible, even as he is seemingly bound by the yoke of the past and located within a much broader network of agents. It is important to not read this as a simple narrative of progress, however. Instead of time as linear here, imagine time in the *Oresteia* as a spiral—circling through cycles of revenge, with each loop building on what passed through the previous iteration. Atreus looping back through Agamemnon; the two of them through to Clytemnestra; Orestes getting swept up in another pass. Each spiral passes through a similar logic of revenge, but picks up new elements, which accrete to the larger assemblage. Moving to time as spiraling instead of linear, we can better appreciate the recurring contingency of action and the fact that the spiral will continue into the future. Orestes and Athena are not *settling* questions of justice, but encompassing the past within a decision point and reshaping the birthright for future Athenians, memorializing— like the Trojan mothers— a set of "ambiguous historical moments" to be interpreted and carried forward by citizens. The momentary tempering of the conflict is not a claim about already established terms of intergenerational justice, but a created product of the assembled actors, one that rests on an orientation that acknowledges both past and future as salient factors in decision-making. In this way, the play *re*stages the tensions between freedom and responsibility, between agency and necessity over multiple cycles, culminating in Orestes' trial and its aftermath.

For much of the *Oresteia*, Orestes attempts to deal with the burden of his inheritance, struggling with those looping claims of necessity. At the most basic level, he was ordered by Apollo to avenge his father and the compulsion was nearly unbearable. In a long speech running from 269–305 in *Libation Bearers*, Orestes details the compulsion:

> The mighty oracle of Loxias . . . bade me brave this peril . . . and it spoke openly of catastrophes that will bring dire chill into my hot heart, if I did not pursue those guilty of my father's death . . . He said that I myself would pay for it with my own dear life, enduring many disagreeable sufferings, enfeebled by penalties that went beyond loss of property. He revealed the effects of the wrath of hostile powers from under the earth against mortals, and spoke of these dreadful afflictions.

These compulsions spring not only from Apollo's command, but from the need of murdered kin for vengeance. Before he fully comes to terms with his inheritance and responsibility, Orestes responds to Clytemnestra's invocation of fate with the assertion that fate is now responsible for her death (911). He also appears to refuse his own capacities as an agent, as well as his own connection to his mother, seeing her only as an object to be destroyed.

Yet, overall, Aeschylus portrays an Orestes who also acknowledges his role much more clearly than the other characters in the trilogy. He confronts both the legacy and the results of his actions in light of that inheritance. We see here the multiplicity of causes for his action—the distributed agency: "the deed still must be done. Many motives join together to point the same way: the command of the god, my great grief for my father, being deprived of my property," as well as the need to liberate Argos from "a pair of women" (a slur on Aegisthus here) (*LB*. 297–304). Orestes wrestles with the decision to murder his mother, for he is aware that what he is about to do is a grave task. His companion Pylades must reinforce Orestes' commitment: "Pylades, what shall I do? Should respect prevent me from killing my mother?" (*LB*. 899) Orestes, to be sure, believes in the justness of his actions—to his mother, he notes, "It is not I that will kill you: *you* will have killed yourself" (emphasis in original) (*LB*. 923). Like his mother in certain ways, Orestes notes that he is fulfilling commands set in motion by elements outside his control. The agency is distributed; the assemblage is an extended network of forces, conditions, and distinct yet interrelated actors. Unlike his mother though, he acknowledges the dual status of his act as a fulfillment and as a violation of justice: "You killed the one whom you ought not; now suffer what you ought not" (930). He goes on later: "I do grieve for her deeds, and for her suffering, and for my whole family, having acquired an unenviable pollution from this victory" (1016–17). His temporary madness at the end of *Libation Bearers* is further testament to his acknowledgment of his own guilt. In this new spiral, in contrast to previous iterations, Orestes knows that what he does is a violation and, like Medea, he grieves at the thought of doing it. Also like Medea, he reminds his victim—and the audience—that these actions are nevertheless not the result of his actions alone. He is part of the larger assemblage, implicated in the dreadful action—not blamelessly suturing the open wound of intergenerational injustices for this family.

Orestes does not try to retain power in Argos, but flees instead to Delphi, quite aware of his crime, but hopeful that Apollo will fulfill his pledge as his protector. Apollo counsels the haunted and terrified Orestes to then proceed to Athens, where he will find "judges to judge these matters, and words that will charm, and we will find means to release you from this misery for good and all" (*E*. 81–3). Apollo promises an end to the familial violence—notably through speech (*muthos*—speech, tale, or story). But Apollo's faith in speech is not a model of democratic intergenerational justice; he means to vanquish the Erinyes who torment Orestes: "why, they were absolutely born for evil, for they dwell in the evil darkness, in Tartarus beneath the earth, and are hateful to men and to the Olympian gods" (*E*. 70–4). He is uninterested in accommodation and, like Zeus over Cronus (and Cronus over his father Uranus), instead maintains the superiority of the Olympian gods over the older ones.[34] Although we see greater acknowledgment of choice in light of conditions not of one's own making in this iteration, the threat of violence has continued. The necessary transformation will depend not on Apollo's wholesale defeat of the Erinyes or Orestes' continued torture, but instead must occur through the cultivation of a larger transgenerational orientation accommodated in new institutional forms. Both Apollo and the Erinyes—the present and the past—demand total victory in this conflict and claim that anything short of it will be unjust. Yet in order to attend to the future, symbolized by Orestes in Athens, the two parties must temper their demands and abide by a transformative democratic procedure (although, to be sure, the compromise is not an equal one, as we see when Athena sides with the male). It is in the responsiveness of the present to the past that we find such democratic openings for the future—not in the enforced priority of one temporal position over and above all others.

Such a transformation will work because Orestes is open to its possibility, although he will not be able to effect it himself. Like his predecessors, Orestes believes he has justice on his side, but, unlike his parents before him, he notes his vulnerability—"for I have no idea how this will end" (*LB*. 1021). We thus see Orestes heading into his adulthood, taking responsibility for his actions and admitting his lack of control over the whole of human life. Instead of the triumphant Clytemnestra at the end of *Agamemnon*, the end of *Libation Bearers* offers the audience only the vision of a hunted and insecure Orestes, reduced to suppliant status. This vision is also a powerful reminder of how the past intrudes on the present, rendering time out of sync with itself, and re-structuring the very rhythm of Orestes' life. This jolt leads to Orestes' acceptance of his profound vulnerability, which in turn drives him to Athens. Haunted by the Erinyes for the murder of his mother, he seeks refuge in a foreign city at Apollo's urging. In this pass through the same logic, Orestes gives up the sovereign fantasy that animated his parents, and submits to the judgment of the citizen assemblage for a crime that was set into motion by a much larger assemblage of forces. Orestes' vulnerability and dependency on others here is indicative of the actual human condition as interdependent members of a shared community. There is no masterful control—only an undeniable need to rely on others. This is a need that is especially clear to those who find themselves in conditions of dependency, for example children, women in patriarchal societies, the disabled, refugees, many elderly. In this case, it is Athena and the citizens of Athens who will found the institutions and community necessary to reshape the birthright of the House of Atreus. This occurs not by erasing the past or starting with a clean slate, but by acknowledging it and forging a new path in light of it, one that sets up future opportunities to make judgments in light of contingency. Here, one generational assemblage openly confronts the past, accepts responsibility (and possibly punishment) for the conditions in which it found itself, and, in so doing, open future potentials for democratic freedom in radical ways. Aeschylus dramatizes this for Athenian audiences, providing a civic education that celebrates the transformative potential of democracy and links the claims of intergenerational justice with those of democracy in an aesthetic display that can motivate the affective energy needed to face such challenges, much as Orestes' own grief and terror (affectively) motivated him to seek out the judgment of the Athenians. At the same time, the trial and aftermath highlight the difficulties and sacrifices that such transformations can require, even in democratic settings.

★★★

It is during Orestes' trial in Athens that the trilogy moves to a fuller picture of the challenges. Led by the goddess Athena, the city establishes the institutions that allow one generational assemblage to accept the conditions inherited from the past and open future potentials. Athena begins this founding by recognizing the complexity of the situation. Neither the demands of the past nor the needs of the present and future can be dismissed easily:

> The matter is too great for any mortal who may think he can decide it; but neither is it proper for me to judge a case of murder which can give rise to fierce wrath—especially since you have approached this temple, disciplined by suffering, as a pure and harmless suppliant, while these beings have an allotted function that is hard to dismiss, and if they do not get a victorious outcome, the poison that will afterwards fall from their outraged pride into the soil that will be an unbearable, unending plague for this land.
>
> (E. 470–9)

Neither can these competing claims be neatly resolved with a technical solution. This is not a matter of fair distribution or uncovering the correct answer, but one that requires attention to issues of recognition amid incommensurable demands.

It also requires attention to other therapeutic techniques—persuasion and aesthetic ritual—to temper the fallout that results when it is impossible to fulfill each claim. Athena therefore convenes a tribunal of Athenian citizens bound by oath to judge the case. It is especially notable that Athena relies on these mortal men to adjudicate the conflict. Although a goddess, she does not act alone. Athena realizes that such conflicts require collective deliberation, and so she institutionalizes a way to deal with future conflict within the polis. Both sides have legitimate and incompatible claims, so coming to a just decision is extremely difficult. Having more perspectives present among those who will judge increases the likelihood of a good decision because the perspective is more likely to be *representative* in Arendt's terms (*not* because there is a single right answer and more minds make it more likely to stumble across it). The collaboration also forces the newly created Athenian democracy to take responsibility for itself. Athenian citizens will decide the city's fate and will continue to do so long into the future. Nothing is truly settled; rather, contestation and judgment find an institutional home. This is especially important since the outcome may engender anger from either Apollo or the Erinyes against the city—anger which the city will bear.

During the proceedings, Athena appears to try to balance each side and then after everyone speaks, she asks, "Shall I now instruct these men to cast a vote in accordance with their honest opinion, on the ground that there has been sufficient argument?" (*E.* 674–5). As voting proceeds, both the Erinyes and Apollo hurl threats of what will happen should their own side lose, intensifying the stakes. Athena exhorts the citizens to judge carefully. Because of the possibility of a tied vote, Athena also judges Orestes; she votes to acquit Orestes, arguing that "I commend the male in all respects (except for joining in marriage) with all my heart: in the fullest sense, I am my Father's child" (*E.* 736–8). Athena takes responsibility for her own judgment, casting her own vote, but remaining part of the larger democratic assemblage. We may hate her reasons, but she offers them. Even though she has power enough to do what she pleases, she partakes in and models democratic accountability, remaining responsible for the outcome of the assemblage's distributed agency here. Meanwhile, freed from his familial legacy through an institution of Athenian citizenship, Orestes finally achieves the freedom from his family's past craved by and promised to the Athenian citizens watching the performance.

The resolution is imperfect, however. In the lengthy aftermath of the trial (about 300 more lines), the Erinyes become enraged at the disrespect they feel has been shown them by the younger gods. Athena tries to calm them: "Let me persuade you not to take this with grief and groaning. You have not been defeated; the result of the trial was a genuinely equal vote, and did you no dishonour" (*E.* 794–6). As the Erinyes persist in their anger, Athena continues her entreaties: "You are *not* dishonoured! And do not yield to excessive anger and, goddesses that you are, afflict mortals with an evil canker on their land" (*E.* 824–5). She reminds them of her power: "I for my part have trust in Zeus. And—what need have I to say more?—and, alone among the gods, I know the keys to the chamber in which his thunderbolt is sealed up" (*E.* 825–9). But she quickly moves from a focus on force to assert her faith in persuasion: "But there is no need for that. Be readily persuaded by me: do not loose off against this land the words of a foolish tongue" (*E.* 829–30). She promises them honors and offerings on behalf of children and marriage if they will agree to the outcome. Athena tries to contain the conflict through persuasive speech.

This passage is complicated in its intertwining of threats of violence alongside the emphasis on persuasion as an alternative. Is Athena modeling the rejection of violence for democratic Athens, noting the fact that violence may always be a possibility but that wisdom lies in renouncing it? Or is she making a subtle threat against the Erinyes, reminding them to accept her offer because otherwise she could make use of Zeus' thunderbolt? My sense is that this statement is neither simply a threat nor simply a noble rejection of the means of violence for higher ends. Athens states the actual conditions at hand—and those conditions afford all those possibilities. The Athenian spectators can then see that even the most powerful goddess relies on persuasion, thus exhorting them also to submit to what happens in their own courts and assembly, even if their faction is the strongest and most powerful. In this case, decision-making is opened up to collective judgment—not just put into the hands of professional experts and designated proxies—and remains accountable to that judgment, committed to addressing the frustration and anger the decision has engendered. This necessitates the move to affective elements—here, the persuasive power of language—to reconstitute the community amidst conflict and division. And although we see here the imperfections of persuasion—it is not the force-free, purely rational medium that we often idealize it to be—even this imperfect medium is critically different from violence, which Athena here explicitly rejects as a worthy alternative. This difference moves us to a democratic approach to the problems of living together. The danger of angered ancient goddesses blighting the city in the future highlights the insufficiency of the recourse to violence and the importance of persuasion, even as we see persuasion bound up with a type of force here. And by honoring the intergenerational anxieties engendered by the outcome of the democratic procedure of the trial, Athena further opens future possibilities for the city, trying to limit the threat of continued violence between opposing forces. She diffuses the language of victory and defeat used by both Apollo and the Erinyes, and instead tries for a mutually acceptable solution—not necessarily the most preferred by either side, but acceptable nonetheless. Aeschylus thus calls the audience's attention to the tensions that remain even at the moment in a which transgenerational orientation finds institutional accommodation.

At first, the Erinyes want no part of it, continuing their laments. Athena defers, acknowledging their anger: "I will be indulgent towards your anger, since you are older than I . . . for that reason you are much wiser than I am" (*E.* 848–9). Athena—the goddess of wisdom—here humbles herself before the older goddesses, offering them the respect they feel they have been denied and acknowledging the sacrifice they would be making by submitting to the collective decision. But Athena also maintains her position of authority: "Still Zeus has given me too a fair degree of intelligence" (*E.* 850). She goes on to detail the special position of Athens, enticing the Erinyes to make their home in this city. She continues soothing the Erinyes, arguing "I will never tire of speaking to you of these goods things I offer . . . If you have reverence for the awesome power of Persuasion, the charm and enchantment of my tongue, well, anyway, please do stay" (*E.* 881–7). The Erinyes are offered an honored place in the city, keeping the city free of internal conflict, unleashing their violence only in war with outsiders. Athena notes the uncertainty of the outcome and credits the powers of speech:

> I am happy that the eyes of Persausion watched over my tongue and lips when they responded to these beings who were savagely rebuffing me. Yes, Zeus of Assemblies has triumphed; and my struggle in the cause of good has won a victory that will last for ever.
>
> (*E.* 970–5)

Speech has a seductive quality here, even as it is associated with wisdom and understanding. It is a combination of reason and emotions, full of aesthetic appeals. Given Athenian anxieties about the dangers of persuasive speech in their own polity, it is not surprising that Aeschylus would include this aspect of persuasion here in the resolution.[35] Yet in light of the earlier actions, we can see speech here as a much preferred option to the violence of the past.

Aeschylus thus presents for the audience the imperfections of democratic procedure, acknowledging that we must act under conditions not of our own making and without the freedom we crave. Like the Erinyes must deal with the younger gods and like Orestes must deal with his family history, we do not choose the circumstances in which we must act. Oftentimes, the choices offered by the circumstances leave no ideal resolution. This is not in itself unjust. It is, rather, a fact of political life. The point, however, is to mitigate present injustices, to acknowledge and honor them and to try to open possibilities for the future.

The play closes with a civic processional escorting the Eumenides to their place of honor beneath the city. Through speech (backed by threats of force), Athena—the patron goddess of the city—expands opportunities for future generations by engaging with the past; the Erinyes must be incorporated, not just vanquished.[36] It is important that Athena, the goddess of wisdom, is Aeschylus' conduit for this transformation. Through her founding act, she symbolically constructs a citizen assemblage wise enough to handle these tensions on their own, guided by their speech and democratic institutions rather than revenge and kin-based authority networks. In future spirals through similar logics, the city will have the institutional resources and democratic orientation to confront the challenge.

"She (and, correspondingly, her city) stands out as a force of intelligence and compromise among warring, purblind gods and men."[37] These new conditions release future generations from the earlier logic of automated revenge, providing institutional means for resolving conflict. The past becomes a resource embedded in the present, rather than cause to renew cycles of violence. Thus, for audience members, the result of Orestes' tragic ordeal is the political culture in which the Athenians live—tying the challenge of intergenerational tension to democracy in their minds, reminding them to face these tensions through the communal judicial processes of the city and the legitimate, if imperfect, power of persuasion. This also helped to fix in their minds the proper attitude of the democratic adult toward the demands of living in an intergenerational world, one marked by both responsibilities and freedoms set in motion by those who came before.

Even as the trilogy offers a democratic model of intergenerational responsibility—an acceptance of the past and a commitment to future politics, anchored in democratic procedures—tensions remain. Given the outcome of the action, it is too easy to slip into the language of progress and resolution—that is, the replacement of the archaic order with democracy, chaos with order, female with male, family with polis—that would obscure the tensions that remain and the fact that the vote was so narrowly decided. Ultimately, the female is completely pushed out of both the public arena and her role in parenthood, thanks to Apollo's infamous exegesis of parenthood and Athena's favor of the male "in all respects." There will be no faction in Athens and generations of citizens can find ways to negotiate these tensions, in part because women no longer have "man-hearts" and must defer to the male. The huge losses instantiated by this "resolution" should remind us of the circularity and spiraling of time; we have not arrived at the linear end of the line, where everything is settled. Instead, we have passed through another loop, another trip through an iterative and generative process of justice. We have more spirals to complete—an unbounded recurrence in which contingent and always incomplete responses to the world find only momentary settling.

In this reading, the play calls on us to consider the tensions inherent in questions of intergenerational justice and the difficulty in confronting the balance between freedom and responsibility. As an artifact of democratic Athens, the trilogy also reminds us that this commitment to intergenerational justice is a fundamental aspect of democracy. The democratic city establishes justice through speech as a way to transform the cycle of revenge that marked the House of Atreus, but the intergenerational tensions do not simply disappear and must continually be renegotiated. The jury was equally divided in their judgment—it was not clear whether old or new should prevail. In return for their reluctant acceptance of the decision, the Erinyes become the Eumenides, protectors of marriage and childbirth in the city, instead of dark forces of revenge. The sacrifices of one generation are acknowledged and honored. Birth and new beginnings are again tied to the democracy, not through a wiping clean of the slate, but via a transformation through speech and a recognition of the past. The present—Orestes' trial in Athens—is the moment in which past and future meet, where a decision made in light of memories of what came before, and sets the stage for future action. In that contingent moment, decided by Athena after a split vote, we can see a vision of politics in which time is "not governed by teleological norms of progress or universal moral imperatives, but rather, time [is] nonlinear, and disrupted, [where memory is] fragmented and present through multiple layers of perception and recollection."[38] Passing through a new spiral, the Athenian court then makes a judgment about the relationship between the past, present, and future—a judgment that could have gone another way and is not universally welcomed, but which nonetheless helps constitute a community. We do not see a full release from the bonds of family in Athens, for parental-directed obligation remains key to Athenian society and citizenship remains based on descent, rather than a territorial birthright. But the city does organize itself based on *demes* rather than kinship networks; myths of autochthony were central to Athenian political practices; and the judicial system allowed any citizen to prosecute another for crimes, not just blood relatives. This system relies not on sovereign authority (like elders or divine authority) nor on technocratic decision-making, but on a specific democratic orientation that requires human judgment. Athena alone cannot decide the case. Judgment here requires an assemblage—a collection of actors with distributed agency (which nonetheless remains individually identifiable). The balancing act between the old and new is key; it occurs through an acceptance of intergenerational responsibility—an orientation that can respond to the past through the democratic procedures of persuasion and collective judgment, thereby opening future potentials.

Thus, the play illustrates how intergenerational justice cannot rest on an ultimately sovereign, presentist self meant to care for, imagine, distribute fairly to, or represent-by-proxy the future. The story of the sovereign individual never adequately captures the actual conditions of our lives—and in fact erases and vilifies the realities—and pleasures—that mark the lives of those bound to care for and be cared for by others, as Chapter 4 demonstrated. Instead, the democratic institutions, legitimated by the agency of broad generational assemblages, and backed up by real power and force (Zeus' thunderbolt) captures the initial motivation to give up the claim to generational sovereignty and attend to future generations. By bringing Athenians into a newly formed generational assemblage, Orestes mobilizes a transgenerational orientation that says: *Enough! We will submit and face the consequences for not only our actions, but all those who came before!* The point is not to discern future interests so that they may be represented accurately, but to mobilize—create—a transgenerational assemblage, buoyed by imaginative, affective engagement with these questions.[39] Like for Orestes, it must involve intergenerational democratic responsibility: taking responsibility not only for the conditions one generation had a hand in making, but also for the unchosen conditions in which it finds itself. For the Athenians, this image of the *demos* was presented in the theater, where everyday citizens had an opportunity to be affectively moved to consider the challenge of intergenerational justice through narratives about their own democratic founding. Thus, the play—both in its own narrative and in its existence as a cultural artifact—highlights aesthetic possibilities for motivating attention to intergenerational concerns. Orestes does not flee to Athens because logic compels him, even if it is Apollo who orders him there. He is tormented by dreadful visions of the Erinyes. The play itself provides the exhortation to Athenians—the affective motivation to embrace this responsibility as part of their commitment to the polis. Why our own generation would move from a comfortable—even if obviously false and lamentable—obsession with (generational) sovereignty and acknowledge its own membership in a much larger transgenerational assemblage is the question that now looms before us.

Notes

1 Portions of this chapter appeared in "Birthrights: Freedom, Responsibility, and Democratic Comportment in Aeschylus' *Oresteia*," *American Political Science Review* 103, no. 2 (August 2009): 427–41.
2 "A relation of cruel optimism exists when something you desire is actually an obstacle to your flourishing." See Laurent Berlant, *Cruel Optimism* (Durham, NC: Duke University Press, 2011), 1.
3 Jason Frank, "The Living Image of the People," 15.
4 Benjamin L. McKean, "What Makes a Utopia Inconvenient? On the Advantages and Disadvantages of a Realist Orientation to Politics," *American Political Science Review* 110, no. 4 (November 2016): 877.
5 See Eric A. Havelock, *The Greek Concept of Justice: From Its Shadows in Homer to Its Substance in Plato* (Cambridge, MA: Harvard University Press, 1978) and Richard Seaford, *Reciprocity and Ritual: Homer and Tragedy in the Developing City-State* (Oxford, UK: Clarendon Press, 1994) for discussions of the development of legal institutions. For discussions of gender, see Aya Betensky, "Aeschylus' Oresteia: The Power of Clytemnestra," *Ramus: Critical Studies in Greek and Roman Literature* 7, no. 1 (1978): 11–25; Peter Euben, *The Tragedy of Political Theory*; Judith Maitland, "Dynasty and Family in the Athenian City State: A View from Attic Tragedy," *The Classical Quarterly* 42, no. 1 (1992): 26–40; Arlene W. Saxonhouse, "Aeschylus' Oresteia: Misogyny, Filogyny and Justice," *Women and Politics* 4, no. 2 (1984): 11–32; R. P. Winnington-Ingram, "Clytemnestra and the Vote of Athena," *The Journal of Hellenic Studies* 68 (1948): 130–47; Froma Zeitlin, "The Dynamics of Misogyny: Myth and Mythmaking in the Oresteia," *Arethusa* 11, no. 1 (1978): 149–74.
6 The first play, *Agamemnon*, recounts the hero's return from Troy and murder at the hands of his wife Clytemnestra. The second play, *Libation Bearers*, follows their son, Orestes, as he grapples with Apollo's command to avenge his father's death by murdering his mother. The final play, *Eumenides*, finds Orestes in Athens, where he will be tried for these crimes and eventually acquitted, thereby establishing Athens as a home for justice and ending the tragic conflict that had followed the family.
7 Havelock, *The Greek Concept of Justice*; Seaford, *Reciprocity and Ritual*.
8 For more, see K. J. Dover, "The Political Aspect of Aeschylus' *Eumenides*," *The Journal of Hellenic Studies* 77, no. 2 (1957): 230–7; Simon Goldhill, "Civic Ideology and the Problem of Difference"; C.W. MacLeod, "Politics and the Oresteia," *The Journal of Hellenic Studies* 102 (1982): 124–44; Anthony Podlecki, *The Political Background of Aeschylean Tragedy* (London: Bristol Classical Press, 1999); Suzanne Said, "Tragedy and Politics."

9. Betensky, "Aeschylus' Oresteia"; Euben, *The Tragedy of Political Theory*; Maitland, "Dynasty and Family in the Athenian City State"; Saxonhouse, "Aeschylus' Oresteia"; Winnington-Ingram, "Clytemnestra and the Vote of Athena"; Zeitlin, "The Dynamics of Misogyny."
10. Also, as Vernant and Vidal-Naquet note in a discussion of the *Oresteia*: "The subject of age groups in Greek tragedy is unfortunately one that has not yet been tackled" (Vernant and Vidal-Naquet, *Myth and Tragedy in Ancient Greece*, 267).
11. These conditions actually form critical non-human elements of the assemblage of which human actors are part, just as other material affordances do (for example, we know that stricter gun or seatbelt laws lead to lower death rates—thus we can say that the physical gun or seatbelt itself also forms part of the assemblage). Yet even as they shape agency and action, materials and other organisms do not bear responsibility in the same way individual humans must. To argue otherwise is simply to deny the unique capacity for deliberation, choice, and self-reflection that higher mammals appear to have—and to deny the outsize capacity for impact that humans in particular have.
12. Krause, *Freedom beyond Sovereignty*, chapter 5.
13. I mean deliberation in the Aristotelian sense, in that we deliberate only about those things with uncertain outcomes and a choice of possible ways to act (*Nicomachean Ethics*, 1112b10).
14. Aristotle, *Nicomachean Ethics*, Book 3, Chapter 2.
15. Book 3, Chapter 5. See Jill Frank, *A Democracy of Distinction: Aristotle and the Work of Politics* (Chicago, IL: University of Chicago Press, 2005), 50–2 for discussion of this circularity.
16. Hirschmann, *The Subject of Liberty*, 34.
17. Vernant and Vidal-Naquet, *Myth and Tragedy in Ancient Greece*, 46–8.
18. Williams, *Shame and Necessity*.
19. Vernant and Vidal-Naquet, *Myth and Tragedy in Ancient Greece*, 77.
20. Williams, *Shame and Necessity*, 141.
21. Ibid., 165.
22. Allen, *Talking to Strangers*, 28.
23. Hannah Arendt, *The Human Condition*, 388.
24. Ibid., 149.
25. Hannah Arendt, *Responsibility and Judgment* (New York: Schocken Books, 2003), 147. Although it is beyond the scope of this work, Arendt has a great deal more to add to discussions of intergenerational justice. See, for example, *The Jewish Writings* (New York: Schocken Books, 2008), especially "The Moral of History." Much thanks to an anonymous reviewer for pointing this out.
26. Krause, *Freedom beyond Sovereignty*, 316.
27. Judith Butler, *Giving an Account of Oneself* (New York: Fordham University Press, 2005), 91.
28. Arendt, *The Human Condition*, 176.
29. Markell, "The Rule of the People," 10.
30. Daniel Tompkins, Paper presented at the 2006 American Political Science Association Meeting (2006): 6; cf. E. R. Dodds, *The Ancient Concept of Progress* (Oxford, UK: Oxford University Press, 1973); Albin Lesky, "Decision and Responsibility in the Tragedy of Aeschylus," *The Journal of Hellenic Studies* 86 (1966): 78–85; Hugh Lloyd-Jones, "The Guilt of Agamemnon," *The Classical Quarterly* 12, no. 2 (1962): 187–99; Williams, *Shame and Necessity* (Berkeley, CA: University of California Press, 1993).
31. Nussbaum, *The Fragility of Goodness*, 33.
32. Euben, *The Tragedy of Political Theory*, 72.
33. N. G. L. Hammond "Personal Freedom and Its Limitations in the *Oresteia*," *The Journal of Hellenic Studies* 85 (1965): 51.
34. Moreover, it is not clear that the Athenians would automatically side with "new" gods like Apollo over the older ones (Apollo had associations with both Persia and Dorian aristocracies). Christopher Rocco, *Tragedy and Enlightenment: Athenian Political Thought and the Dilemmas of Modernity* (Berkeley, CA: University of California Press, 1997), 159.

35 Jon Hesk, *Democracy and Deception in Classical Athens* (New York: Cambridge University Press, 2000); Markovits, *The Politics of Sincerity*, chapter 2.
36 For a view of the *Oresteia*'s ending that instead highlights ways in which the Erinyes are in fact forced into submission, see Markell, *Bound by Recognition*.
37 C. J. Herington, "Athena in Athenian Literature and Cult," *Greece and Rome, 2nd Series* 10 (Supplement: Parthenos and Parthenon, 1963), 69.
38 Rahman, *Time, Memory, and the Politics of Contingency*, 87.
39 In this way, I return, in a roundabout way, to the idea of generational representation. But this is not representation of some bedrock interest of future generations. As Lisa Disch has powerfully argued, "democratic political representation neither simply reflects nor transmits demands; it creates them as it actively recruits constituencies." If we move to Disch's formulation, we see that democratic constituencies are *constituted* through representation; that is, representation produces an effect, rather than reflects some existing state. "In ... representation as mobilization ... acts of representation work together with political practices to configure the social field and to frame the terms of conflict within which the pertinence and cogency of arguments are judged." That is, we might more usefully think of representation here as calling an assemblage into being; agency is emergent, developing out of the interactions among members. Lisa Disch, "Toward a Mobilization Conception of Democratic Representation," *American Political Science Review* 105, no. 1 (February 2011): 102, 110.

6
ART, SPACE, AND POSSIBILITIES FOR INTERGENERATIONAL JUSTICE IN OUR TIME

Berlin. Walking along the streets of Berlin—a city of immigrants, refugees, squats, as well as a city of increasingly rapid gentrification and anti-immigration tension—one might very well miss the small brass cobblestones. Or one might be there looking for them. In a city filled with state memorials to the Jews and others killed during the Nazi Holocaust, each of the thousands of *Stolpersteine* (stumbling stones) is dedicated to the specific memory of the individual taken from the particular address where the stone is placed, and sent to die in the concentration and labor camps of the Third Reich.

The material reality of what took place at that address is briefly thrust into the present, tied to a particular real person. The artist who began the project, Gunter Demnig, imagined people "bowing" to the murdered as they bent to read the names and dates. Others saw people trampling on gravestones. In fact,

FIGURE 6.1   *Stolpersteine* in Weichselstraße 52, Berlin (Photo Credit: Bärbel Ruben/ Neukölln Museum)

the *Stolpersteine* mean many different things to different people; the ambiguity and indeterminacy of meaning is apparent throughout discussions of *Stolpersteine*, especially in German cities where the stones have proved controversial, like Munich.[1] But perhaps this is part of the point. As Elizabeth Kolbert put it in *The New Yorker*, "there was never going to be justice for the Holocaust, or a reckoning with its enormity. The *Stolpersteine*, in a way, acknowledge this. They don't presume to do too much. That is perhaps why they work."[2] The *Stolpersteine* embed the past in the landscape, without a precisely determined meaning. The material concreteness of the stones and the stories they tell might snap a person into awareness about what happened at the site, or they might be ignored. They also draw attention to the passage of time, reminding walkers that this place has a history extending far beyond the present moment. And it is through an engagement with the past that we are able to think more explicitly about the terms we set for the future:

> Through the act of recalling and situating the past through place-based images, the presence or endurance of imagined futures is made possible ontologically. Places are remembered in one's imagination, and through that memory the future is located in the past.[3]

The linearity of time gets disrupted and its out-of-jointness propels reflective thought. The *Stolpersteine* have the potential to be disclosive and reorienting, calling on those who engage them to think through their own responses to the events of Holocaust—and continuing ethnic tensions in Europe. As the present generation interprets and remakes the past, they thereby set the stage for the future, laying out the hopes and possibilities ahead, reckoning (or not) with past injustices. The transgenerational connections are made through these materialized narratives—which literally may trip someone up while they are rushing about in their present. It is an ordinary, everyday experience with affective pull, popping people back into the reality of what took place in their city and the collective political responsibility left to bear in the present.

Berlin is a city rich with memorials (*Denkmale*), many of which resulted from state-sponsored competitions and are now located in the "memory district" in central Berlin—an area pretty much every tourist to the city will visit but which is centralized and thus also avoidable for many people going about their daily lives (Karen Till's excellent *The New Berlin: Memory, Politics, Place* dives deeply into the creation and criticisms of these memorial sites). Dispersed across the city and embedded in the actual streets and sidewalks one must traverse to go about daily activities, the *Stolpersteine* cannot be avoided. As a local, non-state project, there is no obligation for the installers to share the German government's larger vision of memorialization and collective German post-war identity.[4] And although initially conceived by Demnig, the project is a collaborative effort. Each *Stolperstein* requires research—these are communal projects that can be initiated by any community member, with participants digging up more information and engaging with the past. The *Stolpersteine* are highly accessible, community-forging material objects that call to mind the stories of the past, encouraging residents to consider those stories, perhaps (and hopefully) thinking about the terms of the future.

★★★

The previous three chapters all presented different readings of ancient Greek narratives that push us to feel the tragedy of the quest for generational sovereignty and the painful tension between freedom and responsibility in a democracy. The plays, with their concrete descriptions of the burdens imposed by the fact of time and the individual's struggle to negotiate those powerless responsibilities, are themselves a sort of *Stolpersteine*, helping to throw the present out of joint. The plays can provide affectively gripping moments to consider the meaning of time for democracy and the image of citizenship adequate to the challenge of intergenerational justice. I closed the last chapter with a vision of attending to the future by mobilizing a transgenerational orientation, much like the one we see put into play at the close of the *Oresteia*. The call to attend to future-oriented justice requires not only rejecting the unrelenting sovereigntist impulse, but also making room to confront and deal with the psycho-social demands of such work.

Although the Greek plays interpreted here can provide readers with affective motivation for moving forward with this effort, we do not live in the world of ancient Greek theater. A student might read these ancient *Stolpersteine* alongside fellow learners, or a person might read them alone for pleasure, or they might be performed publicly for a community. But these works simply cannot function as they did in 5th-century Athens, a city in which the bulk of the citizenry—limited as it was—took part in that shared narrative experience, reflecting on and judging stories about their own political power and its limits. Of course, the plays continue to exist for us and my arguments here show their continued importance for democratic thought. Each of the readings—and these readings are by no means the only valid interpretations of these texts—highlights themes of intergenerational tension, sovereign power, and distributed agency. Teachers and performers of ancient Greek comedy and tragedy might, I hope, begin to include these interpretations in their work; scholars might build upon or refute them. But surely many people have no interest in or opportunity to study these texts. Thus, these ancient Greek texts lead me to see the ways in which our own democracy needs its own shared and accessible narratives that can help attune citizens to intergenerational justice by feeling the ways in which we are linked generationally, and the tension between freedom and responsibility in a democracy.

In our fragmented, globalized, late capitalist liberal democracy, is a shared narrative experience that might concretely draw our attention to intergenerational responsibility even possible? As Anker argues, many of the narratives around us in the contemporary US come in the form of sovereigntist, melodramatic fantasy. The wave of gentrification in Berlin mentioned at the start attests to the power of this force—historic squats are replaced with high-end condominiums, DDR-era sites are demolished in favor of an antiseptic version of Prussian history.[5] Yet if we are to motivate the needed attention to the future, if we are to minimize the "psychological wage" that the invisible future confers upon us, we need a store of resources beyond the ancient Greek texts, which can only be a starting point. Reviewing my earlier claims about narrative in Chapter 2, not only should these narratives (1) be accessible and widely shared, they should (2) highlight contingency, (3) provide concrete, affective challenge to our current habits, and (4) they must focus our attention on temporal flow in some way, opening our reflection to the potential demands of the future. What contemporary politico-aesthetic efforts can contribute to the development of a new subjectivity, capable of the attunement necessary to make our institutions up to the challenge of the future? What analogues to ancient Greek theater do we have?

★★★

In this chapter, I am not going to turn to the more obvious analogues to ancient Greek theater—blockbuster films or critically acclaimed TV series. Those artifacts are often illuminating and, certainly, they can capture some of the thrill of performance and fantasy that attracted Athenians to the theater.[6] Instead, taking inspiration from ancient Greek theater and the Berlin *Stolpersteine*, I want to start by looking to the ordinary and everyday spaces we occupy—spaces where one might stumble upon affective forces that can help re-shape our sense of self across past and future temporal landscapes. Although ordinary space lacks the excitement of theater, it shapes citizens in critical ways and is obviously accessible—it's just there. What I mean to do here is to establish a parallel between particular artifacts in the contemporary moment and the ancient Greek plays—both in terms of their function and their content. It's not that one *or* the other is necessary or sufficient, but that the specific moment in which we presently find ourselves needs every possible opportunity for an affective jolt into a new vision of and for the future.

In this case, ordinary and everyday have particular meanings. In using them, I am referring to the "the uncatalogued, habitual, and often routinized nature of day-to-day living, what we don't think about while we're living it; it encompasses all those activities whose temporality goes unnoticed . . . Everyday life is a space of routinization, of repetition, of the ordinary."[7] This does not equate to soul-crushing tedium, but instead is meant to draw our attention to the productive forces of ordinary life that shape us. As scholars look to the ordinary and everyday, there is a focused attention on affect—that is, to the psycho-social pushes and pulls that fall into our paths and redirect us. In too many cases, these elements have pushed us further into our fantasy of sovereign freedom. But the ordinary and everyday is never singular and, as I have already argued, the actual lives we lead more often tell us a different story about agency, community, and time—a story that must be heeded in order to take on the challenge of future freedom. In Kathleen Stewart's view:

> The ordinary is a shifting assemblage of practices and practical knowledges, a scene of both liveness and exhaustion, a dream of escape or of the simple life. Ordinary affects are the varied, surging capacities to affect and to be affected that give everyday life the quality of a continual motion of relations, scenes, contingencies, and emergencies. They're things that happen. They happen in impulses, sensations, expectations, daydreams, encounters, and habits of relating, in strategies and their failures, in forms of persuasion, contagion, and compulsion, in modes of attention, attachment, and agency, and in public and social worlds of all kinds that catch people up in something that feels like *some*thing.[8]

The everyday is where we interact with the multiplicity of forces that help produce our subjectivity and thereby our own agency. These are moments where things fall into place or out of joint, where everything is suddenly clear or opaque—where our experience of the world changes in significant but unexceptional ways. We might experience affect in everyday life as "a kind of involuntary and powerful learning and participation . . . Ordinary affects . . . can pull the subject into places it didn't exactly 'intend' to go."[9] The distributed character of our agency—the external and internal production of desire—and our membership in assemblages far outstripping our control—becomes visible to us. By paying attention to the ordinary and everyday, by looking at the reality of our experience, we might be able to jolt ourselves out of the destructive fantasies of generational sovereignty.

In this way, the ordinary and everyday is anything but mundane and repetitive. My point is that looking only to those moments of exception—to the large-scale, official, or monumental—will lead us to miss some of the most critical factors in the shaping of our character—and we will miss important resources for thinking differently about our relationship to time and one another. Of course, ancient Athenian theater provided a place to *disrupt the everyday* routine and taken-for-granted habits of democratic citizenship. It did this as an "institution of exception," to use Honig's phrase, where transgressive ideas could be safely aired and explored. Thus, theater was the opposite of *everyday*. At the same time, it was a widely shared (at least for citizens) and common feature of polis life. It was ordinary in its accessibility and presence as a basic feature of the politico-aesthetic landscape in Athens. There is another parallel as well: just as the ordinary and everyday *can* become a space for affective jolts, theater provided a "dilemmatic space" (again drawing on Honig[10]) where there is no single right choice and where tension, ambivalence, and trying to make sense of incommensurate claims shape the subject's agency, without denying or refusing the pull of the unchosen options. Linking the everyday with the transformational, I look to contemporary claims about space and public art, sussing out the potentials for such dilemmatic spaces that can cultivate new subjectivities, pulling us out of the sovereign imaginary that locks us in the present.

That *space* helps shape who we are is well-established, owing in large part to the work of Henri Lefebvre. A French Marxist associated with the Situationist International and its focus on countering the distracting spectacles of late capitalism with *situations*, Lefebvre's central insight concerns the "production of space"—that is, how space is shaped through our political and social structures—and how that space then shapes us in return. "Every society—and hence every mode of production . . . produces a space, its own space."[11] This is a process of "self-presentation" and "self-representation" over periods of time. And, in turn, that space—the concrete everyday reality of inhabiting a particular society's material space—shapes the individual: "within it they develop, give expression to themselves, and encounter prohibitions."[12] Space is thus both abstract and concrete—and this is how Lefebvre's Marxism connects the material with ideology. Thus, late capitalism has structured physical space, which in turn shapes collective experience and subjectivity. For Lefebvre and others following in his tradition, social change requires changes to the organization of space—and the potential for revolution is shaped and reshaped by the very landscapes, buildings, and geographic spaces we inhabit.[13] Space thus has a disclosive quality, revealing a particular and contingent world to us, one shaped by the choices made by policymakers, artists, engineers, and private individuals over time. And, in turn, this particular world then acts on us, in ordinary, everyday ways, shaping who we are, providing both subtle and unnoticed influence, as well as the occasional dilemmatic moment or obvious affective force (think here of walking to work every day, only to be struck by the incredible height of the usually familiar skyscraper one day, feeling much smaller in the face of it suddenly, but having never really noticed it before).

Picking up on this for political theory, both Susan Bickford and Margaret Kohn have raised the alarm about the connection between spatial practices, the loss of public space, and the potential for democratic political activity.[14] Just as for Lefebvre, both theorists view public space as not simply an aesthetic concern, but a political one. Kohn argues that the intersubjective relations produced by face-to-face interactions in public spaces are key to our democratic health. Public space here is a "cluster concept" with three central components: ownership, accessibility, and intersubjectivity. That is, the term refers "to a place that is owned by the government, accessible to everyone without restriction, and/or fosters communication and interaction."[15] Although this definition takes us a good way in focusing attention on the locales of our shared interactions, many readers will pause on the government-owned requirement—and that's exactly the point. We are facing an alarming loss of public spaces. In fact, more and more of our interactions happen in POPS—privately owned "public" spaces.[16] Instead of a vibrant culture of truly public spaces, we more and more often find ourselves hemmed in by claims of private ownership—of sovereign authority. Bickford

FIGURE 6.2 Coram's Fields, London

connects these transformations with a refusal of the risks of community; it is "an attempt to root out from the lived experience of the privileged both multiplicity and its attendant uncontrollability."[17] Where people once congregated in public areas where anyone could gather together—and potentially speak out, protest, distribute flyers, and so on—they are more and more likely to find themselves in, for instance, a shopping mall where private security can enforce a variety of regulations limiting expression and behavior. More and more, space is owned and organized by capitalist logic. Walking through London, one might come upon a nice park, only to see a sign such as Figure 6.2.

Each particular instance of private or POPS space may, of course, have its own unique history, legitimate reasons for regulating access, and so on. I do not mean to single out Coram's Fields (it became a children's park after the charitable hospital on the site was demolished; the site was sold to a developer but then repurchased for the purpose of a "public" children's park by a group of citizens and philanthropists—hardly a corporate take-over of green space!). But this all has the feeling of a contemporary *enclosure movement*—we are less and less likely to find ourselves in a true commons, where any one person has as much right to be there as the next person. Business Improvement Districts, shopping malls, planned communities like Celebration or The Villages in Florida—all these reflect the neoliberal impulse to use market logic to re-create the public community destroyed by the very thing now marshaled to recreate it. As Honig notes, "In recent years, neoliberals have sought to privatize public things in the name of efficiency, citing waste in public bureaucracy and the unreliability of civil servants unmotivated by private market incentives."[18] Private interests apparently do "public" even better than public ones. We still require spaces for gathering and living together—but they are now limited by the owners' preferences and rules; we conform or leave.

The point is that all this reiterates the claim to sovereign power. When space is private—even if it is functionally open to the public (like a shopping mall), those holding the title can regulate access and activities. As more and more spaces become privatized and consumer-focused, opportunities for such dilemmatic moments—marked by questions, ambiguity, intersubjective vulnerability—decline, cultivating the sovereign individualist view and allowing us to both reduce and ignore interdependence. As Bickford has argued, "the spatial relations built into modern life cannot be thought of primarily as a reflection of desired social relations, for they also produce and form those relations."[19] It also leaves us with fewer truly shared—or share-able—experiences, as we segregate according to class and access. Anxious about a leering and obviously drunk man in Russell Square? Take your child to Coram's Fields—he won't be allowed in! As the female parent of young children, I have seen the appeal of such places. The problem is that this approach to our space reaffirms our desire for sovereign control. As space is structured by social processes, it also shapes those processes—and who we see ourselves to be within those processes. In his work on public monuments, Sanford Levinson argues that political monuments are used by "those with political power within a given society [to] organize public space to convey (and thus to teach the public) desired political lessons."[20] This work is often quite explicit, as Levinson's examples from the former Confederate states and from former Soviet-bloc countries demonstrate. At the same time, Lefebvre, Kohn, and others reveal the much more implicit—and no less powerful—influences on public space more generally. In a landscape marked by late capitalism, a growing precariat class, and increasing privatization, the message of sovereign freedom as the only freedom worth having is reiterated time and time again. That is, the fantasy of freedom as the ability to do whatever we want requires controlling the actions of others, ensuring that they do not muck up our plans and visions for the future. As Kohn notes:

> According to modern conceptions of property rights, ownership also implies control over the range of permissible uses. The saying, "My home is my castle," captures this convergence of privacy and sovereignty. The fantasy of the private realm involves intimacy, safety, and control. According to this fantasy, the home is imagined as a place where the unfamiliar is absent and compromise unnecessary. In a private house one can arrange things the way one wants them. In public she is confronted by visible reminders of the fact that others may want different things.[21]

These smaller scale fantasies are amplified in urban settings. As Nato Thompson, Artistic Director at *Creative Time*, a public art-commissioning organization in Brooklyn, New York, points out:

> The largest victims of privatization . . . are cities and the once-radical spaces within them. Battles over housing, rent, the privatization of space, and zoning are not merely battles over places—they are battles over how meaning is produced in the city . . . all in all, privatization has constrained and contained the variety of infrastructures of resonance available to all of us, thus forcing each participant to scramble for the scraps.[22]

This is why Lefebvre's "right to the city"—the claim that everyone has access to participation in urban life—is such a transgressive and important claim.[23] It undermines the demand for freedom-as-sovereignty in the spatial realm. For Lefebvre, the revolutionary response to late capitalism necessarily had an urban character, since the organization of city life was where capitalism was materially manifest and shaped the subjectivities of citizens. Building on Lefebvre, David Harvey argues:

> The question of what kind of city we want cannot be divorced from that of what kind of social ties, relationship to nature, lifestyles, technologies and aesthetic values we desire. The right to the city is far more than the individual liberty to access urban resources: it is a right to change ourselves by changing the city. It is, moreover, a common rather than an individual right since this transformation inevitably depends upon the exercise of a collective power to reshape the processes of urbanization. The freedom to make and remake our cities and ourselves is, I want to argue, one of the most precious yet most neglected of our human rights.[24]

This revolutionary potential is not just a demand for access to the already existing city. Instead, this is a demand to participate in the world-making potential of space. The focus here is opening spaces for different ways of being—not just gaining access to the promises of capitalism and sovereign freedom. Instead, the right to the city implies alternative worlds, in which our very subjectivities might be reconstituted. The point is to develop "heterotopic spaces": everyday social spaces, but ones in which "something different" is possible.

> This "something different" does not necessarily arise out of a conscious plan, but more simply of out what people do, feel, sense, and come to articulate as they seek meaning in their daily lives. Such practices create heterotopic spaces all over the place.[25]

This view of public space and its potential echoes the view of ancient Greek theater as a space for democratic education and working through the anxieties engendered by the contingency of the democratic project. The theater was a central institution of the regular political life of the polis, and our cities are likewise central features of our daily political lives, both constituting and expressing our understanding of self and community. Once people have some space to imagine the world differently, to not fall into line with the fantasy of sovereign freedom—and the illusion of legitimate and actual generational sovereignty that comes along with that—the possibility of a new image of self, citizenship, and community comes into view. One possibility for expanding the space for alternative imaginaries rests with a particular kind of public art. This is art that refuses the solidity necessary for commodification and co-optation by the forces so problematic for the development of alternatives to claims of generational sovereignty (and the sovereign individual underwriting such claims). Drawing on Lefebvre's work, the Situationist International first described this type of art as focused on "the situation, as a created, organized moment . . . includes perishable instants, ephemeral and unique . . . production breaks radically with durable works. It is inseparable from its immediate consumption as a use value essentially foreign to conservation as a commodity."[26] From here, "moments constructed into 'situations' might be thought of as moments of rupture, of acceleration, *revolutions in individual everyday life.*"[27] Think here of non-permanent installations, street art and graffiti, performances, and similarly non-enduring art in public space. Not everything that appears in the city and claims to be art would necessarily work as a *situation* in this sense, but the point is that such art is distinct from the painter's canvas hung in a gallery.

As we move through ordinary and everyday spaces—spaces that are increasingly privatized or marked by capitalist logics (billboards surrounding us in a public park), we might happen upon *situations*, moments of exception, where "power snaps into place"[28] and new ways of being are glimpsed, practiced, and affirmed. Unlike Orestes, we are not tormented by the Erinyes and forced to deal with our relationships across time. Moreover, the structural character of intergenerational injustice makes it fairly easy to ignore. But by cultivating spaces that can provide dilemmatic moments—moments that require us to consider the future and the costs of both attending to and ignoring intergenerational justice claims—we might be able to combat the sovereigntist pull of the increasingly privatized landscape around us. These spaces might take us backward or forward in time. They may push us to think in terms of connection to others, assemblages, our own vulnerability. They should be widely shared in public space and provide a concrete, affective experience, but never with a predetermined, closed meaning for the community. In this way, city spaces and public art sites may become texts—providing affective accounts of the past, present, or possible futures, offering space for reflection and judgment, and generating the transgenerational orientation capable of confronting the challenges ahead.

★★★

Edgard, Louisiana. You can walk all over the historic French Quarter in New Orleans, imagining the antebellum Creole city, and never be reminded that it was home to the largest slave market in the US. A person could have a nice steak dinner at the Rib Room on St. Louis Street (in the French Quarter) and never realize that the hotel in which it is housed was once a prominent slave auction site. There are no markers, no memorials. A similar dissonance happens on the plantation tours on Louisiana's historic "River Road," just outside the city, where the genteel lives of the country's wealthiest antebellum families is on full display. However, on the tour of the Whitney Plantation, visitors do not

FIGURE 6.3 Haydel House, Whitney Plantation

begin with the "Big House." In sharp contrast to the usual plantation tour, the guided tour at the Whitney begins in a historic African-American church, then proceeds through a memorial to the slaves who died on the plantation grounds, then to their living quarters, and then finally to the "Big House." The African slaves' experience is the central narrative at the Whitney, not the sprawling oaks or interior paintings or silver collections. When visitors finally come to the "Big House," they are led into the bedroom once occupied by Marie Azélie Haydel, one of the largest slaveowners in the state at the time of her death in 1860. Instead of looking at the linens and furniture as in most plantation tours, spectators find Woodrow Nash's sculpture of Anna, Haydel's "companion servant" (slave), who slept on the floor so as to be at Azélie's beck and call.

Throughout the Whitney Plantation, Nash's sculptures and Prof. Ibrahima Seck's stories of the African children enslaved at the Haydel plantation take center stage.[29] The agency of grief—the memorialization, the reckoning with the past—allows no possibility to prevent the catastrophe that befell the Africans shipped to Louisiana but does demand a taking up of responsibility nevertheless. Like the *Trojan Women*, the tour's narrative of what happened on the site moves spectators to consider the tragedy of the powerless responsibility of parents for their children, the limits of lament, and the obligation to attend to the past and future in our time. On my own tour, the guide pushed visitors to consider the connections between the enslaved children and contemporary social justice movements like Black Lives Matter—and how the "ugly things" happening today in our country result, at least in part, from ignorance about the history of the enslaved experience (and the fact that it generated so much of the wealth that propelled the US into the industrial revolution). Looping and spiraling through the past and present, the (non-linear) threads linking generations become critical for understanding what needs to happen in the future.[30]

Art, Space, Intergenerational Justice **159**

FIGURE 6.4 Slave Quarters, Whitney Plantation

★★★

London. Walking into the courtyard of Somerset House in downtown London on a summer day in 2016, visitors were greeted with an invitation to imagine the future.

Part of a longer program marking the 500th anniversary of Thomas Moore's *Utopia*, the Utopia Fair brought together more than 30 community groups from across the United Kingdom to explore what the idea of utopia means to them. Interactive booths and installations asked people to imagine the future. They might make a single wish for the future and write it on a flag to be strung across the courtyard or to consider the costs of social isolation of the elderly by sitting alone in a small black shelter with "Loneliness Is. . ." written across the outside. The Caer Heritage Project (based in Cardiff) generally focuses on community-building through archeology, but here invited young people to imagine their ideal village. Working with artists and community organizers, children created

FIGURE 6.5 Utopia Fair, Somerset House Courtyard, London

160 Art, Space, Intergenerational Justice

FIGURE 6.6 Caer Heritage Project, Utopia Fair, London (Photo credit: Viv Thomas, Caer Heritage Project)

cartoon characters to populate the village and developed narratives, which were then made into short films. A multigenerational group of whoever happened by the courtyard worked together to create a vision of how they want to live in the future, spurring conversations about responsibility to future generations. Drawing connections between generations in the present, developing narratives about future possibilities here provides an opportunity to joyfully negotiate those tensions between freedom and responsibility, to work through the powerless responsibility for the future, and to build an affective community of citizens attuned to the urgency of these tasks.

★★★

Brooklyn. Entering the elevator toward the end of the *Doomocracy*, an immersive haunted house created in Fall 2016 by Pedro Reyes and *Creative Time*, participants are surrounded by reflective mylar and greeted by an elevator operator in an aluminized radiation suit. Red light floods the small space. As the elevator begins, the display reads 2016, where the temperature is a lovely 72.8 Fahrenheit. Hot air blows through the elevator. As the elevator moves through time—and the temperatures spike—the warnings become more and more dire, with a campy excitement about irrecoverable habitat loss and the need for a cool drink of water. By the time the elevator hits 2060, the average US temperature is 88.8 degrees and the elevator operator is selling bottles of water for $500 a piece. More hot air fills the small space. In another 40 more years, the temperature has gone up another 10 degrees and "the wealthy live inside domes which they cannot leave. And the poor. Well. The poor burn to death."[31] The elevator operator again asks if anyone wants a drink, but it doesn't matter because he drank it. In any case, everyone in my group is looking away, shamed by the whole thing. Throughout the haunted house, participants have been engaged as rightsless people—pulled out

Art, Space, Intergenerational Justice   **161**

FIGURE 6.7   Climate Change Elevator, *Doomocracy*, Brooklyn (Photo credit: Will Star, courtesy of Creative Time)

of a van at the start, stop-and-frisked in the dark; ballots shredded in secret rooms alongside polling places—and as consumers, with a playful but damning invitation to judge. Will you take the "golden parachute" at the Board Meeting (or end up working as a verbally abused cater-waiter in the next room)? Would you like some artisanal oxygen? Will you help the strung-out prescription drug addict begging you for a few pills or look away? The Climate Change Elevator comes near the end, after participants have seen the worst of the American Dream and where it might lead. Finally released from the Climate Change Elevator, participants move into "Apocalypse Park," where a cheerful guide from a privatized version of the National Park Service leads people through a virtual reality tour of nature—the next best thing—and the only "nature" left in a fully corporate US in an era of climate change. There's nothing to be done, only a tragic apocalyptic vision to witness.

★★★

Bristol. If you walk into the garden by the Life Sciences building at the University of Bristol (UK), you'll find a small structure.

FIGURE 6.8   *Hollow*, Exterior, Bristol

FIGURE 6.9 *Hollow*, Interior, Bristol

You walk inside and are surrounded by a seemingly infinite small sample of wood. Inside, it is silent and smells like a woodshop set into a forest. Commissioned by the Bristol-based public art organization *Situations*, *Hollow* is made up of samples from 10,000 trees, from some of the oldest forests on earth to newly emergent species, and soon-to-be-extinct ones. Working with scientists and wood libraries across the globe, artist Katie Paterson took samples not only from trees but also from wooden structures that might spark memories or reflection: a railroad tie from the Panama Canal Railway, the Atlantic City Boardwalk damaged in Hurricane Sandy. Making thousands of times present at once, the samples draw attention to the passage of time—and its immensity. With room for only one or two people, the experience is intimate and overwhelming. The hyperobjects of geologic time and biodiversity are brought into a collapsed, cathedral-like space, surrounding the observer, connecting with all the senses—sight, sound, smell, touch. A sort of *Stolpersteine* in the middle of the university campus, *Hollow* calls on individuals to slow down and to consider the linkages across generations, the enormity of time, and the possibilities of a deforested future.

★★★

The preceding four sites all provide affective experiences and spaces for reflection and judgment, pulled away from the present, but firmly rooted in the everyday—houses, work, consumer choices, village life, university studies. The sites and installations do not mean the same thing for each participant, and each changes over time, depending on the guides, the weather, the other participants. They are not all explicitly focused on the future, but they connect with time and contingency in central ways. Although most were free, public events, some, like the Whitney Plantation or *Doomocracy* required a ticket (*Doomocracy* tickets were free but quickly "sold" out). Nevertheless, they all engage people to think critically about community and power, oftentimes by eliciting responses that form the basis for conversation within a community that has been called into being by the performance, site, or exhibit. Indeed, this is often an explicit goal. Most of the projects here fall within the "new public art" framework, which aims to call forth community, reshape spaces, and generate dialogue.[32] Inspired in part by the Situationist International, among other movements, artists working in this tradition do not have the beautification of spaces as their primary purpose. Instead:

> [t]he aim of critical public art is neither a happy self-exhibition nor a passive collaboration with the grand gallery of the city, its ideological theatre and architectural social system. Rather, it is an engagement in strategic challenges to the city structures and mediums that mediate our everyday perception of the world: an engagement through aesthetic-critical interruptions, infiltrations and appropriations that question the symbolic, psycho-political and economic operations of the city.[33]

This engagement will not lead to any pre-determined outcome, just as no ancient playwright or contemporary interpreter can pronounce a final meaning for any of the plays discussed here. Instead, the indeterminacy of all these narratives animates their potentials as sites of democratic attunement to the future. Although critical of the ways in which ambiguity can often shelter and hide the capitalist logic underlying cultural production, Nato Thompson also draws attention to its importance: "in an ambiguous cultural intervention, the inability for a viewer to pin down a work's intentions is the very thing that makes the dynamic significant."[34] Because they are not determined and *require* reflection and judgment, they help forge a:

> [c]ollective sense of becoming . . . the encounters enact a range of transformations that exceed mere words. They are somatic. They are lived. These encounters come with feeling as well as ideas. This is a politics of doing that provides an entirely unique and powerful set of potentialities.[35]

Of course, beauty is important, but the power relations and community around these projects is critical. This is not just the artistic genius presenting for the individual spectator, but an affective community *formed* by the performance or art moment. The artist here is part of the assemblage—not the head of some organic whole. Analogous to ancient Greek theater, the new public art appeals to me because of its ability to forge connections among individuals and to move them to think about their place in time. This is art that can help develop new understandings of subjectivity, ones that deny the primacy of sovereign freedom, precisely because of the challenge to claims of ownership/authorship. Its often explicitly political character ensures a focus on power relations.

Echoing some of the civic functions of the Great Dionysia, community organizing with the potential audience as true collaborators is key to much of this new public art. Projects are not a single moment or exhibit, envisioned and produced by a special genius. For the *Situations*-sponsored work by Chicago-based Theaster Gates, *Sanctum*, Gates began by asking the community: what is missing here? The goal was to provide space for Bristol's voices (not just Gates' own).[36] Without knowing what exactly would happen, they opened up an abandoned church in the city and issued a call for programming, with the idea that the space would have continuous sound—spoken word, music, dance—continuously for 24 days or 552 hours. Performance groups, refugee organizations, school groups, and others engaged in the project. People got a small badge after visiting, which then sparked conversations in coffee shops and the wider community. People were welcome day or night. For some, it became part of their daily routine for the month it existed. And, for many projects like this, the durational quality—the specialness conferred on it by virtue of it ending—is part of the beauty of the thing. The performance is intentionally impermanent, drawing attention to time and its passage, to the ephemeral nature of community and connection. This is the connection to a new subjectivity—one that does not demand sovereign control, especially in the face of the passage of time. The projects rely on community—not just for reception but for their very character—and then, as the community shifts, the project dissipates. The memories and history created by the event remain, and shape the future. But the art itself has faded again, with no owner to claim it and resell it. There is no claim to sovereignty here and the ephemeral nature of action in time—momentary but generating memory and affect—is inescapable. The meaning is ambiguous and multiple. The judgment to which the participant or viewer is invited helps connect that person with others, forming an affective community by appealing to the *sensus communis* in each person and requiring reflection in order to be shared. The community formed by the project shapes and reshapes the work in the end, helping to dissolve that sense of sovereign control that this book has argued is so troublesome. Agency is distributed across the assemblage, and emerges over time.

In this way, just as for Greek plays, the aesthetic qualities provide an entry point, and the political effect lies in how these projects engender reflection and the formation of new visions of peoplehood. This is where the potential for motivating the kind of transgenerational mobilization might come in. By making accessible and widely shared "texts," these new public art movements can highlight time and intersubjective space, and provide a concrete, affective challenge to our present (bad) habits. Even as there is no guarantee that these works will be widely shared in the same way as Greek plays (neither is our scale analogous), they are accessible in their public-ness, generally located outside of museums and dedicated arts spaces. Indeed, location choice often reiterates the anti-sovereign, community-focused, and time disjointedness claims of the art.[37] This brief catalog of possibilities rests on my belief that cultivating a democratic comportment toward the future must be prior to the institutional engagement with the issue. In order to acknowledge the future for what it is—a potential assemblage of which we are part, composed of equally democratically worthy individuals—we must develop new forms of subjectivity that reject sovereign claims to freedom. In this conclusion, I have tried to begin to survey the alternative imaginative resources that might unsettle the current sensibility that renders the future invisible and privileges demands for generational sovereignty. The concrete, practical condition of our lives—our assembled selves, our membership in transgenerational assemblages, our lack of control over what we inherit from the past—requires forging communities in new ways. For the ancient Athenians, there was the monumental art of the theater, widely shared narratives that, according to my readings, might have generated the affective motivation to attend to intergenerational concerns. For us, untimely engagement with those texts can take us to new places. But we must also find our own texts and narratives, cultivating them and seeing the democratic potentials they contain. Rejecting claims to generational sovereignty, accepting the reality of our powerless responsibility for the future, and encouraging the mobilization of a transgenerational orientation that can negotiate the tensions between freedom and responsibility will depend upon our willingness to see beyond the very near future, to open ourselves to the radical realities of our lives.

Notes

1 "Stolperstein-Befürworter scheitern vor Münchner Gericht," *Spiegel Online*, May 31, 2016, www.spiegel.de/panorama/gesellschaft/stolpersteine-in-muenchen-weitere-schlappe-fuer-befuerworter-a-1095047.html. Last accessed 1 January 20, 2017.
2 Elizabeth Kolbert, "A Stone for My Great-Grandmother." *The New Yorker*, March 16, 2015. www.newyorker.com/magazine/2015/02/16/last-trial. Last accessed January 20, 2017.
3 Karen E. Till, *The New Berlin: Memory, Politics, Place* (Minneapolis, MN: University of Minnesota Press, 2005), 39.
4 Kirsten Harjes, "Stumbling Stones: Holocaust Memorials, National Identity, and Democratic Inclusion in Berlin," *German Politics & Society* 23, no. 1 (74, Spring 2005): 138–51.
5 Kate Connelly, "From People's Palace Back to Prussian Palace," *The Guardian*, November 28, 2008. www.theguardian.com/world/2008/nov/29/berlin-prussian-palace-reconstruction-germany. Last accessed February 13, 2017. Michael Kimmelman, "Rebuilding a Palace May Become a Grand Blunder," *The New York Times*, December 31, 2008. www.nytimes.com/2009/01/01/arts/design/01abroad.html?_r=1. Last accessed February 13, 2017.
6 See especially Peter Euben's work on *The Simpsons* cartoon in *Platonic Noise* (chapter 4: "Aristophanes in America").
7 Lawrence Grossberg, *Cultural Studies in the Future Tense* (Durham, NC: Duke University Press, 2010), 278.
8 Kathleen Stewart, *Ordinary Affects* (Durham, NC: Duke University Press 2007), 1–2.
9 Ibid., 40.
10 Bonnie Honig, "Difference, Dilemmas, and the Politics of Home," *Democracy and Difference: Contesting the Boundaries of the Political*, ed. Seyla Benhabib, 257–77.
11 Henri Lefebvre, *The Production of Space*, trans. Donald Nicholson-Smith (Oxford, UK: Blackwell, 1992), 31.

12 Ibid., 34.
13 Ibid., 59.
14 Susan Bickford, "Constructing Inequality: City Spaces and the Architecture of Citizenship," *Political Theory* 28, no. 3 (2000): 355–76; Margaret Kohn. *Brave New Neighborhoods: The Privatization of Public Space* (New York: Routledge, 2004).
15 Ibid., 11.
16 See Jerold S. Kayden, The New York City Department of City Planning, and The Municipal Art Society of New York, *Privately Owned Public Space: The New York City Experience* (New York: John Wiley & Sons, 2000).
17 Bickford, "Constructing Inequality," 362.
18 Bonnie Honig, "The Politics of Public Things: Neoliberalism and the Routine of Privatization," *No Foundations: An Interdisciplinary Journal of Law and Justice* 10 (2013): 59.
19 Bickford, "Constructing Inequality," 366.
20 Sanford Levinson, *Written in Stone: Public Monuments in Changing Societies* (Durham, NC: Duke University Press, 1998), 10.
21 Kohn, *Brave New Neighborhoods*, 7.
22 Nato Thompson, *Seeing Power: Art and Activism in the 21st Century* (Brooklyn, NY: Melville House, 2005), 78.
23 Note: the focus here is on urban space, which is especially important as more and more people live in urban areas. But I think many of the claims work for rural areas (like the one I live in), where public, not to mention community, space often feels even harder to come by, even if open space is relatively plentiful.
24 David Harvey, "The Right to the City," *New Left Review*, 53 (September-October 2008): 23.
25 David Harvey, *Rebel Cities: From the Right to the City to the Urban Revolution* (New York: Verso, 2013), xvii.
26 Situationist International, "The Theory of Moments and the Construction of Situations," *Internationale Situationniste* 4 (June 1960).
27 Ibid.
28 Stewart, *Ordinary Affect*, 16.
29 Ibrahima Seck, *Bouki Fait Gombo: A History of the Slave Community at Habitation Haydel (Whitney Plantation) Louisiana, 1750–1860* (New Orleans, LA: UNO Press, 2014).
30 Although the tour is not free—and is located well outside of the city of New Orleans—the curators have made a distinct effort to open it as a public space to young people in the surrounding area.
31 Paul Hufker, *Pedro Reyes' Doomocracy: The Script* (Brooklyn Army Terminal: Creative Time, October 7 to November 6, 2016).
32 See Claire Doherty, *Out of Time Out of Place: Public Art (Now)* (London: Art Books Publishing, Inc., 2015). That is, these projects are not undertaken to beautify and gentrify neighborhoods. The art and the community springing up around it is the point. To be sure, this has political implications (and intent), just as using art to persuade people to buy things or to "revitalize downtown" does. For a broader discussion of these dynamics, see Nato Thompson, *Culture as Weapon: The Art of Influence in Everyday Life* (Brooklyn, NY: Melville House, 2017).
33 Krysztof Wodiczko, "Strategies of Public Address: Which Media? Which Publics?" in *Situation: Documents of Contemporary Art*, ed. Claire Doherty (Cambridge, MA: MIT Press, 2009), 124.
34 Thompson, *Seeing Power*, 48.
35 Ibid., 137, 145.
36 Interview with Owen Kim, *Situations*. June 23, 2016.
37 Many of the projects from *Creative Time* and *Situations* take place in neglected spaces—the abandoned Temple Church (*Sanctum*; Bristol, UK), Folkestone Beach (*Folkestone Digs*; Folkestone, UK) or a Domino Sugar Factory (*A Subtlety*; Brooklyn). Or they

might be located in the most common of spaces: public parks, city streets, and neighborhoods (*Waiting for Godot*; New Orleans), across highways and in open spaces (*It Is What It Is*; US), university campuses (*Hollow*; University of Bristol), or a forest in the middle of nowhere (*Future Library*; Norway). The point is that this is not specialized art space. One might happen upon it or one might intentionally go out to this derelict building, but now see it in a new light. These spaces are mundane, unexceptional places where the everyday and ordinary occur. The performance or artwork becomes part of the space's history, giving the place new meaning beyond its market value, an increasingly important claim given the privatization of the contemporary landscape.

BIBLIOGRAPHY

Aeschylus. *Oresteia*, translated by Alan H. Sommerstein. Cambridge, MA: Harvard University Press/Loeb Editions, 2009.
Albert, Elisa. *After Birth*. New York: Mariner Books, 2016.
Alcoff, Linda. "The Problem of Speaking for Others," *Cultural Critique* 20 (Winter 1991–2): 5–32.
Allen, Danielle. *Talking to Strangers: Anxieties of Citizenship since Brown V. Board of Education*. Chicago, IL: University of Chicago Press, 2004.
Anker, Elisabeth. *Orgies of Feeling: Melodrama and the Politics of Freedom*. Durham, NC: Duke University Press, 2014.
Arendt, Hannah. *The Jewish Writings*. New York: Schocken Books, 2008.
_____. *Responsibility and Judgment*. New York: Schocken Books, 2003.
_____. *The Human Condition*. Chicago, IL: University of Chicago Press, 1998.
_____. *Between Past and Future: Eight Exercises in Political Thought*. New York: Penguin, 1993.
_____. *Lectures on Kant's Political Philosophy*. Chicago, IL: University of Chicago Press, 1992.
_____. "Freedom and Politics," *Chicago Review* 14, no. 1 (Spring 1960): 28–46.
Aristophanes. *Acharnians, Knights*, translated by Jeffrey Henderson. Cambridge, MA: Harvard University Press/Loeb Editions, 1998.
_____. *Clouds. Wasps. Peace*, translated by Jeffrey Henderson. Cambridge, MA: Harvard University Press/Loeb Editions, 1998.
Aristotle. *Nicomachean Ethics*. Cambridge, UK: Cambridge University Press, 2014.
Aslam, Ali. *Ordinary Democracy: Sovereignty and Citizenship beyond the Neoliberal Impasse*. New York: Oxford University Press, 2016.
Attius-Donfut, Claudine and Sara Arber, eds. *The Myth of Generational Conflict: The Family and State in Aging Societies*. New York: Routledge, 2000.
Barry, Brian. *Justice as Impartiality*. New York: Oxford University Press, 1995.
_____. *Theories of Justice*. Berkeley, CA: University of California Press, 1989.
Barry, John and Marcel Wissenburg, *Sustaining Liberal Democracy*. New York: Palgrave, 2001.

Beauvoir, Simone de. *The Second Sex*. New York: Vintage, 1949/2011.
———. *The Coming of Age*, translated by Patrick O'Brian. New York: W.W. Norton, 1996.
Benhabib, Seyla. *Another Cosmopolitanism*. With commentaries by Jeremy Waldron, Bonnie Hong, Will Kymlicka, edited and introduced by Robert Post. New York: Oxford University Press, 2006.
———. "Toward a Deliberative Model of Democratic Legitimacy." In *Democracy and Difference: Contesting the Boundaries of the Political*, edited by Seyla Benhabib, 67–94. Princeton, NJ: Princeton University Press, 1996.
Benjamin, Jessica. *The Bonds of Love: Psychoanalysis, Feminism, and the Problem of Domination*. New York: Pantheon Books, 1988.
Bennett, Jane. *Vibrant Matter: A Political Ecology of Things*. Durham, NC: Duke University Press, 2010.
Berger, Harry. *Situated Utterances: Texts, Bodies, and Cultural Representations*. New York: Fordham University Press, 2005.
Berlant, Lauren. *Cruel Optimism*. Durham, NC: Duke University Press, 2011.
Betensky, Aya. "Aeschylus' Oresteia: The Power of Clytemnestra," *Ramus: Critical Studies in Greek and Roman Literature* 7, no. 1 (1978): 11–25.
Bickford, Susan. "Emotion Talk and Political Judgment," *Journal of Politics* 73, no. 4 (2011): 1025–37.
———. "Constructing Inequality: City Spaces and the Architecture of Citizenship," *Political Theory* 28, no. 3 (2000): 355–76.
———. *The Dissonance of Democracy: Listening, Conflict, and Citizenship*. Ithaca, NY: Cornell University Press, 1996.
Bohman, James. *Democracy across Borders: From Dêmos to Dêmoi*. Cambridge, MA: MIT Press, 2004.
———. "Deliberative Democracy and Effective Social Freedom." In *Deliberative Democracy: Essays on Reason and Politics*, edited by James Bohman and William Rehg, 321–48. Cambridge, MA: MIT Press, 1997.
Booth, W. James. "Communities of Memory: On Identity, Memory, and Debt," *American Political Science Review* 93, no. 2 (June 1999): 249–63.
Brock, R. W. "The Double Plot in Aristophanes' *Knights*," *Greek, Roman, and Byzantine Studies* 27 (1986): 15–27.
Burke, Edmund. *Reflections on the Revolution in France*. London: Penguin, 2004.
Butler, Judith. *Giving an Account of Oneself*. New York: Fordham University Press, 2005.
Butler, Octavia. *Lillith's Brood*. New York: Aspect, 2000.
———. *Kindred*. Boston, MA: Beacon Press, 1979.
Caney, Simon. "Two Kinds of Climate Justice: Avoiding Harm and Sharing Burdens," *Journal of Political Philosophy* 22, no. 2 (June 2014): 125–49.
Carmola, Kateri. "Noble Lying: Justice and Intergenerational Tension in Plato's *Republic*," *Political Theory* 31, no. 1 (February 2003): 39–62.
Cartledge, Paul. "'Deep Plays': Theatre as Process in Greek Civic Life." In *The Cambridge Companion to Greek Tragedy*, edited by P. E. Easterling, 3–35. Cambridge, UK: Cambridge University Press, 1997.
———. *Aristophanes and His Theatre of the Absurd*. London: Duckworth, 1995.
Cha, Ariana Eunjung. "It Turns Out Parenthood Is Worse than Divorce, Enemployment—Even the Death of a Partner." *The Washington Post*, August 11, 2015. www.washingtonpost.com/news/to-your-health/wp/2015/08/11/the-most-depressing-statistic-imaginable-about-being-a-new-parent/?tid=sm_fb&utm_term=.94d25712812e. Last accessed March 2, 2017.

Chiaet, Julianne. "Novel Finding: Reading Literary Fiction Improves Empathy," *Scientific American*. October 4, 2013.

Clifford, Stacy. "Making Disability Public in Deliberative Democracy," *Contemporary Political Theory* 11 (2012): 211–28.

Clough, Patricia Ticento. "Introduction," in *The Affective Turn: Theorizing the Social*, eds. Patricia Ticento Clough and Jean Halley, 1–33. Durham, NC: Duke University Press, 2007.

Cocks, Joan. *On Sovereignty and Other Political Delusions*. London: Bloomsbury, 2014.

Connelly, Kate. "From People's Palace Back to Prussian Palace." *The Guardian*, November 28, 2008. www.theguardian.com/world/2008/nov/29/berlin-prussian-palace-reconstruction-germany. Last accessed February 13, 2017.

Connolly, William. *Identity/Difference*. Ithaca, NY: Cornell University Press, 1991.

Cooper, Davina. "Against the Current: Social Pathways and the Pursuit of Enduring Change," *Feminist Legal Studies* 9, no. 2 (2001): 119–48.

DeLanda, Manuel. *A New Philosophy of Society: Assemblage Theory and Social Complexity*. London: Continuum, 2006.

Didion, Joan. *Slouching towards Bethlehem* (New York: Farrar, Straus and Giroux, 2008), 139.

Disch, Lisa. "Toward a Mobilization Conception of Democratic Representation," *American Political Science Review* 105, no. 1 (February 2011): 100–14.

———. "Please Sit Down, but Don't Make Yourself at Home: 'Visiting' and the Prefigurative Politics of Consciousness-Raising." In *Hannah Arendt and the Meaning of Politics*, edited by Craig Calhoun and John McGowan, 132–65. Minneapolis, MN: Minnesota University Press, 1997.

———. "More Truth Than Fact: Storytelling as Critical Understanding in the Writings of Hannah Arendt," *Political Theory* 21, no. 4 (1993): 665–94.

Dobson, Andrew, ed. *Fairness and Futurity: Essays on Environmental Sustainability and Social Justice*. New York: Oxford University Press, 1999.

———. "Representative Democracy and the Environment." In *Democracy and the Environment: Problems and Prospects*, edited by W. Lafferty and J. Meadowcroft, 124–39. Cheltenham, UK: Edward Elgar, 1996.

Dodds, E. R. *The Ancient Concept of Progress*. Oxford, UK: Oxford University Press, 1973.

Doherty, Claire. *Out of Time Out of Place: Public Art (Now)*. London, UK: Art Books Publishing Inc., 2015.

Dover, K. J. "The Political Aspect of Aeschylus's *Eumenides*," *The Journal of Hellenic Studies* 77, no. 2 (1957): 230–7.

Dryzek, John S. *Foundations and Frontiers of Deliberative Governance*. New York: Oxford University Press, 2012.

Dunn, Francis M. "Beginning at the End in Euripides' *Trojan Women*," *Rheinishes Museum für Philologie*. Neue Folge 136. Bd. H. 1 (1993): 22–35.

Eckersley, Robyn. "Deliberative Democracy, Ecological Representation, and Risk: Towards a Democracy of the Affected." In *Democratic Innovation: Deliberation, Representation, and Association*, edited by Michael Saward, 117–32. New York: Routledge, 2000.

Eckersley, Robyn and Andrew Dobson, eds. *Political Theory and the Environmental Challenge*. Cambridge, UK: Cambridge University Press, 2006.

Edmunds, Lowell. *Cleon, Knights, and Aristophanes' Politics*. Washington, DC: University Press of America, 1987.

———. "The Aristophanic Cleon's 'Disturbance' of Athens," *The American Journal of Philology* 108, no. 2 (Summer 1987): 233–63.

Ekeli, Kristian Skagen. "Green Constitutionalism: The Constitutional Protection of Future Generations," *Ratio Juris* 20, no. 3 (September 2007): 378–401.

———. "Giving a Voice to Posterity: Deliberative Democracy and Representation of Future People," *Journal of Agricultural & Environmental Ethics* 18, no. 5 (September 2005): 429–50.

Espejo, Paulina Ochoa. *The Time of Popular Sovereignty: Process and the Democratic State*. University Park, PA: Penn State University Press, 2011.

Euben, Peter. *Platonic Noise*. Princeton, NJ: Princeton University Press, 2003.

———. *Corrupting Youth: Political Education, Democratic Culture, and Political Theory*. Princeton, NJ: Princeton University Press, 1997.

———. *The Tragedy of Political Theory: The Road Not Taken*. Princeton, NJ: Princeton University Press, 1990.

———. *Greek Tragedy and Political Theory*. Berkeley, CA: University of California Press, 1986.

Euripides. *Trojan Women. Iphigenia among the Taurians. Ion*, translated by David Kovacs. Cambridge, MA: Harvard University Press/Loeb Editions, 1999.

———. *Cyclops. Alcestis. Medea*, translated by David Kovacs. Cambridge, MA: Harvard University Press/Loeb Editions, 1994.

Eylon, Yuval and David Heyd. "Flattery," *Philosophy and Phenomenological Research* 77, no. 3 (November 2008): 685–704.

Finley, M. I. "The Elderly in Classical Antiquity," *Greece & Rome* 28, no. 2 (October 1981): 156–71.

Foley, Helene. "The Conception of Women in Athenian Drama." In *Reflections of Women in Antiquity*, edited by Helene Foley, 127–68. New York: Gordon and Breach, 1981.

Frank, Jason. "The Living Image of the People," *Theory & Event* 18, no. 1 (2015): https://muse.jhu.edu/article/566086.

Frank, Jill. *A Democracy of Distinction: Aristotle and the Work of Politics*. Chicago, IL: University of Chicago Press, 2005.

Fraser, Nancy. "Recognition without Ethics?" *Theory, Culture & Society* 18, no. 2–3 (2001): 21–42.

———. "From Redistribution to Recognition?" In *Justice Interruptus: Critical Reflections on the Post-Socialist Condition*, 11–40. New York: Routledge, 1996.

Goldhill, Simon. "Civic Ideology and the Problem of Difference: The Politics of Aeschylean Tragedy, Once Again," *The Journal of Hellenic Studies* 120 (2000): 34–56.

———. "The Dionysia and Civic Ideology." In *Nothing to Do with Dionysos? Athenian Drama in Its Social Context*, edited by John J. Winkler and Froma I. Zeitlin, 97–129. Princeton, NJ: Princeton University Press, 1990.

Goodin, Robert E. *Reflective Democracy*. Oxford, UK: Oxford University Press, 2003.

———. "Democratic Deliberation Within," *Philosophy and Public Affairs* 29, no. 1 (Winter 2000): 81–109.

———. "Political and Ecological Communication," *Environmental Politics* 4, no. 4 (1995): 13–30.

Gosseries, Alex and Lukas H. Meyer, eds. *Intergenerational Justice*. New York: Oxford University Press, 2009.

Grossberg, Lawrence. *Cultural Studies in the Future Tense*. Durham, NC: Duke University Press, 2010.

Habermas, Jürgen. *The Future of Human Nature*. New York: Polity, 2003.

———. *On the Pragmatics of Social Interaction: Preliminary Studies in Theory of Communicative Action*. Cambridge, MA: MIT Press, 2001.

Bibliography

———. *The Postcolonial Constellation*. Cambridge, MA: MIT Press, 2001.

———. *Between Facts and Norms: Contributions to a Discourse Theory of Law and Democracy*. Cambridge, MA: MIT Press, 1996.

———. *A Theory of Communicative Action, Vol. 2, Lifeworld and System: A Critique of Functionalist Reason*. Boston, MA: Beacon Press, 1987.

———. *A Theory of Communicative Action: Vol. 1, Reason and the Rationalization of Society*. Boston, MA: Beacon Press, 1984.

Habermas, Jürgen and Joseph Ratzinger. *On the Dialectics of Secularization*. San Francisco, CA: Ignatius Press, 2006.

Halliwell, Stephen. *Greek Laughter: A Study of Cultural Psychology from Homer to Early Christianity*. New York: Cambridge University Press, 2008.

———. "Comic Satire and Freedom of Speech in Classical Athens," *The Journal of Hellenic Studies* 111 (1991): 48–70.

———. "The Uses of Laughter in Greek Culture," *The Classical Quarterly* 41, no. 2 (1991): 279–96.

Hammond, N. G. L. "Personal Freedom and Its Limitations in the *Oresteia*," *The Journal of Hellenic Studies* 85 (1965): 42–55.

Hancock, Ange-Marie. *The Politics of Disgust: The Public Identity of the Welfare Queen*. New York: New York University Press, 2004.

Harjes, Kristen. "Stumbling Stones: Holocaust Memorials, National Identity, and Democratic Inclusion in Berlin," *German Politics & Society* 23, no. 1 (Spring 2005): 138–51.

Harvey, David. *Rebel Cities: From the Right to the City to the Urban Revolution*. New York: Verso, 2013.

———. "The Right to the City," *New Left Review*, 53 (September-October 2008): 23–40.

Havelock, Eric A. *The Greek Concept of Justice: From Its Shadows in Homer to Its Substance in Plato*. Cambridge, MA: Harvard University Press, 1978.

Havercroft, Jonathan. *Captives of Sovereignty*. New York: Cambridge University Press, 2011.

Heath, Malcolm. *Political Comedy in Aristophanes*. Göttingen, Germany: Vandenhoeck & Ruprecht, 1987.

Held, Virginia. *Feminist Morality: Transforming Culture, Society, and Politics*. Chicago, IL: University of Chicago Press, 1993.

Henderson, Jeffrey. "Attic Old Comedy, Frank Speech, and Democracy." In *Democracy, Empire, and the Arts in Fifth-Century Athens*, edited by Deborah Boedeker and Kurt A. Raaflaub, 255–73. Cambridge, MA: Harvard University Press, 1998.

———. "The *Demos* and Comic Competition." In *Nothing to Do with Dionysos? Athenian Drama in Its Social Context*, edited by John J. Winkler and Froma I. Zeitlin, 271–313. Princeton, NJ: Princeton University Press, 1990.

———. "Older Women in Attic Old Comedy," *Transactions of the American Philological Association* 117 (1987): 105–29.

Herington, C. J. "Athena in Athenian Literature and Cult," *Greece and Rome, 2nd Series* 10 (1963): 61–73.

Hesk, Jon. *Democracy and Deception in Classical Athens*. New York: Cambridge University Press, 2000.

Heyd, David. "A Value or an Obligation? Rawls on Justice to Future Generations." In *Intergenerational Justice*, edited by Axel Gosseries and Lukas H. Meyer, 167–88. New York: Oxford University Press, 2009.

Hill Collins, Patricia. *Black Feminist Thought*. New York: Routledge, 2000.

Hirschmann, Nancy J. *The Subject of Liberty: Toward a Feminist Theory of Freedom*. Princeton, NJ: Princeton University Press, 2003.
Honig, Bonnie. *Antigone Interrupted*. New York: Cambridge University Press, 2013.
_____. "The Politics of Public Things: Neoliberalism and the Routine of Privatization," *No Foundations: An Interdisciplinary Journal of Law and Justice* 10 (2013): 59–76.
_____. "Antigone's Laments, Creon's Grief: Mourning, Membership, and the Politics of Exception," *Political Theory* 37, no. 1 (February 2009): 5–43.
_____. "Difference, Dilemmas, and the Politics of Home." In *Democracy and Difference: Contesting the Boundaries of the Political*, edited by Seyla Benhabib, 257–77. Princeton, NJ: Princeton University Press, 1996.
Hopman, Marianne. "Revenge and Mythopoiesis in Euripides' *Medea*," *Transactions of the American Philological Association* 138, no. 1 (Spring 2008): 155–83.
Howes, Dustin Ells. *Freedom Without Violence: Resisting the Western Political Tradition*. New York: Oxford University Press, 2016.
Hubbard, Thomas K. *The Mask of Comedy: Aristophanes and the Intertextual Parabasis*. Ithaca, NY: Cornell University Press, 1991.
Hufker, Paul. *Pedro Reyes Doomocracy: The Script*. Brooklyn Army Terminal, NY: Creative Time, October 7–November 6, 2016.
Jamieson, Dale. *Reason in a Dark Time: Why the Struggle against Climate Change Failed—and What it Means for Our Future*. New York: Oxford University Press, 2014.
Jefferson, Thomas. *Political Writings*. New York: Cambridge University Press, 1999.
Johnson, Paul, Christoph Conrad, and David Thompson, eds. *Workers versus Pensioners*. New York: St. Martin's Press, 1989.
Kasimis, Demetra. "The Tragedy of Blood-Based Membership: Secrecy and the Politics of Immigration in Euripides' *Ion*," *Political Theory* 41, no. 2 (2013): 231–56.
Kavka, Gregory. "The Paradox of Future Individuals," *Philosophy and Public Affairs* 11, no. 2 (Spring 1982): 93–112.
Kayden, Jerold S., The New York City Department of City Planning, and The Municipal Art Society of New York. *Privately Owned Public Space: The New York City Experience*. New York: John Wiley & Sons, 2000.
KHOU. "Mom charged with abandonment said kids were never out of sight." *Tegna*, July 18, 2015. Last accessed February 5, 2017. www.khou.com/news/local/mom-charged-with-abandonment-said-kids-were-never-out-of-sight/148484566.
Kim, Owen. Interview with author. *Situations*, June 23, 2016.
Kimmelman, Michael. "Rebuilding a Palace May Become a Grand Blunder," *The New York Times*, December 31, 2008. www.nytimes.com/2009/01/01/arts/design/01abroad.html. Last accessed February 3, 2017.
Kittay, Eva Feder. *Love's Labor: Essays on Women, Equality, and Dependency*. New York: Routledge, 1999.
Kohn, Margaret. *Brave New Neighborhoods: The Privatization of Public Space*. New York: Routledge, 2004.
Kolbert, Elizabeth. "A Stone for My Great-Grandmother." *The New Yorker*, March 16, 2015. www.newyorker.com/magazine/2015/02/16/last-trial. Last accessed January 20, 2017.
Kompridis, Nikolas. "Turning and Returning: The Aesthetic Turn in Political Thought." In *The Aesthetic Turn in Political Thought*, edited by Nikolas Kompridis, xiv–xxxvii. New York: Bloomsbury, 2014.
Kotlikoff, Lawrence and Scott Burns. *The Coming Generational Storm: What You Need to Know about America's Economic Future*. Cambridge, MA: MIT Press, 2005.

Krause, Sharon. *Freedom beyond Sovereignty: Reconstructing Liberal Individualism*. Chicago, IL: University of Chicago Press, 2015.

———. "Bodies in Action: Corporeal Agency and Democratic Politics," *Political Theory* 39, no. 3 (2011): 299–324.

Lane, Melissa. *Eco-Republic: What the Ancients Can Teach Us about Ethics, Virtue, and Sustainable Living*. Princeton, NJ: Princeton University Press, 2012.

Lanier, Jaron. *Who Owns the Future*. New York: Simon & Schuster, 2013.

Lara, María Pía. *Narrating Evil: A Postmetaphysical Theory of Reflective Judgment*. New York: Columbia University Press, 2007.

Laslett, Peter and James S. Fishkin, eds. *Justice between Age Groups and Generations*. New Haven, CT: Yale University Press, 1992.

Lauriola, Rosanna. "Aristophanes' Criticism: Some Lexical Considerations," *AION* 32 (2010): 25–61.

———. "Athena and Paphlagonian in Aristophanes' '*Knights*': Reconsidering '*Equites*' 1090–5," *Mnemosyne* 59, no. 1 (2006): 75–94.

Laymon, Kiese. *Long Division*. Chicago, IL: Agate Publishing, 2013.

Lefebvre, Henri. *The Production of Space*, translated by Donald Nicholson-Smith. Oxford, UK: Blackwell, 1992.

Lesky, Albin. "Decision and Responsibility in the Tragedy of Aeschylus," *The Journal of Hellenic Studies* 86 (1966): 78–85.

Levett, Bradley Morgan. "Verbal Autonomy and Verbal Self-Restraint in Euripides' *Medea*," *Classical Philology* 105, no. 1 (January 2010): 54–68.

Levine, Caroline. *Forms: Whole, Rhythm, Hierarchy, Network*. Princeton, NJ: Princeton University Press, 2015.

Levinson, Sanford. *Written in Stone: Public Monuments in Changing Societies*. Durham, NC: Duke University Press, 1998.

Liebell, Susan. "The Text and Context of 'Enough and as Good': John Locke as the Foundation of an Environmental Liberalism," *Polity* 43, no. 2 (April 2011): 210–41.

Lindh, Thomas, Bo Malmberg, and Joakim Palme. "Generations at War or Sustainable Social Policy in Ageing Societies?" *The Journal of Political Philosophy* 13, no. 4 (2005): 470–89.

Lloyd-Jones, Hugh. "The Guilt of Agamemnon," *The Classical Quarterly* 12, no. 2 (1962): 187–99.

Locke, John. *Second Treatise of Government*. Indianapolis, IN: Hackett, 1980.

Loraux, Nicole. *Mothers in Mourning*. Ithaca, NY: Cornell University Press, 1998.

McIvor, David W. *Mourning in America: Race and the Politics of Loss*. Ithaca, NY: Cornell University Press, 2016.

McKean, Benjamin L. "What Makes a Utopia Inconvenient? On the Advantages and Disadvantages of a Realist Orientation to Politics," *American Political Science Review* 110, no. 4 (November 2016): 876–88.

MacKinnon, Catherine. *Feminism Unmodified: Discourses on Life and Law*. Cambridge, MA: Harvard University Press, 1987.

McKittrick, Katherine. "Unparalleled Catastrophe for Our Species? Or, to Give Humanness a Different Future: Conversations." In *Sylvia Winter: On Being Human as Praxis*, edited by Katherine McKittrick, 9–89. Durham, NC: Duke University Press.

MacLeod, C. W. "Politics and the Oresteia," *The Journal of Hellenic Studies* 102 (1982): 124–44.

Maitland, Judith. "Dynasty and Family in the Athenian City State: A View from Attic Tragedy," *The Classical Quarterly* 42, no. 1 (1992): 26–40.

Markell, Patchen. "The Rule of the People: Arendt, Archê, and Democracy," *American Political Science Review* 100, no. 1 (February 2006): 1–14.

———. *Bound by Recognition*. Princeton, NJ: Princeton University Press, 2003.

Markovits, Elizabeth. *The Politics of Sincerity*. University Park, PA: Penn State University Press, 2008.

Markovits, Elizabeth and Susan Bickford. "Constructing Freedom: Institutional Pathways to Changing the Gender Division of Labor," *Perspectives on Politics* 12, no. 1 (March 2014): 81–99.

Martell, James R. "Can There Be Politics Without Sovereignty? Arendt, Derrida, and the Question of Sovereign Inevitability," *Law, Culture and the Humanities* 6, no. 2 (2010): 153–66.

———. "The Rule of the People: Arendt, Archê, and Democracy," *The American Political Science Review* 100, no. 1 (2006): 1–14.

Mastronarde, Donald J. *The Art of Euripides: Dramatic Technique and Social Context*. New York: Cambridge University Press, 2010.

Meyer, Lukas H., ed. *Justice in Time: Responding to Historical Injustice*. Baden-Baden, Germany: Nomos, 2004.

Meyer, Lukas H. and Dominic Roser, "Enough for the Future." In *Intergenerational Justice*, edited by Axel Gosseries and Lukas H. Meyer, 219–48. New York: Oxford University Press, 2009.

Michelina, Ann. "Euripides: Conformist, Deviant, Neo-Conservative?" *Arion: A Journal of Humanities and the Classics* 4, no. 3 (Winter 1997): 208–22.

Miller, Jon and Rahul Kumar, eds. *Reparations: Interdisciplinary Inquiries*. Oxford, UK: Oxford University Press, 2007.

Monoson, S. Sara. *Plato's Democratic Entanglements: Athenian Politics and the Practice of Philosophy*. Princeton, NJ: Princeton University Press, 2000.

Morrison, Toni. *Beloved*. New York: Vintage, 2004.

Morton, Timothy. *Hyperobjects: Philosophy and Ecology after the End of the World*. Minneapolis, MN: University of Minnesota, 2013.

Muñiz-Fraticelli, Victor M. "The Problem of Perpetual Constitution." In *Intergenerational Justice*, edited by Axel Gosseries and Lukas H. Meyer, 377–410. New York: Oxford University Press, 2009.

Nehamas, Alexander. *The Art of Living: Socratic Reflections from Plato to Foucault*. Berkeley, CA: University of California Press, 1998.

Norton, Bryan. "Intergenerational Equity and Environmental Decisions: A Model Using Rawls' Veil of Ignorance," *Ecological Economics* 1, no. 2 (May 1989): 137–59.

Nussbaum, Martha C. *Frontiers of Justice: Disability, Nationality, Species Membership*. Cambridge, MA: The Belknap Press of Harvard University Press, 2006.

———. *The Fragility of Goodness: Luck and Ethics in Greek Tragedy and Philosophy*. Cambridge, UK: Cambridge University Press, 1986.

O'Brien, Mary. *The Politics of Reproduction*. Boston, MA: Routledge and Kegan Paul, 1981.

Okin, Susan Moller. *Justice, Gender, and the Family*. New York: Basic Books, 1989.

Parfit, Derek. *Reasons and Persons*. New York: Oxford University Press, 1984.

Park, Shelley M. *Mothering Queerly, Queering Motherhood: Resisting Monomaternalism in Adoptive, Lesbian, Blended, and Polygamous Families*. Albany, NY: State University of New York Press, 2013.

Partridge, Ernest, ed. *Responsibilities to Future Generations: Environmental Ethics*. Buffalo, NY: Prometheus Books, 1981.

Pew Research Center. "Modern Parenthood: Roles of Moms and Dads Converge as They Balance Work and Family." 2013: www.pewsocialtrends.org/2013/03/14/modern-parenthood-roles-of-moms-and-dads-converge-as-they-balance-work-and-family. Last accessed June 27, 2017.

Podlecki, Anthony. *The Political Background of Aeschylean Tragedy*. London: Bristol Classical Press, 1999.

Pucci, Pietro. *The Violence of Pity in Euripides' Medea*. Ithaca, NY: Cornell University Press, 1980.

Purdy, Jedidiah. *After Nature: A Politics for the Anthropocene*. Cambridge, MA: Harvard University Press, 2015.

Raaflaub, Kurt. *The Discovery of Freedom in Ancient Greece*. Chicago, IL: University of Chicago Press, 2004.

Rahman, Smita A. *Time, Memory, and the Politics of Contingency*. New York: Routledge, 2014.

Rawls, John. *Political Liberalism*. New York: Columbia University Press, 1993.

———. *A Theory of Justice*. Cambridge, MA: The Belknap Press of Harvard University Press, 1971.

Rich, Adrienne. *Of Woman Born: Motherhood as Experience and Institution*. New York: W.W. Norton, 1995.

Ricoy, Iñigo González and Axel Gosseries. *Institutions for Future Generations*. New York: Oxford University Press, 2016.

Roberts, Dorothy. *Killing the Black Body: Race, Reproduction, and the Meaning of Liberty*. New York: Vintage, 1998.

———. *Shattered Bonds: The Color of Child Welfare*. New York: Basic Civitas Books, 2003.

Robinson, Kim Stanley. *Green Earth: The Science in the Capital*. New York: Del Ray, 2015.

Rocco, Christopher. *Tragedy and Enlightenment: Athenian Political Thought and the Dilemmas of Modernity*. Berkeley, CA: University of California Press, 1997.

Rhodes, P. J. "Nothing to Do with Democracy: Athenian Drama and the Polis," *Journal of Hellenic Studies* 123 (2003): 104–19.

Ruddick, Sara. *Maternal Thinking: Toward a Politics of Peace*. Boston, MA: Beacon Press, 1989.

Said, Susan. "Tragedy and Politics." In *Democracy, Empire, and the Arts in Fifth-Century Athens*, edited by Debora Boedeker and Kurt Raaflaub, 275–95. Cambridge, MA: Harvard University Press, 1998.

Salkever, Stephen. "Teaching Comparative Political Thought: Joys, Pitfalls, Strategies, Significance," *Political Science Faculty Research and Scholarship*. Paper 26.

Saxonhouse, Arlene. *Fear of Diversity: The Birth of Political Science in Ancient Greek Thought*. Chicago, IL: University of Chicago Press, 1992.

———. "The Tyranny of Reason in the World of the Polis," *American Political Science Review* 82, no. 4 (December 1988): 1261–75.

———. "Aeschylus' *Orestia*: Misogyny, Filogyny and Justice," *Women and Politics* 4 (1984): 11–32.

———. "Men, Women, War, and Politics: Family and Polis in Aristophanes and Euripides," *Political Theory* 8, no. 1 (1980): 65–81.

Schell, Jonathan. *The Fate of the Earth and the Abolition*. Stanford, CA: Stanford University Press, 2000.

Schiff, Jade. *Burdens of Political Responsibility: Narrative and the Cultivation of Responsiveness*. New York: Cambridge University Press, 2014.

———. "Inclusion and the Cultivation of Responsiveness," *The Good Society* 18, no. 1 (2009): 63–9.

———. "Confronting Political Responsibility: The Problem of Acknowledgement," *Hypatia* 23, no. 3 (2008): 99–117.
Scholtz, Andrew. "Friends, Lovers, Flatterers: Demophilic Courtship in Aristophanes' *Knights*," *Transactions of the American Philological Association* 134 (2004): 63–93.
Seaford, Richard. *Reciprocity and Ritual: Homer and Tragedy in the Developing City-State.* Oxford, UK: Clarendon Press, 1994.
Seck, Ibrahima. *Bouki Fait Gombo: A History of the Slave Community at Habitation Haydel (Whitney Plantation) Louisiana, 1750–1860.* New Orleans, LA: UNO Press, 2014.
Segal, Charles. *Euripides and the Poetics of Sorrow: Art, Gender, and Commemoration in Alcestis, Hippolytus, and Hecuba.* Durham, NC: Duke University Press, 1993.
Shapiro, Ian. *Democratic Justice.* New Haven, CT: Yale University Press, 1999.
Shulman, George. "American Political Culture, Prophetic Narration, and Toni Morrison's *Beloved*," *Political Theory* 24, no. 2 (May 1996): 295–314.
Sikora, R. I. and Brian Barry, eds. *Obligations to Future Generations.* Philadelphia, PA: Temple University Press, 1978.
Silk, M. S. *Aristophanes and the Definition of Comedy.* New York: Oxford University Press, 2000.
Singer, Peter. *One World: The Ethics of Globalization.* New Haven, CT: Yale University Press, 2002.
Situationist International. "The Theory of Moments and the Construction of Situations," *Internationale Situationniste* 4 (June 1960), http://www.cddc.vt.edu/sionline/si/moments.html. Last accessed August 7, 2017.
Slater, Niall W. *Spectator Politics: Metatheatre and Performance in Aristophanes.* Philadelphia, PA: University of Pennsylvania Press, 2002.
Sontag, Susan. "At the Same Time: The Novelist and Moral Reasoning." In *At the Same Time: Essays and Speeches*, edited by Paolo Dilonardo and Anne Jump, 210–32. New York: Picador, 2007.
Soss, Joe, Richard C. Fording, and Sanford F. Schram. *Persistent Power of Race.* Chicago, IL: University of Chicago Press, 2011.
Spinner-Halev, Jeff. *Enduring Injustice.* New York: Cambridge University Press, 2012.
Stengel, Richard. *You're Too Kind: A Brief History of Flattery.* New York: Touchstone Books, 2000.
Stewart, Kathleen. *Ordinary Affects.* Durham, NC: Duke University Press, 2007.
"Stolperstein-Befürworter scheitern vor Münchner Gericht," Spiegel Online, May 31, 2016, www.spiegel.de/panorama/gesellschaft/stolpersteine-in-muenchen-weitere-schlappe-fuerbefuerworter-a-1095047.html. Last accessed January 20, 2017.
Stowe, Simon. *Republic of Readers? The Literary Turn in Political Thought and Analysis.* Albany, NY: State University of New York Press, 2007.
Suter, Ann. "Lament in Euripides' *Trojan Women*," *Mnemosyne* 56, no. 1 (2003): 1–28.
Taylor, Charles. "The Politics of Recognition." In *Multiculturalism: Examining the Politics of Recognition*, edited by Amy Guttman. Princeton, NJ: Princeton University Press, 1994.
Taylor, John Wilson. "The Athenian Ephebic Oath," *The Classical Journal* 13, no. 7 (April 1918): 495–501.
Tessitore, Aristide. "Euripides' *Medea* and the Problem of Spiritedness," *The Review of Politics* 53, no. 4 (1991): 587–601.
Thompson, Dennis F. "Representing Future Generations: Political Presentism and Democratic Trusteeship," *Critical Review of International and Political Philosophy* 13, no. 1 (2010): 17–37.
Thompson, Janna. "Identity and Obligation in a Transgenerational Polity." In *Intergenerational Justice*, edited by Axel Gosseries and Lukas H. Meyer, 33–8. New York: Oxford University Press, 2015.

———. *Intergenerational Justice: Rights and Responsibilities in an Intergenerational Polity*. New York: Routledge Press, 2009.

Thompson, Nato. *Culture as Weapon: The Art of Influence in Everyday Life*. Brooklyn, NY: Melville House, 2017.

———. *Seeing Power: Art and Activism in the 21st Century*. Brooklyn, NY: Melville House, 2005.

Thomson, David. *Selfish Generations? How Welfare States Grow Old*. Wellington, New Zealand: White Horse Press, 1996.

Thucydides. *History of the Peloponnesian War, Vol. 1*, translated by C.F. Smith. Cambridge, MA: Harvard University Press/Loeb Editions, 1919.

Till, Karen E. *The New Berlin: Memory, Politics, Place*. Minneapolis, MN: University of Minnesota Press, 2005.

Toffler, Alvin. *Future Shock*. New York: Bantam, 1984.

Tompkins, Daniel. Paper presented at the 2006 American Political Science Association Meeting, Philadelphia. September 2006.

Toqueville, Alexis de. *Democracy in America: Volume 2*. New York: Vintage Classic, 1990.

Tronto, Joan. *Caring Democracy*. New York: New York University Press, 2013.

———. *Moral Boundaries: A Political Argument for an Ethic of Care*. New York: Routledge, 1994.

Vernant, Jean-Pierre. *Myth and Thought among the Greeks*. New York: Zone Books, 2006.

Vernant, Jean-Pierre and Pierre Vidal-Naquet. *Myth and Tragedy in Ancient Greece*. New York: Zone Books, 1990.

Weheliye, Alexander G. *Habeas Viscus: Racializing Assemblages, Biopolitics, and Black Feminist Theories of the Human*. Durham, NC: Duke University Press, 2014.

Williams, Bernard. *Shame and Necessity*. Berkeley, CA: University of California Press, 1993.

Winnington-Ingram, R. P. "Clytemnestra and the Vote of Athena," *The Journal of Hellenic Studies* 68 (1948): 130–47.

Winnington-Ingram, R. P., John Gould, and Bernard M. W. Knox, "Tragedy." In *The Cambridge History of Classical Literature*, edited by P. E. Easterling and Bernard M. W. Knox, 258–345. New York: Cambridge University Press.

Wodiczko, Krysztof. "Strategies of Public Address: Which Media? Which Publics?" In *Situation: Documents of Contemporary Art*, edited by Claire Doherty, 124–7. Cambridge, MA: MIT Press, 2009.

Wolin, Sheldon. "Norm and Form: The Constitutionalizing of Democracy." In *Athenian Political Thought and the Reconstruction of American Democracy*, edited by J. Peter Euben, John R. Wallach, and Josiah Ober, 29–58. Ithaca, NY: Cornell University Press, 1994.

———. *The Presence of the Past: Essays on the State and the Constitution*. Baltimore, MD: Johns Hopkins University Press, 1989.

Young, Iris Marion. *Responsibility for Justice*. New York: Oxford University Press, 2011.

———. "Responsibility and Global Justice: A Social Connection Model," *Social Philosophy and Policy* 23, no. 1 (January 2006): 137–65.

———. *On Female Body Experience: "Throwing Like a Girl" and Other Essays*. New York: Oxford University Press, 2005.

———. *Inclusion and Democracy*. New York: Oxford University Press, 2000.

———. *Justice and the Politics of Difference*. Princeton, NJ: Princeton University Press, 1990.

Zeitlin, Froma. "Foreword." In *The Children of Athena: Athenian Ideas about Citizenship and the Division between the Sexes* by Nicole Loraux, xi–xvii. Princeton, NJ: Princeton University Press, 1993.

———. "The Dynamics of Misogyny: Myth and Mythmaking in the Oresteia," *Arethusa* 11, no. 1 (1978): 149–74.

Zerilli, Linda. "'We Feel Our Freedom': Imagination and Judgement in the Thought of Hannah Arendt." In *The Aesthetic Turn in Political Thought*, edited by Nikolas Kompridis, 29–60. New York: Bloomsbury, 2014.

Zumbrunnen, John. *Aristophanic Comedy and the Challenge of Democratic Citizenship*. Rochester, NY: University of Rochester Press, 2012.

INDEX

accountability 19–21, 29, 42, 57, 61 n. 52, 122, 132, 140
acknowledgement 26, 46–7, 54
Aegisthus, 123, 137
Aeschylus 1, 5–7, 55, 82; and gender conflict 122, 135, 143; and necessity 121, 125–32; and political context 122, 125; and responsibility 132–9; and transgenerational orientation 139–45
aesthetics, political 31, 40, 42, 121, 139–42, 151–7, 162–5
affect: and assemblages 3, 109; and climate change 3–4, 41–2; definition of 60 n. 42; and freedom 81–3; and Greek theater 56, 64, 71, 150; and lament 97–8, 107; and narrative 5, 48, 51–2, 54, 141–5; and the ordinary 149, 151–2; and public art 163–5; and space 151–60, 162; and transgenerational orientation 7, 122, 139, 164–5
Agamemnon 121–4, 127, 132–6
Agamemnon 122–8, 132–5, 145
agency 5–6, 28, 32–3; distributed agency 4, 7, 31, 77–8, 84, 98–9, 104–105, 108–11, 120–3, 128–30, 133, 137, 140, 144; emergent quality 7, 77, 147 n. 39, 164; and freedom 1–2, 31, 34, 125; intergenerational agency 87–9, 98; and intergenerational time 52, 54, 88; as involvement 102, 104; of lament 97, 102, 107, 116, 158; and necessity 121, 132, 136; non-human 118 n. 46, 146 n. 11; and the ordinary 152; sovereign agency 6, 24–5, 30, 114
aging: de Beauvoir on 73; *see also* elderly
Allen, Danielle 25, 83, 128–9
anangke see necessity
Andromache 96, 99–102, 107
Anker, Elisabeth 7, 30–1, 34, 74, 150
Anthropocene 41
Apollo 106, 124, 136–8, 140–1, 143, 145, 145 n. 6, 146 n. 34
Apology 57
archê 78, 80–2, 85–6 n. 35, 130
Arendt, Hannah: and *archê* 80–1, 85 n. 35; and freedom 6, 28–9; and generations 9, 120, 129, 146 n. 25; and judgment 42–7; and "problem of the new" 40–2; and representative thinking 43–5, 140; and responsibility; 129–30; and sovereignty 8 n. 12, 28–9, 39 n. 76, 39 n. 86; and storytelling 45–7
Aristophanes: and affect 64, 83; and Athenian politics 5–6, 57–8, 64, 66, 69, 85 n. 34; and Cleon 57, 66; as anti-political 6, 74, 82, 84, 88, 121; and flattery 65–9; and intergenerational dynamics 64–5, 78–83; and old age 69–74, 88
Aristotle 3, 55, 126, 131, 146
Aslam, Ali 30
assemblages: definition 77; and democracy 120, 138, 140–4, 147 n. 39;

and distributed agency 128–9; family as 6, 87–8, 98–116, 127, 133–6; non-human elements 146 n. 11; and public art 163–4; self as 40, 78–8, 84, 87, 126; and space 152, 157; transgenerational assemblage 7, 120–2, 128–30, 136–9, 145, 165
Astyanax 96, 99, 101–2, 107
Athena 33, 93, 95, 136, 138–47
Athens: analogies to contemporary era 117 n. 16, 150; as decaying city 64–6; and democracy 124, 136, 139; intergenerational themes in 58–9, 120, 143–4; leadership of 67–8, 73–4, 92; and mothers 6, 92–4; and mourning 93, 97, 103, 107; nostalgia in 71, 74; theater in 2, 4, 54–8, 64, 136, 152; as vigorous 72–3
attunement 90–1, 151, 163; *see also* orientation
autochthony 74, 92–3, 144
autonomy: and assemblages 100; and democracy 83; and gender 88, 94, 113, 114; and old age 73, 88; as sovereignty 31, 99

Benjamin, Jessica 90
Bennett, Jane 98, 118 n. 46
Berlant, Lauren 120
Berlin 148–51
Bickford, Susan 44, 51, 153–5
birthright 15, 25, 58, 136, 139, 144
bomolochos 65
Bodin, Jean 29
Bristol 161–2, 164
Brooklyn 155, 160–1
Burke, Edmund 12, 14
Butler, Judith 130
Butler, Octavia 34 n. 1, 53

Cartledge, Paul 56, 70
Cassandra 95–7, 102, 105–7, 134–5
children: in art 158, 159; in Athens 58, 59, 93–7; care of 88–92, 104–5, 113; deaths of 58, 94–5, 101, 107–15, 123, 133–4; as part of assemblage 98–100, 115, 135; power over 32, 39 n. 93; qualities of 73, 123–4, 139; as saviors 124; *see also* motherhood, youth
City Dionysia *see* Great Dionysia
Cleon 57, 64–9, 71–4, 85 n. 22
climate change 1–4; 13, 23, 32–3, 40, 41–2, 51, 103, 105, 161

Clouds 71, 75, 78–9, 81–5, 88, 120
Clytemnestra 121, 123, 133–8
Cocks, Joan 29–31, 86 n. 39
comedy: comedic voyaging 64; *parrhesia* 57, 62 n. 65; political function 57–8, 62 n. 65, 74, 83–4
Creative Time 155, 160–1, 166 n. 37
critical race theory 31
cosmopolitan theory 4, 10

De Beauvoir, Simone 73, 89
DeLanda, Manuel 98–9
deliberation 18–21, 42–3, 126, 131–2, 140, 146 n. 11
demagoguery 64–69, 71–2, 74, 85 n. 22
Demnig, Gunter 148–9
democracy: aspiration to rule 25; deliberative democracy 18–19; radical models 10, 57; *see also* autonomy, agency, freedom
demophilia 66
Demos 64–8, 70–8, 88
demos 29, 70–4, 144; fickleness of 71
dependence 31, 69, 73, 89, 92, 98, 99, 104, 108, 139
Didion, Joan 77
Disch, Lisa 44–5, 47, 147 n. 39
distribution, generational 15–18
Dobson, Andrew 19
Doomocracy 160–2
DuBois, W.E.B. 24
Dunn, Francis 96

Eckersly, Robyn 19
Ekeli, Kristian 19–20
elderly 64–5, 67, 69–78, 88, 159
Elektra 124, 135
Ephebic oath 58, 62 n. 71, 120
Erinyes 105, 122, 124, 138–45, 147 n. 36, 157
ethics: care ethics 34–5 n. 2, 88–92, 104–5; environmental 3, 9–10, 15, 19–20
Euben, J. Peter 53, 82, 85 n. 34, 165 n. 6
Eumenides 33, 61 n.52, 122, 124, 138–43, 145 n. 6
Euripides: portrayal of Greek gods 94–5; women in 95

fathers 54, 58, 88; *see also* Agamemnon, Jason, Strepsiades
feminist theory 4, 8, 34–5 n. 2, 89–92, 98, 104–5

182 Index

finitude 2, 5, 26, 76–9, 83–4, 85 n. 29, 88, 122, 125
Fishkin, James 16
flattery 65–73, 85 n. 22
Foley, Helene 92
Frank, Jason 4
Frank, Jill 146 n. 15
freedom: and democracy 10–11, 28–31, 69, 75–6, 83–4; and desire 126–7; of the future 13–14, 33–4, 40, 81, 116, 142–3, 164–5; and intergenerational responsibility 128–39; limits of 25, 32, 42, 59, 76, 79, 111; natural freedom 86 n. 39; plural freedom 28, 32, 125; as responsiveness/non-sovereign 32, 110, 112; as sovereignty 6, 13, 18, 21, 25–34, 64, 74–5, 114–15, 150, 155–6; tension with responsibility 7, 26, 46, 81, 121, 124–5, 132–9, 150; and time 11, 27, 78, 81; as tyranny 14, 75–6; women and 96, 98, 100, 101; *see also* agency, necessity
Furies *see* Erinyes
future: invisibility of 22–5; non-identity problem 19; popular writing about 9–10, 34 n. 1; sacrifices endured by 128–9

Gates, Theaster 164
generations: cleavages within 8 n. 2, 12
gerontas 64
Goodin, Robert 19
Gosseries, Alex 16, 35 n. 7
guilt 33, 129, 133, 137

Habermas, Jürgen 18, 37 n. 46
Halliwell, Stephen 57, 62 n. 65
Hammond, N. G. L. 136
Harvey, David 156
Hecuba 96–103, 105–7, 109, 114
Helen 96, 105–6, 123
Henderson, Jeffrey 57, 67, 70
Hirschmann, Nancy 98, 126
Hollow 161–2, 167 n. 37
Honig, Bonnie 93–4, 152, 154
hyperobject 14, 52, 162

identity: and agency 32, 118 n. 46; in assemblage 98, 101–2, 104–5, 108–9, 115–16; *see also* orientation, recognition imagination 2–4, 30–3, 40, 44–5, 50, 52, 149
individualism 2, 5, 12, 29, 34, 88, 91, 122

inheritance 9, 24, 33, 46, 130, 136–7
injustice: historical injustice 34 n. 2; as misrecognition 24–6; structural injustice 23, 25, 40, 46–7, 50, 103, 108, 129
intergenerational justice: generational sovereignty 12–15; generational distribution 15–18; generational representation 18–21; as misrecognition 21–6; as problem of sovereignty 26–7, 32–4; as structural injustice 23; *see also* orientation (transgenerational)
intergenerational tensions 5, 54, 78–83, 65 n. 35, 121, 123–4, 143, 150; conflict among gods 123–4, 138, 140–2
intersubjectivity: intersubjective vulnerability 24–6, 33, 42, 46, 138–9, 155; temporal intersubjectivity 12, 46, 122–3, 157
invisibility 22–5

Jamieson, Dale 41–2
Jason 108–16
Jefferson 2, 12–15, 17, 24, 26, 36 n. 20, 78, 120, 124; perpetual constitution 2, 13
judgment 41–7, 51, 54, 69, 74, 121, 139, 140; and art 157, 162–4; collective judgment 54, 128, 132, 141–4; and Greek theater 55–9, 69, 74; *see also* intergenerational justice

Kasimis, Demetra 54, 93
Knights 5, 63–74
Kohn, Margaret 153, 155
kolakeia see flattery
Krause, Sharon 32–3, 39 n. 82, 102, 118 n. 46, 125, 129

lament 118 n. 37, 123, 135, 141, 158; agency of 107; in Athens 93–4; in *Medea* 111–12, 114, 115; in *Trojan Women* 96–103
Lane, Melissa 3
Lara, María Pía 45
Laslett, Peter 16, 36 n. 36
LeFebvre, Henri 153–7
legitimacy 10, 20, 32–3, 51
Levine, Caroline 50, 52
Libation Bearers 122, 124, 135–8, 145 n. 6
Liebell, Susan 15

Locke, John 12, 15
London 154, 159–60
Loraux, Nicole 92–3, 112–13

McKean, Benjamin 121
Marathon 65, 69, 79
Markell, Patchen 24–6, 32–3, 46, 80–1, 85 n. 35, 103, 131, 147 n. 36, McIvor, David 56–7
Mastronarde, Donald 94
Medea 6, 87, 108–16; Platonic irony in 116
Medea 95, 97, 108–16, 133, 134, 137
memory 34 n. 2, 51, 94, 101, 106, 108, 110, 113, 144, 148–9, 164; monuments 101, 155
Menelaus 106–7, 123–4
Meyer, Lukas 16, 34 n. 2
misrecognition 22–4, 32, 44, 46, 50–1, 90, 95, 103, 114
Monoson, Sara 56
Morton, Timothy 14
motherhood: ambivalence about 91–2; in assemblage 98–100; in Athens 92–4; body-memory of 94, 110, 113; connection to children 88–92, 98–100, 104–5, 109, 111–2, 115, 124, 135; as constraint 87–91; and essentialism 88, 91; maternal thinking 89–92; in *Medea* 108–16; and responsibility 87, 97–8; in *Trojan Women* 96–103, 105–8; *see also* Andromache, Hecuba, Medea, Clytemnestra
motivation 3, 16, 21, 48, 50–1, 95, 99, 122, 126, 144–5, 150, 165
mourning 93–4, 97, 103; *see also* lament
Muñiz-Fraticelli, Víctor 13
Mytilenean Debate 71

narrative 5, 7, 40, 83, 95, 135, 145; ancient Greek theater 55–7; definition 60 n. 17; qualities of 41, 45–54, 64; sovereignty as a narrative 31; space as 149–51, 163–5
natality 81, 131
necessity 89, 100, 104, 107, 121, 125–32, 135–6
New Orleans 78, 157–8, 167 n. 37
Nietzsche, Friedrich 53
non-identity problem 19
nostalgia 53, 72
Nussbaum, Martha 16, 48–9, 97, 133

Oedipus 75–6
ordinary 47, 149, 151–2, 153, 157, 167 n. 37; definition of 151–2
Oresteia 121–145; alternate interpretation of ending 147 n. 36; backstory 123; gender conflict in 122, 134, 145 n. 5; political significance of 122
Orestes 7, 121, 124, 135–45, 157
orientation: definition of 121; transgenerational 3, 7, 116, 121–2, 125, 136, 138, 141, 144, 150, 157, 164–5

pandering *see* flattery
Paphlagon 64–72
Park, Shelley 77, 98
parrhesia 57, 62 n. 65, 71
Paterson, Katie 162
Phidippides 79, 82
Plato 75, 80–1, 116, 119 n. 70
plurality 12, 24, 28, 32–3, 75, 81, 120, 125
poets 57, 71–2, 82
powerlessness: in Aristophanes 56, 68–9; in Euripides 6, 95, 97, 101, 103, 107, 110, 114, 116;
powerless responsibility 87–8, 92, 101, 103, 116, 120, 150, 158, 160, 165
presentism 10, 17, 37 n. 46, 40, 52, 53, 64
problem of the new 40–5, 47
prohairesis 126
public art 55, 57, 153–7, 162–4
Purdy, Jedidiah 3

race in the United States: Black Lives Matter 2, 53, 55, 158; racism 15, 131; slavery 2, 14, 157–9; Whitney Plantation 157–9
Rahman, Smita 27, 35 n. 10
Rawls, John 4, 15–16, 36 n. 30; original position 15; veil of ignorance 16
recognition *see* misrecognition
representation: generational 18–21; surrogate 20–1; representatives 10, 19–21, 44, 116
representative thinking 43–5
responsibility: intergenerational responsibility 4–5, 7, 121, 123, 128, 130–2, 135, 143–4, 140; versus guilt 33, 129; as liability 23, 104, 129; and necessity 121, 125–32, 136; powerless responsibility 87–8, 92, 101, 103,

116, 120, 150, 158, 160, 165; social connection model 23, 104; tension with freedom 7, 26, 46, 81, 121, 124–5, 132–9, 150
Reyes, Pedro 160
Rich, Adrienne 40, 87, 103
Ruddick, Sara 89–90

sacrifice: of children 115; by Clytemnestra 135; in democracy 6, 128–30, 139, 142–3; of Iphigenia 123–4, 127, 132–4; by Medea 6, 114–16; by mothers 92, 105
Salkever, Stephen 49, 55
Sausage Seller 66–71, 74
Saxonhouse, Arlene 75
Schell, Jonathan 10
Schiff, Jade 23, 46–7, 51–2
Scholtz, Andrew 65
science fiction 34 n. 1, 46, 53
sensus communis 43, 164
Situationist International 153, 157, 163
Situations (Bristol) 162, 164, 166 n. 37
Socrates 57, 64, 78–9, 82, 119 n. 70
sovereignty 4, 5, 6, 7, 109, 164; *archê* 80–2; definition 29–30; and democracy 83–4; freedom as 2, 17, 18, 28–34, 75, 120, 155–6; generational 2, 7, 11, 12–15, 18, 21, 24, 27, 31–2, 35 n. 8, 37 n. 42, 94, 124–5, 144–5, 150, 152, 156–7, 165; and vulnerability 25, 103
space 7, 151–6, 166 n. 23, 166–7 n. 37; dilemmatic 152–3, 157; heterotopic 156–7, 164; production of 153–5, 163; privatization of 153–5
speech 44, 66–8, 107, 130, 138, 141–43; *see also parrhesia*
Stewart, Kathleen 152
Stolpersteine 148–51, 162
storytelling *see* narrative
Stowe, Simon 48
Strepsiades 64, 78–9, 82–3, 88–9
sustainability 3, 13, 20
Suter, Ann 96–7

Taylor, Charles 22
temporality 13, 46, 77, 88, 122, 151

theater: and citizenship 54–9; and democratic orientation 121, 125; intergenerational conflict in 58; as *Stolpersteine* 150
Thompson, Dennis 10, 20, 38 n. 53, Thompson, Janna 14–5, 36 n. 36
Thompson, Nato 155, 163
threnos see lament
Thucydides 66, 69, 72
time: out-of-jointness 27, 35 n. 10, 52–3, 77, 149, 150, 152, 164; progressivist frame 27; as spiral 7, 136–7, 142–4, 158
tragedy: family in 58; as institution of exception 94, 97, 152; political function 53–7, 59, 61 n. 52
transgenerational: assemblage 7, 120–1, 145, 149, 165; orientation 3, 7, 116, 121–2, 125, 136, 138, 141, 144, 150, 157, 164–5; projects 13–5, 18, 78
Trojan Women 6, 57, 87, 96–108, 111, 114, 116, 158
tyranny 14, 70, 75–6

universal moral respect 10
untimeliness 4, 5, 53, 55, 165

Vernant, Jean-Pierre 127, 146 n. 10
Vidal-Naquet, Pierre 127, 146 n. 10
vulnerability 24–6, 33, 42, 46, 138–9, 155; and climate change 1, 23; and dependency 6, 75, 79–80, 97, 102, 108–9; intersubjective temporal intersubjective vulnerability 12, 46, 122–3, 157

welfare state politics 9, 10, 15
Whitney Plantation 157–9, 162
Wolin, Sheldon 10, 15, 25, 62 n. 64, 75, 76, 81
Wynter, Sylvia 31

Young, Iris Marion 17, 22–3, 50, 104, 105, 129
youth 59, 64, 70–4

Zerilli, Linda 41–3